# LORD OF THE ELVES AND ELDILS

RICHARD PURTILL

# LORD OF THE
# ELVES AND ELDILS

*Second Edition*

IGNATIUS PRESS    SAN FRANCISCO

First edition © 1974 by
the Zondervan Corporation,
Grand Rapids, Michigan

Cover art: © iStockphoto.com

Cover design by John Herreid

© 2006 by Richard Purtill
All rights reserved.
Published in 2006 Ignatius Press, San Francisco
ISBN 978-1-58617-084-4
ISBN 1-58617-084-8
Library of Congress Control Number 2005938825
Printed in the United States of America ∞

*This book is dedicated to*
J. R. R. TOLKIEN
*in gratitude for the many hours*
*of enchantment I have received*
*from his work since as a boy*
*I first took* The Hobbit
*from a library shelf*


*and to*
*Gord Wilson*
*and the other students*
*in my*
*Philosophy and Fantasy class*
*in gratitude*
*for what I have learned*
*from them*

# CONTENTS

Introduction                                        ix

LITERATURE AND LANGUAGE

1   Why Fantasy?                                      3
2   Fantasy and Literature                           20
3   Language, Mind, and Character                    41

GOOD, EVIL, AND GOD

4   Good and Evil in Lewis                           63
5   Good and Evil in Tolkien                         85
6   Religion in Tolkien                             105
7   Religion in Lewis                               134

CONCLUSIONS

8   The Baptism of the Imagination                  153
9   The Christian Intellect                         168
10  The Continuing Battle                           185

APPENDICES

Appendix A: Forerunners and Friends                199
Appendix B: *That Hideous Strength*: A Double Story  209
Appendix C: Did C. S. Lewis Lose His Faith?        227
Appendix D: A Basic Lewis–Tolkien Bibliography     253

Acknowledgments                                     257
Index                                               259

# INTRODUCTION

In this book I write about the ideas and imaginings of two men. The men are C. S. Lewis and J. R. R. Tolkien, and their books range from fantasies, some highly popular, to scholarly works of little interest except to specialists in their fields. Both men taught at Oxford, and they met regularly, with or without other friends, over a period of years, both for conversation and conviviality and to read to each other their works in progress. They agreed on many matters, not the least on religion, and on a general attitude toward literature and life. One perceptive observer and sometime junior member of their circle described them as having "a corporate mind, as all effective groups must", and there is at least an element of truth in this. But in other respects they were almost comically dissimilar, and their shared assumptions were expressed in very different ways.

One important way in which their books are alike is that both found it best to create, for the purposes of their fiction, other worlds—not Utopias or dystopias but *different* worlds—what Tolkien was to call "secondary worlds". This sort of writing raises certain little-discussed problems, which this book explores. Both also wrote *about* literature or at least about certain aspects of it. Tolkien, who was primarily a philologist, did very little of this sort of writing, but what he did do was original and suggestive. Lewis, whose professional field was English literature, of course wrote a great deal on such subjects, some of it highly specialized but all worth reading. Part of my task in this book is to examine the ideas expressed by my authors on these subjects, ideas that are often in disagreement with the prevailing orthodoxy. I seek to weigh the consistency and defensibility of these ideas and also to see to what extent they are applicable to my authors' own writings.

Since I am a philosopher by profession, my interest in these authors is primarily in their ideas, not only in their ideas about literature but in their ethical and religious ideas and their views about language. Where these views are implicit in a work, I will try to make them explicit; where they are stated rather than argued, I will try to see how they might be criticized and defended.

I know no more of the personal lives of my authors than can be found in the books written by or about them and available to anyone, so it has not seemed worthwhile merely to summarize such secondhand information in this book. Somewhat more complicated is the question of whether to summarize those of their books I discuss. While it is doubtful whether many people will be interested in a discussion of Lewis and Tolkien who have not read at least some of their work, some of my readers may have read Tolkien but not Lewis or vice versa. I have concluded that any adequate summary of the works I am interested in would take an inordinate amount of space and be a poor substitute for reading the works themselves.

Thus I presume at least some familiarity with the fictional works of both Lewis and Tolkien. A reader who lacks such familiarity would do well to pause here and read the works listed in the "essential" section of the Basic Lewis-Tolkien Bibliography (Appendix D).

Since I have hopes that this book will be of some interest both to scholars of Lewis and Tolkien and to ordinary readers, I have tried to reach a workable compromise between the pedantic accuracy of reference of a scholarly book and the less rigorous standards of a popular book. Thus, instead of citing the first publication of a book, I have usually cited the cheapest and most accessible edition, generally a paperback. When I refer to the same book a number of times, I give its title in full the first time I cite it and the usual publication information. When I discuss the same book again in another chapter I cite the title and publication information again in full. I hope this will be neither too pedantic for the common reader nor too lacking in rigor for the scholar.

In Appendix A, I say something about those who have influenced my authors and a little about those who have been influenced by them. But I also take a critical look at the whole idea of the importance of "influences" that bulks so large in most writing about literature. I also say something about critics of Tolkien and Lewis, but not in the sense of a formal "reply to the critics". To tell the truth, very few of Tolkien's critics deserve a formal reply, and very few of Lewis' need one. Rather, I have used the critics as taking-off points for my own discussions. But if this book can provoke a better critic to do better what I have tried to do, to correct my misunderstandings, and to replace them with better interpretations, I will be quite happy.

The great importance of my authors, it seems to me, is that they have succeeded in restating certain traditional values, including traditional religious values, in such a way that they make an imaginative appeal to a very wide audience, young and old, traditionalist and untraditionalist. The wide appeal of Tolkien's *Lord of the Rings* trilogy on college campuses is perhaps the most striking example of this, but Lewis' fantasies have a similar audience.

Those who look with gloom at the contemporary scene (and who can avoid a certain amount of gloom at what is to be seen?) often fall into one of two groups. The first group declares that old values have failed us, and we must create new ones. The second group, to which my authors belong, declares that values are not the sort of thing that can be created. Certain values exist whether we will or not, and to these values we must conform or perish. To enable people to see these values and love them is the task to which Lewis and Tolkien set themselves. Their methods were unconventional; their success, though partial, was real.

## A Note to the New Edition

*Lord of the Elves and Eldils* (Zondervan, 1974; Ignatius Press, 2006) was my first book on Lewis and Tolkien. It was followed by C. S. Lewis' *Case for the Christian Faith* (Harper and Row, 1981; Ignatius Press, 2005) and *J. R. R. Tolkien: Myth, Morality, and Religion* (Harper and Row, 1984; Ignatius Press, 2003). Ignatius Press has reprinted these in reverse order.

After the publication of *Lord of the Elves and Eldils*, I had some standing as a "Lewis and Tolkien scholar" and was invited to give lectures on one or the other author, rarely both, at various meetings and universities. My lectures on Lewis were mostly incorporated into *C. S. Lewis' Case for the Christian Faith*, and my lectures on Tolkien were mostly incorporated into *J. R. R. Tolkien: Myth, Morality, and Religion*. Now that *Lord of the Elves and Eldils* is being reprinted, I have two additional essays on Lewis that bear reprinting, but unfortunately none on Tolkien. I have, however, added to Chapter 6 some notes on *The Simarillion*.

The first essay (found here in Appendix B) is "*That Hideous Strength*: A Double Story", a very detailed analysis of the last book of Lewis' "space trilogy". This essay I think defends the depth and clarity of this book, which has been undervalued even by sympathetic critics. The second essay (Appendix C below) is "Did C. S. Lewis Lose His Faith?" This essay has to do with certain biographical facts about Lewis that have been distorted and misused by some of his critics. I would not willingly bring up these old controversies except that they still have a certain currency in writings about Lewis, especially on the Internet, which is a great source of half-informed or ill-informed opinion.

The inclusion of these essays and the revision of all the references to Lewis' and Tolkien's books to what is currently available make this a new and perhaps better edition of *Lord of the Elves and Eldils*. Many people over the years have spoken of enjoying and learning from this book, some as recently as a few months ago. I hope that this new edition will meet with an equally favorable response.

—Richard Purtill
Bellingham, Washington
2006

# LITERATURE AND LANGUAGE

I

# Why Fantasy?

Those who enjoy reading and discussing Lewis and Tolkien often encounter an impatient, even irritated, reaction from friends or acquaintances. Why read fantasies or fairy stories? Aren't such things for children? Shouldn't grown-ups read about "real life"? (One literary critic called Tolkien's trilogy a "children's story which got out of hand".) A former student of Lewis, novelist and critic John Wain, once challenged Lewis' own praise and enjoyment of fantasy.

> A writer's task, I maintained, was to lay bare the human heart, and this could not be done if he were continually taking refuge in the spinning of fanciful webs. Lewis retorted with a theory that, since the Creator had seen fit to build a universe and set it in motion, it was the duty of the human artist to create as lavishly as possible in his turn. The romancer, who invents a whole world, is worshipping God more effectively than the mere realist who analyses that which lies about him. Looking back across fourteen years, I can hardly believe that Lewis said anything so manifestly absurd as this, and perhaps I misunderstood him; but that, at any rate, is how my memory reports the incident.[1]

[1] John Wain, *Sprightly Running: Part of an Autobiography* (New York: St. Martin's Press, 1963), p. 182.

Here we have very neatly the whole basis of the conflict between Lewis and Tolkien on the one hand and many modern writers and critics on the other. Wain maintains, and many moderns would agree, that a writer's task is to "lay bare the human heart". Judged by this standard, practically nothing written by Tolkien and only a few things written by Lewis carry out "the writer's task". The theory attributed to Lewis, which is a recognizable caricature of the theory developed by Tolkien in his essay "On Fairy-Stories", is dismissed as "manifestly absurd". Before discussing who is more nearly right, let us first try to understand more thoroughly the theory proposed by Lewis to Wain.

The theory, presumably, is that espoused by Tolkien in his essay "On Fairy-Stories". According to Tolkien, "the story-maker proves a successful 'sub-creator.' He makes a Secondary World which your mind can enter. Inside it, what he relates is 'true': it accords with the laws of that world. You therefore believe it while you are, as it were, inside." [2] This could be said of other forms of writing, but fantasy has special characteristics.

> The achievement of the expression, which gives (or seems to give) "the inner consistency of reality," is ... Art, the operative link between Imagination and the final result, Sub-creation. For my present purpose I require a word which shall embrace both the Sub-creative Art in itself and a quality of strangeness and wonder in the Expression, derived from the Image: a quality essential to fairy-story. I propose ... to use Fantasy for this purpose.... Fantasy (in this sense) is, I think, not a lower but a higher form of Art, indeed the

[2] J. R. R. Tolkien, "On Fairy-Stories", in *Tree and Leaf*, in *The Tolkien Reader* (New York: Ballantine Books, 2001), p. 60.

most nearly pure form, and so (when achieved) the most potent.[3]

Note several things to begin with. First, this is a theory about *one kind* of writing. Tolkien indeed suggests that it may, if properly handled, be the "most potent" form of narrative art or story-making. But this is not to say that it is the only allowable form even of narrative art, much less the only allowable form of writing. Wain, on the other hand, seems to suggest that the purpose of all "writing" (presumably by "writing" he means primarily "fiction") is to lay bare the secrets of the human heart. Second, the two views are not necessarily in conflict, even considered at their most extreme. One might consistently hold both that the purpose of fiction is to lay bare the secrets of the human heart and that the "most potent" way of doing this is to create a "secondary world" in Tolkien's sense.

This could be done in various ways. In *strict allegory* (e.g., Bunyan's *Pilgrim's Progress*), every figure, incident, or place in your secondary world will stand for some person, emotion, or idea in the primary world. In a well-worked-out strict allegory, it should be possible to say what each person, place, or incident "stands for" (its *significatio*), and the whole story *could* be retold without the use of a secondary world (though it would lose something by this, or the allegory is useless).

In a *loose allegory*, on the other hand, it is impossible to find a *significatio* for each person, place, or incident, but the secondary world as a whole is intended to give a general impression or idea—for example, an idea of "the human condition". (Kafka and Beckett are good examples.) A work may be classified as loose allegory if the author seems to

---

[3] Ibid., p. 68.

be saying, or trying to make us say, "That is what life is like."

With *illustrative fantasy*, the author wishes to make a point about some aspect of the primary world that can best be made by isolating or exaggerating certain aspects of that world by the use of a secondary world (as in Golding's *Lord of the Flies*). The author of illustrative fantasy is saying, "This couldn't happen, of course; but if it did, this is how people would behave."

But there is a fourth use of secondary worlds that does not seem suited to "laying bare the heart". In *appreciative fantasy* (for example, *Alice in Wonderland*), the secondary world is enjoyed purely for its own sake. The characters, places, and incidents do not have a *significatio*, do not "stand for" anything in the primary world. The secondary world is not intended to show what "life is like", and there is no attempt to show that people would behave in a certain way given certain improbable occurrences. So although the first three of these sorts of allegory and fantasy can be used to "lay bare the secrets of the heart", this last sort of fantasy seems unsuited to that purpose. To write appreciative fantasy is, in fact, to "spin fanciful webs".

Now Lewis and Tolkien do not in the main write strict allegory or even loose allegory, nor do they write illustrative fantasy.[4] By their own statements, they aim at writing largely appreciative fantasy. Legolas the Elf or Tumnus the Faun have no *significatio*, illustrate no possible or plausible reaction of human nature, no views of what life is like. Tolkien writes about Legolas, Lewis about Tumnus, because they enjoy contemplating elves and fauns. They like to think about them and

---

[4] The exception for Lewis is *The Pilgrim's Regress*, a strict allegory, and for Tolkien, "Leaf by Niggle", a loose allegory found in *Tree and Leaf*.

write about them. If such tastes were to disqualify them as "significant" writers, they would be undisturbed. They would rather write about Faërie than about "modern problems". And why not, if they and others enjoy it? This statement may seem somewhat surprising. Surely both Tolkien and Lewis illustrate all kinds of religious values—and even, in Tolkien, Catholic values. But we must distinguish between the intent of the authors and its effect on their readers. Neither Tolkien nor Lewis set out to write books that were Christian or Catholic "propaganda". They wrote the kind of stories that they enjoyed reading. Being the kind of men they were, the kind of stories they wrote were very Christian. This was not, however, the purpose for which they wrote the stories: they wrote them to enjoy them.

The idea that Lewis, for example, was writing Christian apologetics in his Narnia books (an accusation that was made on the release of the recent *Narnia* film) is absurd. If Lewis wanted to write Christian apologetics, he could do it quite effectively (e.g., in *Mere Christianity*, *Miracles*, or *The Problem of Pain*). But a fictional presentation of a story with strong underlying Christian values is not an apologetic. Fiction can prove nothing because the "fictional facts" it contains are wholly up to the author. What fiction *can* do is to illustrate what it is like to have the values it embodies. A story written from a Buddhist perspective or even a Nazi perspective would give you an understanding of that perspective: it wouldn't necessarily convince you to become a Buddhist or a Nazi. If you want to say that Lewis' and Tolkien's works are, in a certain sense, illustrative as well as appreciative, you may, if you like.

May we then merely say "laying bare the secrets of the human heart" is one legitimate purpose of literature and the creation of secondary worlds is another? I fear that reconciliation is not likely to be so easy. For Wain, the creator of secondary worlds is "*taking refuge* in the spinning of fanciful webs". Tolkien's reply to this is that "fantasy is a natural human activity. It certainly does not destroy or even insult Reason; and it does not either blunt the appetite for, nor obscure the perception of, scientific verity. On the contrary. The keener and the clearer is the reason, the better fantasy will it make. . . . For creative Fantasy is founded upon the hard recognition that things are so in the world as it appears under the sun; on a recognition of fact, but not a slavery to it." [5]

Of course, fantasy, like everything else, can be abused.

> Fantasy can, of course, be carried to excess. It can be ill done. It can be put to evil uses. It may even delude the minds out of which it came. But of what human thing in this fallen world is that not true? Men have conceived not only of elves, but they have imagined gods, and worshipped them, even worshipped those most deformed by their authors' own evil. But they have made false gods out of other materials: their notions, their banners, their monies; even their sciences and their social and economic theories have demanded human sacrifice. *Abusus non tollit usum.* Fantasy remains a human right: we make in our measure and in our derivative mode, because we are made: and not only made, but made in the image and likeness of a Maker.[6]

What Tolkien says here is connected with his theory about the uses of fantasy, which is to say the uses of creating secondary worlds. In his view, fantasy has three purposes: Recovery, Escape, and Consolation. By Recovery, he means

[5] Tolkien, "On Fairy-Stories", pp. 74–75.
[6] Ibid., p. 75.

a "regaining of a clear view . . . 'seeing things as we are (or were) meant to see them' ".[7] Familiarity has dulled our sense of the wonder and mystery of things; fantasy restores it. "You will be warned that all you had (or knew) was dangerous and potent, not really effectively chained, free and wild; no more yours than they were you."[8] Notice that this implies two things. First, that many of us fail to see any wonder and mystery in things, which is undeniable. Second, that in so failing we are failing to see the truth, and this I suppose some would dispute.

By Escape, Tolkien means nothing especially original. We must define Escape as the turning of our thoughts and affections away from what is around us to something else—the past, the future, a secondary world. Tolkien's originality lies in defending Escape when so many have deprecated it. His reasons are several. First, the modern world is preeminently something desirable to escape *from*. "Why should a man be scorned if, finding himself in prison, he tries to get out and go home? Or if, when he cannot do so, he thinks and talks about other topics than jailers and prison-walls?"[9] And the modern world is, to Tolkien, prisonlike: ugly, cruel, and unjust.

A deeper reason for Escape, however, is the human longing to flee from our limitations. First is the hardness of life even at its best; but beyond this is our isolation from each other and from the living world around us. Finally, the great limit, Death, is something that men have tried to escape from in many fashions.

Here Tolkien's discussion of Escape merges into a discussion of the third use of fantasy. Consolation is secondarily the

[7] Ibid.
[8] Ibid., p. 78.
[9] Ibid., p. 79.

imaginative satisfaction of ancient desires, such as the desire really to communicate with species other than our own. But primarily it centers on the happy ending, the "eucatastrophe", the "sudden joyous 'turn'".[10] This Consolation arises from the denial of "universal final defeat and in so far is *evangelium*, giving a fleeting glimpse of Joy, Joy beyond the walls of the world, poignant as grief".[11]

In fantasy we have a happy ending, a joyous "turn" within the secondary world, to which we give secondary belief, and it gives such consolation as such things may, which is a good worth seeking. But Tolkien concludes by discussing the "Christian Story" as "a story of a larger kind which embraces all the essence of fairy-stories".[12] This is a eucatastrophe in the primary world, a happy ending to which primary belief can be given. Such belief leads to true Consolation. "There is no tale ever told that men would rather find was true, and none which so many sceptical men have accepted as true on its own merits. For the Art of it has the supremely convincing tone of Primary Art, that is, of Creation. To reject it leads either to sadness or to wrath."[13]

So we see in the end that Tolkien's view of fairy stories is not just a view about literature, but a view about life. Tolkien could, if he liked, use Wain's formula about "laying bare the secrets of the human heart". But Tolkien would not agree with Wain or with most moderns on what those secrets are. For in Tolkien's view the important secret of the human heart is this longing for the real happy ending. And the most important thing about this longing is that it can be satisfied.

[10] Ibid., p. 86.
[11] Ibid.
[12] Ibid., p. 88.
[13] Ibid., p. 89.

Indeed, no matter how "pure", how "appreciative" in our sense, a fantasy is, it is bound to reflect to some extent the views or ideas of its writer, for several reasons. Lewis and Tolkien create secondary worlds. Because they are Christians, because they are British, even because they are Oxford dons, they create different secondary worlds than they otherwise might have.

For, of course, the sort of secondary world you create will depend on the sort of things you believe possible. Not scientifically possible, however—a secondary world may often have scientific laws quite different from those of the primary world—but what we might call "morally possible". Orwell could write *Nineteen Eighty-Four* because, although he didn't *want* such a state of affairs to be true, he thought such a state of affairs was "morally possible" in my sense. "A heel pressing down on the neck of Man—forever" [14] was a real possibility for Orwell. But for many humanists as well as theists, such a fate for man is unthinkable. To take another example at random, a pacifist would not find a secondary world in which violence and killing are good and noble morally possible. In other words, each of us has certain expectations about how bad (or good) things could be, and any secondary world we create will be influenced by these expectations.

Now a Christian will not necessarily create a Christian secondary world—Tolkien did not. (Although perhaps a theist may be unable to conceive of a Godless world, because of the nature of theism.) But if he does, what then? Christians will quite possibly find this world one they can enter with special enjoyment (or perhaps not, as we shall see).

---

[14] The quote is from *1984* in *George Orwell, The Complete Novels* (London: Penguin Classics, 2000), p. 898.

But for non-Christians, is the Christian nature of such a world a bar to enjoyment? Well, why should it be? A secondary world created by a Buddhist, a Zuñi, a Communist would certainly give us all sorts of insights into Buddhism, the Zuñi religion and outlook, or Communism. As Lewis says in *An Experiment in Criticism,*

> The mark of strictly literary reading, as opposed to scientific or otherwise informative reading, is that we need not believe or approve the Logos [the thing said]. Most of us do not believe Dante's universe is at all like the real one. . . . None of us can accept simultaneously Housman's and Chesterton's views of life, or those of Fitzgerald's *Omar* and Kipling. What then is the good of—what is even the defence for—occupying our hearts with stories of what never happened and entering vicariously into feelings which we should try to avoid having in our own person? . . .
>
> The nearest I have got yet to an answer is that we seek an enlargement of our being. We want to be more than ourselves. . . . We want to see with other eyes, to imagine with other imaginations, to feel with other hearts as well as with our own.[15]

Elsewhere Lewis says, "I read Lucretius and Dante at a time when (by and large) I agreed with Lucretius. I have read them since I came (by and large) to agree with Dante. I cannot find that this has much altered my experience, or at all altered my evaluation, of either."[16]

Thus we will find that although Lewis' and Tolkien's fantasies may be read purely as appreciative fantasy, enjoyed simply for their own sake, yet certain views of the world,

---

[15] C. S. Lewis, *An Experiment in Criticism* (Cambridge, Eng.: Cambridge University Press, 1961), pp. 136–37.
[16] Ibid., p. 86.

certain ideas about life, will be discernible in them. It is these views and these ideas that I am especially interested in extracting and analyzing. We will find that such views and ideas often appear in the form of broad "themes" that can be discerned in the fantasies of Lewis and Tolkien.

We have seen in this discussion certain key themes in Tolkien, which we will see echoed in Lewis. They are, first, that we ought to see the world as a place of wonder and mystery; second, that the modern world seems increasingly to tend to become a place of ugliness and misery; and, finally, that the Christian Story gives us consolation by showing us that the world ends in eucatastrophe. Let us call these The World of Wonder Theme, The Modern Failure Theme, and The Happy Ending Theme. Both our authors use secondary worlds, yet each uses them in ways of his own and for purposes of his own. But in each of their secondary worlds these three themes can be found, modified by the author's own way of doing things and by the purposes of that particular story.

Let us look first at the sort of secondary world created by each author. Tolkien created—initially in his children's book *The Hobbit* and then in his trilogy *The Lord of the Rings*—a secondary world of imaginary prehistory. It is inhabited by a number of rational species, not only Men and other more or less manlike beings such as Elves, Dwarves, Hobbits, Ents, Orcs (or goblins), and trolls,[17] but also beasts

---

[17] This volume follows Tolkien's *general* use of capitals (which was not terribly consistent). He usually capitalized racial terms: Elvish, Dwarf, Ents. But when it came to "hobbits", he usually left the word lowercase, by and large capitalizing it only when speaking of them as a race in the Prologue and Appendices. He often, but not always, capitalized "Men" in the plural, but rarely in the singular. And while he usually capitalized "Orcs", he never capitalized "goblins" and rarely "trolls".

Lewis was even less consistent, so we are capitalizing words that he usually capitalized in the Chronicles: Dwarves, Talking Beasts, Owls, etc.—Ed.

that can think and talk, among them dragons and Wargs (a sort of wolf). There is an alignment of good and evil forces. Some species of beings, such as Elves, are almost wholly on the side of good; some, such as Orcs, almost wholly on the side of evil. But most species are both corruptible and perfectible; individual Men, Hobbits, and Dwarves may be on the side of good or of evil and may change from one side to the other. Some beings are preternaturally good (like Gandalf the Wizard) or preternaturally evil (like Sauron in *The Lord of the Rings* trilogy, and to some degree Smaug in *The Hobbit*), but the focus of attention is never on such beings. The real heroes, and to some extent even the real villains of Tolkien's books, are capable of both good and evil. They stand in danger of corruption, like Bilbo and Frodo, or have a chance (which they can accept or reject) of salvation, like Gollum and Saruman.

Nature is generally seen as beneficient. Where particular places (the Misty Mountains, Mirkwood, Mordor) are evil or unfriendly, this is due to the presence, seen or unseen, of evil beings; such places have been good in the past and can be cleansed and restored by the expulsion of the evil beings. Conversely, the presence of good beings, especially Elves, can make a region or territory better and more beautiful. Places like Mirkwood, Lothlórien, the Shire, and Mordor have almost the status of characters in their own right. Technology in the sense of architecture or handicraft is good in itself, but subject to corruption. Uncorrupted technology tends to be associated with a golden age in the past, while manifestations of modernity, such as factories, are sinister.

C. S. Lewis created two major secondary worlds, that of his interplanetary trilogy—*Out of the Silent Planet, Perelandra*, and *That Hideous Strength*—and that of his Chronicles of Narnia, seven stories written for children but enjoyed by many adults. Lewis' secondary worlds are like that of Tolkien's in many respects. There are a number of nonhuman, rational species in the trilogy, especially the three Martian species described in *Out of the Silent Planet* and the eldils who appear in all three books. In the Narnia stories, there are men, Dwarves, Giants, and Talking Beasts of many species as well as a host of evil beings such as Hags and Wer-Wolves. There is an alignment of good and evil forces in each story, but it is often a different group. Ransom, the hero of *Out of the Silent Planet*, is also the hero of *Perelandra*, but in *That Hideous Strength*, he is a remote, demigod-like figure, not unlike Gandalf in the last part of Tolkien's trilogy. The real heroes of *That Hideous Strength* are perhaps Mark and Jane Studdock, both of whom nearly fail under testing. The child heroes and heroines of the Narnia tales are an overlapping group, with changes from book to book; one of the early heroines has "dropped out" by the end of the series. The villains in the two worlds change also, though there is again some overlap. Weston, one of the villains of *Out of the Silent Planet*, is the vehicle of demonic forces in *Perelandra*, and Devine, the other villain of the first book, is a minor figure in the gallery of villains in *That Hideous Strength*. The Witch Jadis is the villainess of two of The Chronicles of Narnia, another witch the villainess of another, and evil men and beasts are the villains of others. There are preternaturally good and evil beings: good and evil eldils in the space trilogy, and in the Narnia stories, Aslan on the one hand and the witches and their allies on the other. But, as with Tolkien, the real focus is on the corruptible or perfectible characters.

As in Tolkien, nature is almost a character in the drama: Malacandra (Mars) and Perelandra (Venus) are parts of the stories set on them, not mere backgrounds. In *That Hideous Strength*, a mythical Arthurian Britain gives a "depth" to the English setting. The land of Narnia and its neighboring kingdoms are similarly important in the Chronicles. Although Lewis' supposed antiscientific attitude has been exaggerated by critics, there is some tendency in his books to idealize the bucolic and primitive and to show the dangers of science and technology. Because of the nature of the secondary worlds in question, there is more of this in the space trilogy than in Tolkien and less of it in The Chronicles of Narnia.

These brief descriptions suggest two more themes that should be added to our previous list. The first, which we will call The Good versus Evil Theme, is that the world is in a state of conflict between good and evil. The second, a corollary of this, is that each of us can and must choose his side in this conflict. We will call this The Choice Theme.

It may now be clear how Tolkien and Lewis embody the first three themes we listed in their secondary worlds. The World of Wonder Theme is introduced indirectly by describing secondary worlds in such a way that we return to contemplate the primary world with new eyes. The Modern Failure Theme is introduced by isolating certain undesirable features of the modern world and showing them in contrast with other values. In contrast to the greenness of the Shire, for example, Mordor's blackness is more apparent, and we realize with a shock that the modern world is closer to Mordor than to the Shire. Associating ugliness and misery with moral evil has some dangers, which we shall examine, but it is an association Tolkien and Lewis believed in and could argue for. Thus the combination of these elements in the secondary worlds begs no questions that they are not prepared to answer elsewhere.

The Happy Ending Theme is embodied by our authors in their secondary worlds in two ways. Lewis confronts it most directly in The Chronicles of Narnia, which contain events parallel (though not always in an obvious fashion) to the creation of the world, the death and Resurrection of Christ, and the Final Judgment. The space trilogy contains an averted fall of man in *Perelandra* and an apocalyptic ending in *That Hideous Strength*. Tolkien—who found the Narnia stories, at least, "too allegorical"—attacks this theme in a much more indirect way. However, as we shall see, he manages to give a new expression to one of the most difficult yet most important ideas in Christianity, the idea of vicarious atonement.

The Good versus Evil Theme is obviously present in *The Lord of the Rings*, to such an extent that novelist critic Edmund Wilson accused Tolkien of having an oversimplified "black and white" picture of morality.[18] Most of the Narnia books and all of the space trilogy similarly describe battles between good and evil forces. Perhaps the books in which the struggle is the least clear are *The Hobbit*, where the original motives of the "good guys" are somewhat mixed, and *The Voyage of the Dawn Treader*, one of the most delightful of the Narnia series but the most episodic. (There is not one clear-cut confrontation between good and evil, but a number of tests of courage and moral stamina.) Yet, even with these exceptions, all the books we have been discussing could be described as stories of a conflict between good and evil forces.

The Choice Theme is presented in a variety of ways by Lewis and Tolkien, sometimes explicitly, as for example in some of the things Gandalf says to Frodo. Sometimes this is implicit, as in the moral struggles that go on in the heroes

[18] Edmund Wilson, "Oo Those Awful Orcs!" *Nation* (April 14, 1956).

and in the subsidiary characters. Indeed, this moral struggle is, in a way, the main focus of much of the story. When Ransom in the space trilogy and Frodo in *The Lord of the Rings* are to some degree lifted above the moral struggle, the focus of the stories shifts away from them to other characters.

Let us consider the Lewis–Tolkien view in relation to its "anti-view", the view consisting of the opposites of the five themes we have been discussing. We can state these roughly as follows. The world is pointless and absurd, and therefore, like all pointless and absurd things, ultimately dull and boring. The modern world with its physical comfort and technological marvels is as near to paradise as we are likely to come; the urgent problem is to extend this "high standard of living" to as many people as possible and make it last as long as possible. Far from having a happy ending, the world will ultimately end "not with a bang but a whimper", and no matter how great the triumphs of the human race, that race will ultimately die. The universe will outlast us, but our story will inevitably end in futility. "Good" and "evil" are purely emotional reactions to the universe; they have no ground in the nature of the universe and are at best the shibboleths of our tribe or nation. There is no great moral drama in which the individual has a part: at best, our moral choices can make life somewhat more livable for ourselves and those close to us. Such a view is in many respects the characteristic "modern" view of the universe. Not all who call themselves modern would share it in all respects, but they would recognize that in challenging any of its tenets they are challenging the prevailing orthodoxy.

The strong person, facing such a view of the universe, may find consolation in work or in personal relationships, or in working to give others what happiness he can. Even he may sometimes falter and find a certain hollowness in triumphs doomed to eventual futility. The weaker person will turn to drugs or submerge himself in sex or violence, pulling the covers over his head to hide the bleak picture. But that, too, is ultimately unsuccessful. Hiding under the covers doesn't remove the bogey, if real, or the fear of the false bogey. If this is the way things are, then we must face the knowledge as best we can. But the good news from Narnia and Middle-earth is that the modern view is false in whole and in part. The story they tell is "Fear not, I have overcome the world." And to those who have drunk the bitterness of the modern view, "There is no tale told which we would rather find is true."

To return to the question opening this chapter, "Why fantasy?" we can now see that there are three answers to this question. First, "fantasy remains a human right"; the mind demands "vacations" as well as the body, and after our mental holiday we may return to our tasks in the world refreshed, renewed, and with a new vision. But second, appreciative fantasy, just because it makes no direct statement about the world, paradoxically is the best way to see the beauty and danger of the real world. By recovering the vision and appreciation that fantasy gives us, we learn to see again the world as it is. And finally, it is the consolation of fantasy, the echo in our hearts of the greatest Happy Ending, which makes the fantasy of Lewis and Tolkien so valuable to so many of us. Escape, Recovery, Consolation: these are answers enough, and more than enough, to the question "Why fantasy?"

# 2

# Fantasy and Literature

Even though we can now see that fantasy serves important purposes—Escape, Recovery, Consolation—we may still wonder about the *literary* value of the fantasies of Lewis and Tolkien. Are these fantasies to be considered as literature, or are they subliterary or at least nonliterary? The difficulty in answering these questions is that there are many theories as to what gives a work literary value. Those who are quick to condemn works they dislike as "not literature" are not always equally ready to give a clear and coherent theory of what is and what is not literature.

In his capacity as a professor of English literature, Lewis himself gave a clear and interesting account of how to distinguish literature from nonliterary works. Lewis' theory, as expressed in his book *An Experiment in Criticism*, runs contrary to much that has recently been thought and said about literature. However, like all of Lewis' writing, the book is vigorous and provocative; even those who do not agree with Lewis will find his views a stimulus to think out their own views more clearly. Let us first look at the essentials of Lewis' theory and then see how it applies to his own work and that of Tolkien.

The "experiment" spoken of in the book's title is a reversal of the usual process, in which we judge the worth of a book by some set of criteria and then judge readers by the sort of books they enjoy. Lewis suggests that, instead, we look at different sorts of readers and the sort of reading they do and judge books by the sort of reading they receive. "Let us try to discover", Lewis says, "how far it might be plausible to define a good book as a book which is read in one way, and a bad book as a book which is read in another".[1] Lewis points out that the "nonliterary" reader, whom he is careful to distinguish from the uneducated or the vulgar, reads books in quite a different way from the "literary" reader.

On the most obvious level, the nonliterary reader (who, remember, might be a great saint, a great scientist, or a great statesman) never reads anything twice, turns to reading only as a last resource, and does not seem to be greatly affected by any literary experience. A more important contrast between the literary "few" and the nonliterary "many", however, is that

> as a result of their different behavior in reading, what they have read is constantly and prominently present to the mind of the few, but not to that of the many. The former mouth over their favorite lines and stanzas in solitude. Scenes and characters from books provide them with a sort of iconography by which they interpret or sum up their own experience. They talk to one another about books, often and at length. The latter seldom think or talk about their reading.
>
> It is pretty clear that the majority, if they spoke without passion and were fully articulate, would not accuse us of liking the wrong books, but of making such a fuss about any books at all.[2]

[1] C. S. Lewis, *An Experiment in Criticism* (Cambridge, Eng.: Cambridge University Press, 1961), p. 1.
[2] Ibid., p. 3.

A further analysis of the reading of the nonliterary discloses some less obvious characteristics, which may be summed up as a preference for pure narrative and a disregard for rhythm, style, description, character, and the like. In fact, Lewis says, "they enjoy narratives in which the verbal element is reduced to the minimum—'strip' stories told in pictures, or films with the least possible dialogue.... [The unliterary reader] ignores nearly all that the words before him are doing; he wants to know what happens next".[3] It is important to emphasize that Lewis does not mean to deprecate the narrative element in literature—he elsewhere defends it strongly. In *An Experiment in Criticism* Lewis says, "Let us be quite clear that the unliterary are unliterary not because they enjoy stories in these ways, but because they enjoy them in no other. Not what they have but what they lack cuts them off from the fulness of literary experience."[4]

In exploring the proper place of narrative in literature, Lewis makes a digression—highly relevant for our purposes—on myth and fantasy. Myth he describes as "a particular kind of story which has a value in itself—a value independent of its embodiment in any literary work.... The pleasure of myth depends hardly at all on such usual narrative attractions as suspense or surprise.... Human sympathy is at a minimum.... The experience may be sad or joyful but it is always grave ... [and] not only grave but awe-inspiring. We feel it to be numinous. It is as if something of great moment had been communicated to us."[5]

---

[3] Ibid., p. 30.
[4] Ibid., p. 38.
[5] Ibid., pp. 41, 43, 44.

In addition, "myth is always, in one sense of that word, 'fantastic'. It deals with impossibles and preternaturals." [6] This leads Lewis to a discussion of fantasy. He distinguishes the literary and psychological senses of fantasy: "As a literary term a fantasy means any narrative that deals with impossibles and preternaturals." In the psychological sense, Lewis identifies fantasy as "an imaginative construction which in some way ... pleases". Where such a construction is mistaken for reality, it becomes delusion; where it is "entertained incessantly and to his injury" by the subject, Lewis calls it "Morbid Castle-building"; and where it is "indulged in moderately and briefly as a temporary holiday or recreation, duly subordinated to more effective and outgoing activities", Lewis calls it "Normal Castle-building". [7]

This normal castle-building may be "Egoistic" or "Disinterested". If egoistic, the daydreamer is the hero of the story and derives satisfaction from imaginary triumphs. If disinterested, the daydreamer merely amuses himself by stories or pictures. "There is thus, if the day-dreamer has any talent, an easy transition from disinterested castle-building to literary invention". [8] Lewis notes that the unliterary reader often uses fiction for the purposes of egoistic castle-building, identifying himself with a book's heroic or fortunate characters. Thus the unliterary reader does not like literary fantasy. "Though they do not mistake their castle-building for reality, they want to feel that it might be.... A story which introduces the marvellous, the fantastic, says by implication 'I am merely a work of art. You must take me as such.' ... The more completely a man's

[6] Ibid., p. 44.
[7] Ibid., pp. 50–52.
[8] Ibid., p. 53.

reading is a form of egoistic castle-building the more he
will demand a certain superficial realism, and the less he
will like the fantastic." [9]

The mention of realism leads to a distinction between
realism of presentation and realism of content. A fantasy
may have great realism of *presentation*: "the dragon 'sniffling
along the stone' in *Beowulf*; ... the pinnacles in *Gawain*
that looked as if they were 'pared out of paper'; ... the
fairy bakers in *Huon* rubbing the paste off their fingers".[10]
In fact, "the two realisms are quite independent. You can
get that of presentation without that of content, as in medieval romance: or that of content without that of presentation, as in French (and some Greek) tragedy; or both
together, as in *War and Peace*; or neither, as in the *Furioso* or
*Rasselas* or *Candide*.

"In this age it is important to remind ourselves that all
four ways of writing are good and masterpieces can be produced in any of them." [11]

Lewis points out that many examples of great literature
(*The Iliad*, *Oedipus Rex*, *Hamlet*, *The Miller's Tale*) are not
"true to life" in the sense of telling about the sort of thing
that normally or expectably happens. "Even if the stories
permit the conclusion 'Life is such that this is possible', can
anyone believe that they invite it ... ? ... They are not, in
any sense that matters, representations of life as we know
it, and were never valued for being so." [12] Literary fantasy
does not "give a false picture of life" in the sense of deceiv-
ing the reader. "The real danger lurks in sober-faced novels
where all appears to be very probable, but all is in fact

---

[9] Ibid., pp. 55–56.
[10] Ibid., pp. 57–58.
[11] Ibid., pp. 59–60.
[12] Ibid., pp. 64, 66.

contrived to put across some social or ethical or religious or anti-religious 'comment on life'." [13]

Having noted some parts of Lewis' theory important for my purposes, I can more briefly describe his conclusions. Lewis shows that on his theory "the ideally bad book is one of which a good reading is impossible. The words in which it exists will not bear close attention, and what they communicate offers you nothing unless you are prepared either for mere thrills or for flattering day-dreams." [14] The good book, on the other hand, permits, invites, and ideally *compels* good reading. "We start from the assumption that whatever has been found good by those who really and truly read probably is good." [15]

How does Lewis' theory apply to his own works and Tolkien's? I would argue that the readers of these works read them in a way that marks them as "literary" rather than "nonliterary" readers; that none of these works as a whole is a "myth" in Lewis' sense, although portions of them have the qualities Lewis ascribes to myth; [16] and that though these works lack realism of content, in very different ways they make use of realism of presentation to achieve their ends. I would also claim that on Lewis' theory, his own and Tolkien's imaginative works are very good books indeed, and Lewis' theory, though not without faults, has considerable advantages over any rival theory.

To begin with the weakest and most indirect evidence that Lewis' and Tolkien's works are "literary", a major portion

[13] Ibid., pp. 67, 68.
[14] Ibid., pp. 113–14.
[15] Ibid., p. 112.
[16] These works are, of course, fantasies in the literary sense of fantasy, but do not characteristically inspire delusion, morbid castle-building or egoistic castle-building, for reasons that are clear enough from Lewis' discussion.

of the sale of Tolkien's *Lord of the Rings* trilogy and Lewis' space trilogy is in college bookstores, and a great number of college students and faculty members seem to have read and enjoyed one or both. But this, it might be argued, is true also of *Playboy*. More important is the evidence from various sources that many who have read either Tolkien's or Lewis' fictional works return to them for frequent rereadings and find in them a reading experience of great importance. As Peter Beagle, a brilliant young novelist and observer of the American scene,[17] writes in an introduction to a collection of Tolkien's shorter pieces:

> *The Lord of the Rings* and its prologue, *The Hobbit*, belong, in my experience, to a small group of books and poems and songs that I have truly shared with other people. The strangest strangers turn out to know it, and we talk about Gandalf and mad Gollum and the bridge of Khazad-dûm while the party or the classroom or the train rattles along unheard. Old friends rediscover it, as I do—to browse through any book of the *Ring* trilogy is to get hooked once more into the whole legend—and we talk of it at once as though we had just read it for the first time, and as though we were remembering something that had happened to us together long ago. Something of ourselves has gone into reading it, and so it belongs to us.[18]

Stella Gibbons, a novelist perhaps best known for her wickedly delightful satire *Cold Comfort Farm*, says of Lewis' imaginative writing that science fiction

[17] To substantiate the first claim, look at his novels, *A Fine and Private Place* and *The Last Unicorn*. For the second, see his *I See by My Outfit*. All are published by Ballantine Books, New York.

[18] Peter Beagle, "Tolkien's Magic Ring", an introduction to *The Tolkien Reader* (New York: Ballantine Books, 2001), pp. ix–xii. The piece originally appeared in *Holiday* (1966).

in the right hands . . . can appear what she truly is: Poetry's younger sister. Lewis had those right hands. His three novels of science fiction . . . hold all that we ask of this kind of story and they are also poetry; of a very old, pure, and satisfying kind, and packed with allegory and myth. . . .

Lewis as a writer of imaginative fiction had superb authority. . . . What can be more astonishing than to imagine the soil and scents and noises on a speck of fire millions of miles from the Earth so vividly that the reader can actually feel a nostalgia for them, as if they had been personally experienced? But even more marvelous are Lewis's accounts of the creatures that live on Malacandra. In their creation, his gift soars until it touches the fringes of that region in Shakespeare's nature out of which the poet drew Ariel and Caliban.[19]

It would be easy enough to multiply such testimony, but it is also easy enough to prove to yourself that Lewis' and Tolkien's books permit and invite good reading.

Perhaps surprisingly, none of the works as a whole is a myth in Lewis' sense. Beagle describes Tolkien's book as embodying "a legend". Gibbons describes Lewis' books as "packed with allegory and myth". But it is fairly obvious that neither set of stories is "extra-literary" in the sense that its plot has a value completely independent of its embodiment. Other criteria of Lewis are not satisfied: neither human sympathy nor the comic element is lacking. I think, however, that we are tempted to use such words as "myth" or "legend" (both in their dictionary sense appropriate only to "a traditional story of unknown authorship . . . handed down for generations"), because both Lewis' stories and Tolkien's satisfy the last criterion Lewis lists for

[19] Stella Gibbons, "Imaginative Writing", in *Light on C. S. Lewis*, ed. Jocelyn Gibb et al. (New York: Harcourt, Brace and World, 1966), pp. 87, 89.

myth: "We feel it to be numinous. It is as if something of great moment had been communicated to us." We may note, however, that myths in Lewis' sense may be part of the total machinery of a Lewis or Tolkien story. In discussing myth, Lewis gives among his examples the conception of the Ents and of Lothlórien from *The Lord of the Rings* trilogy. Similar mythical substructures could easily be found in Lewis' books.

Tolkien and Lewis use, in different ways, realism of presentation. This is obvious enough in Lewis' case. His vivid descriptions of extraterrestrial scenes and nonhuman entities, the acute observation of character, the realism of the dialogue, all make it easy to suspend disbelief. Stella Gibbons notes with delight, "How skillfully he introduced what may be called the 'stiffening' into these tales, the introduction of *invented fact*—in some cases of actual fact—to give credibility to the incredible!" [20]

One amusing instance of this is the way in which Ransom, the imaginary hero of *Out of the Silent Planet*, is linked to the real Lewis, who appears as a minor character in the last chapter of the story. Lewis supposedly writes to Ransom, a philologist, and asks him about the word *Oyarses*, which occurs in the twelfth-century Platonist Bernardus Silvestris: "I asked C.J. about it and he says it ought to be *Ousiarches*. That of course would make sense, but I do not feel quite satisfied. Have you by any chance ever come across a word like *Oyarses*?" [21] Ransom has, in the story: Oyarsa is the title of the tutelary spirit or "intelligence" of the planet Malacandra (Mars). Now look at Lewis' perfectly serious and scholarly work, *The Allegory of Love*, which made

---

[20] Ibid., p. 88.
[21] C.S. Lewis, *Out of the Silent Planet* (New York: Scribner, 2003), p. 151.

his reputation as a scholar of medieval and Renaissance literature. "In Bernardus Sylvestris, on reaching the *aplanon* or sphere of the fixed stars, we have the following: Illic Oyarses quidem erat at genius.... The name *Oyarses*, as Professor C. C. J. Webb has pointed out to me, must be a corruption of ουσιαρχης; and he has kindly drawn my attention to Pseudo-Apuleius Asclepius (xix), where the ousiarch of the fixed stars ..." [22]

This is almost art for art's sake—not one out of a hundred of the readers of *Out of the Silent Planet* would be likely to know that passage from *The Allegory of Love*. But it helps the air of authenticity Lewis created so well that people often wrote him to ask if *Out of the Silent Planet* was a true story. This was part of the same element in Lewis' character that made him translate passages from Latin authors into sixteenth-century English, since "[w]hen passages from Calvin, Scalinger or Erasmus in modern English jostle passages from vernacular authors with all the flavour of their period about them, it is fatally easy to get the feeling that the Latinists are somehow more enlightened, less remote, less limited by their age than those who wrote English." [23] How few authors, other than Lewis, could have seen the danger, remedied it so brilliantly, or have thought to apologize that he had not done the translation to sixteenth-century English "simply for the fun of it"!

With Tolkien we get apparently a rather different situation. One criticism made of Tolkien is that his language is general, unspecific, not evocative of particular images unlike

[22] C. S. Lewis, *The Allegory of Love* (New York: Oxford University Press, 1925), p. 362.

[23] C. S. Lewis, *English Literature in the Sixteenth Century excluding Drama* (New York: Oxford University Press, 1954), preface.

that of D. H. Lawrence, for example.[24] But Tolkien writes in this way on theory and of set purpose. As some scattered remarks make clear, Tolkien distrusts overspecific description in fantasy for the same reason he is wary of pictures in such books: both have the effect of dragooning the imagination, forcing us to see the scene in a certain way.

> However good in themselves, illustrations do little good to fairy-stories. The radical distinction between all art (including drama) that offers a *visible* presentation and true literature is that it imposes one visible form. Literature works from mind to mind and is thus more progenitive. It is at once more universal and more poignantly particular. If it speaks of *bread* or *wine* or *stone* or *tree*, it appeals to the whole of these things, to their ideas; yet each hearer will give to them a peculiar personal embodiment in his imagination. Should the story say "he ate bread," the dramatic producer or painter can only show "a piece of bread" according to his taste or fancy, but the hearer of the story will think of bread in general and picture it in some form of his own. If a story says "he climbed a hill and saw a river in the valley below," the illustrator may catch, or nearly catch, his own vision of such a scene; but every hearer of the words will have his own picture, and it will be made out of all the hills and rivers and dales he has ever seen, but specially out of The Hill, The River, The Valley which were for him the first embodiment of the word.[25]

On this view Tolkien understandably avoids specificity of description. In this rather compressed discussion (it occurs

---

[24] Cf. Burton Raffell, "*The Lord of the Rings* as Literature", in *Tolkien and the Critics*, ed. Neil D. Isaacs and Rose A. Zimbardo (Notre Dame, Ind.: University of Notre Dame Press, 1968), p. 223.

[25] J. R. R. Tolkien, "On Fairy-Stories", in *Tree and Leaf*, in *The Tolkien Reader* (New York: Ballantine Books, 2001), p. 96.

in a note to the essay) Tolkien perhaps exaggerates the difference between pictorial art and literature in general. But
certainly the generality of his descriptions is intentional, at
worst the result of a mistaken theory, not of a failure to
realize a need or satisfy a felt need. Incidentally, his critic
gives an unintentional example of the pitfalls of overspec-
ificity; the critic's example of vivid description is "shiny
new Grand Rapids furniture". In an informal poll of my
students, none knew what Grand Rapids furniture was or
might be like!

Tolkien, like Lewis, provides "stiffening" to his fantasy
by linking it with his own scholarly interests—the study of
ancient manuscripts and ancient languages. In the Appendices to *The Lord of the Rings*, Tolkien provides an elaborate
background to the main story: its supposed sources in such
imaginary manuscripts as the Red Book of Westmarch, the
full story of legends and histories alluded to in the story,
and a discussion of the languages, names, and alphabets used
in the story. Part of the story's delight, whether we read the
Appendices or not, is the careful work that has gone into
this background. Imitators of Tolkien merely give us a mosaic
of strange names and strange stories, drawn from various
sources, which do not "hang together" in the way in which
Tolkien's names do. An Elvish name in Tolkien is perspic-
uously Elvish, a Dwarvish name noticeably unlike Elvish
names and like other Dwarvish ones. Tolkien's characters
always speak and act in character, not only personally (Gandalf always acts Gandalflike) but, so to speak, *racially* (Legolas and Galadriel are both in their own way Elvish). The
customs, legends, and histories of the Rohirrim are of a
piece with each other and with their names. (Tolkien helps
himself here by drawing some of the Rohan material from
real Anglo-Saxon words and customs.) Some of us enjoy

"going behind the scenes" and seeing the careful work that gives us this sense of authenticity. But all who enjoy Tolkien are enjoying in part the fruits of this meticulous preparation. Tolkien's realism of presentation, though unlike Lewis' in some ways, is equally striking.

On Lewis' theory, the imaginative works of Tolkien and of Lewis himself come out with very high marks, and that is clear enough; certainly they are read in the "literary" way by many readers and have values far beyond those of simple narrative. But, one might cynically claim, the theory may have been designed for just that purpose and have no real support. On the theory, the books are good, but is the theory good? Lewis' thesis in *An Experiment in Criticism* is essentially that any book that allows and invites good reading is a good book. Many people would admit the converse of this, that any good book allows and invites good reading. It would seem hard to defend the contradictory, that some good books neither allow nor invite good reading. But some people might want to claim that some books that allow and invite good reading are not good books.

Let us see how this may be done. We must reject at the outset any confusion of the contradictory of Lewis' thesis with the mere assertion that some books that are read with enjoyment are not good books. Lewis' discussion explicitly allows for this—a book may be enjoyed because it satisfies a desire for egoistic castle-building, or a desire for mere thrills, and so on. But such motives for enjoyment will not satisfy the criteria Lewis has set down for good reading. For example, those who read merely for thrills will not reread, and those who read for egoistic castle-building will not choose fantasy.

Any theory, however, which denied *any* connection between enjoyment and literature would thereby reduce itself to absurdity. So it must be that any viable criticism of Lewis' theory would have to show that there are enjoyable experiences of reading—not reducible to ego satisfaction or thrill-seeking and therefore superficially like "genuine" literary experience—which fail some important test of genuineness. Notice that such a criticism cannot deny the enjoyment or reduce it to the *obviously* nonliterary (thrill-seeking, etc.) without conflicting with fact. Thus, such a criticism is not like the accusation that Jack is not attracted to Jill at all, or the accusation that he merely lusts after her. It is, rather, like the accusation that he does not *really* love her. (Perhaps he is merely "in love with love" or is in love with an imaginary person of his own creation.)

It seems to me there are several grounds on which critics have argued that the works of Lewis and Tolkien give merely "pseudoliterary" enjoyment and that these would cover most of the plausible grounds for calling enjoyment of a book "pseudoliterary". It might be alleged that one's enjoyment of a book was pseudoliterary (1) because of banality, (2) because of propaganda, or (3) because while purporting to satisfy literary needs it is, in fact, valued for satisfying psychological or emotional needs (e.g., for reassurance). We will consider these accusations in turn.

1. *The accusation of banality.* The word "banal" neatly wraps up a series of accusations made against Tolkien and Lewis by their critics. "Banal" can mean "trite", "hackneyed", "commonplace", or "trivial". Furthermore, the accusation of banality may refer to either language or ideas. The basic assumption behind the accusation of banality seems to be that new ways of expression and new ideas are always to be preferred to old. Now "this is newer than that, therefore this is superior to that" is, as it stands, a plain non sequitur.

With regard to language, presumably the bridge between "this is newer" and "this is better" is the supposed principle that new ways of expression invariably do a better job of conveying ideas, impressions, and emotions. But this principle seems to be merely false. Aside from the difficulties it leads to in dealing with much recognized great literature (e.g., the use of stock epithets in Homer), the principle seems to be simply an expression of naïve, chronological provincialism: "You must not make people in your book talk that way because this is not the way people talk now."

An allied accusation is that the language in, for example, *The Lord of the Rings* is "derivative", full of echoes of other literature. This general type of accusation was elegantly put by Samuel Johnson. Boswell questioned him about some poems. "Boswell: Is there not imagination in them, Sir? Johnson: Why Sir, there is in them what *was* imagination, but it is no more imagination in *him* than sound is sound in the echo. And his diction too is not his own. We have long ago seen *white-robed innocence* and *flower-bespangled meads*." [26] Of course, this is a highly relative matter. If you have not read the other literature you will miss the echoes, and if you read *The Hobbit* before *Beowulf*, the dragon in *Beowulf* is likely to remind you of Smaug rather than vice versa. But again there is a principle behind the accusation, the principle that originality is valuable in itself and lack of originality vitiates any other merits a work may have. Yet, prevalent as this assumption is, it seems also to be false. Originality in itself does not make a work good, for a work can be a failure in an entirely new way. Complete originality is impossible; any work has a great deal in common with works that have gone before. Furthermore, originality

---

[26] *Boswell's Life of Johnson*, Tuesday, July 5, 1763.

is a matter of degree; a completely unoriginal work would have to be an exact copy of another work. Traditional material traditionally treated occurs in many admittedly great works of literature. The idea that interesting work can no longer be done in some traditional form is always open to refutation by counterexample.

But there is also a confusion here between two kinds of unoriginality. Tolkien is unoriginal in his images in one way, original in another. He is unoriginal in that he uses familiar associations—light with goodness, darkness with evil, for example. And as Lewis says in *The Allegory of Love*: "It is of the very nature of thought and language to represent what is immaterial in picturable terms. What is good or happy has always been high like the heavens and bright like the sun. Evil and misery were deep and dark from the first. Pain is black in Homer and goodness is a middle point for Alfred no less than for Aristotle. To ask how these married pairs of sensibles and insensibles first came together would be a great folly; the real question is how they ever came apart." [27]

However, the use Tolkien makes of these familiar images is far from unoriginal. Lewis, in *A Preface to Paradise Lost*, makes a similar point about Milton.

> There is, furthermore, a special reason why mythical poetry ought not to attempt novelty in respect of its ingredients. What it does with the ingredients may be as novel as you please. But giants, dragons, paradises, gods, and the like are themselves the expression of certain basic elements in man's spiritual experience. In that sense they are more like words— the words of a language which speaks the else unspeakable— than they are like the people and places in a novel. To give

[27] Lewis, *Allegory of Love*, p. 44.

them radically new characters is not so much original as ungrammatical.... The whole art consists not in evoking the unexpected, but in evoking with a perfection and accuracy beyond expectation the very image that has haunted us all our lives. The marvel about Milton's Paradise or Milton's Hell is simply that they are there—that the thing has at last been done—that our dream stands before us and does not melt. Not many poets can thus draw out leviathan with a hook. Compared with this the short-lived pleasure of any novelty the poet might have inserted would be a mere kickshaw.[28]

Perhaps the strongest accusation that can be made under the head of banality of language may be seen by looking at the dictionary meaning of "trite"—"worn out by constant use, no longer having freshness, originality or novelty; hackneyed, stale". But certainly such an accusation completely fails to apply to Tolkien or Lewis; far from being worn out by *constant* use, the "high style" sometimes used by Tolkien and Lewis is almost never seen in other contemporary literature. In Tolkien especially there are parallels to what Lewis, in discussing Milton, describes as

the "grandeur" or "elevation" of the style.... This grandeur is produced mainly by three things. (1) The use of slightly unfamiliar words and construction, including archaisms. (2) The use of proper names, not solely nor chiefly for their sound, but because they are the names of splendid, remote, terrible, voluptuous, or celebrated things. They are there to encourage a sweep of the reader's eye over the richness and variety of the world—to supply that *largior aether* which we breathe as long as the poem lasts. (3) Continued allusion to all the sources of heightened interest in our sense

[28] C. S. Lewis, *A Preface to Paradise Lost* (London: Oxford University Press, 1942), pp. 57–58.

experience (light, darkness, storm, flowers, jewels, sexual love, and the like).[29]

Archaisms, richness, and variety of proper names and imagery taken from sense experiences are all highly characteristic of Tolkien's works.

When we come to supposed banality of ideas, the idea that novelty or originality is the sole criterion is even sillier. Presumably anyone given a choice between truth or originality would choose truth. But both Lewis and Tolkien have been accused of putting forward ideas that are banal in the sense of being commonplace or trivial, on the order of "good is nice and evil is nasty." That this is false can be seen simply by looking at the list of themes in the last chapter. Every one of the themes we found in Tolkien and Lewis, far from being a commonplace, was directly contradicted by the characteristic modern view of the world. And the differences, far from being trivial, went to the root of one's view of life. Furthermore, the view that Tolkien and Lewis utter mere trivial commonplaces is completely contradictory to the next accusation—propagandizing— though it is often made by the same critics. Let us, then, examine this second charge.

2. *The accusation of propaganda.* The accusation that the works of Tolkien, or more especially those of Lewis, are vitiated by propagandistic aims can hardly be the accusation that they contain a characteristic view of life or that they take a position for or against certain things. For if this prevented a work from being literature, many admittedly great works of literature (Lucretius, Dante, and Dostoyevsky, for example)

[29] Ibid., pp. 40–41.

would be disqualified. The accusation, then, must be that the propaganda is so overdone that it detracts from the literary value of the work and can be applauded only by partisans of a cause. This accusation is at least partly refuted by the fact that Lewis and Tolkien are admired by intelligent readers and critics who are entirely out of sympathy with their basic assumptions and ideas. Since Tolkien is less explicit than Lewis about some of his deep convictions, critics sometimes attempt to interpret him as "really" sympathetic in whole or in part to their views. This is much harder to do with Lewis, but many readers totally out of sympathy with his ideas have nevertheless admired him.[30]

In fact, the accusation of propaganda seems to come most often from those violently opposed to Lewis' and Tolkien's basic conviction and afraid of their apparent success in making them attractive to others. It is thus not really a literary criticism at all but a philosophical one: "These ideas are false and you do a disservice by propagating them." But philosophical criticism must be backed by argument, and those who accuse Lewis and Tolkien of propaganda are notably short of arguments for their view. Indeed, their main techniques seem to be direct and indirect sneers and more or less flat assertions that certain ideas cannot be believed.[31] Such devices are unlikely to persuade any person not already persuaded, and even he may

[30] See, for example, Gilbert Highet's "From World to World" in *People, Places and Books* (New York: Oxford University Press, 1953).

[31] Some notable practitioners of these techniques are Catherine Stimpson, *J. R. R. Tolkien* (New York: Columbia University Press, 1969); William Ready, *Understanding Tolkien and the Lord of the Rings* (New York: Warner Paperback Library, 1973), orig. title: *The Tolkien Relation*; and Mary Ellman, "Growing Up Hobbitic", *New American Review*, no. 2, New American Library (1968). Their main target is Tolkien, but there are oblique attacks on Lewis, especially in Ready.

feel some embarrassment if this is the best his champion can do.

3. *The accusation of wish-fulfillment.* This is a curious accusation, for presumably hardly anyone gives primary belief to Tolkien's Middle-earth or its inhabitants, and those who believe in explicitly Christian ideas occurring in Lewis have ground for their belief outside of Lewis' fictional works. Those who seek reassurance will surely look for it in new or established religions or philosophies, which make a claim to primary belief, and not in explicitly fictional works, which lay claim only to secondary belief. Of course, any vividly imagined work may produce primary belief in the unsophisticated or unstable, but this is as true of Homer as of Tolkien, or as true of Dante as of Lewis.

I think these sorts of accusations do point to some weak places in Lewis' theory, some possibilities he has not considered. Someone may read a book in the "literary" way, yet it may be true that the book he enjoys is a mere imitation of better works with which he is unfamiliar. Someone may misunderstand his delight in seeing agreeable views well expressed, or his pleasure in wishful thinking for literary enjoyment. But these holes in Lewis' theory are easily plugged, and when they are, the theory is left stronger than before. The approach of judging books by the kind of reading they admit and invite seems more and more attractive as we probe and test it.

And after all, what alternative is there to Lewis' theory? Even if we were ready to hand over our judgment of literature to experts, the experts disagree. If there are clear criteria (different from Lewis') of literary worth, what are they and who has managed to state and support them? The philosopher, used to clear distinctions and exhaustive argumentation, finds a notable lack of both in most writers about literature. He finds a plethora of confident assertions and a paucity of reasonable backing—except in Lewis.

Of course, to substantiate this point fully would lead us into a complete survey of the present state of aesthetics and the philosophy of literature, which is too much to undertake here. Still, lacking such a survey I fling out at least a challenge: Lewis' theory is clear and well reasoned; it seems to cover the facts on which there is general agreement and to argue persuasively for its distinctive theses. No alternative theory known to me is a serious rival to Lewis'. There may be better theories, but one would have to see the argument.

Finally, as we have seen, both Lewis' and Tolkien's imaginative works come off well by the standards of Lewis' theory. For some readers, at least, if any theory of literature ruled out Lewis' and Tolkien's imaginative works as good books this would in itself be a damaging criticism of that theory. Books are good in different ways, but in their own way the books of Lewis and Tolkien are very good indeed.

# 3

# Language, Mind, and Character

In any voyage from world to world, language is a problem. If you go to Mars or to elfland, are the Martians or elves to speak English or are you to speak their language? If the first, how do you explain the fact to them? And if the second, how do you prevent the learning of the alien language from delaying or obstructing your story? In a children's book you need not face this problem. In Lewis' Chronicles the Talking Beasts of Narnia, the Witch Jadis from the dying world of Charn, the Persianlike Calormenes all apparently speak English (or, if not, the English children who are the heroes and heroines of the stories magically understand whatever they do speak). In *The Hobbit*, Elves, Dwarves, trolls, and goblins all speak a language intelligible to each other and to Bilbo the hobbit. But in an adult world this will not do. The "language problem" must be solved.

Lewis and Tolkien solve it, each in characteristic ways. Tolkien supposes a "Common Speech" spoken by Hobbits and Men, but constantly uses invented languages with characteristic proper and place names, so that snatches of identifiable Elvish or Orcish language can be used for literary effect. Lewis makes Ransom's learning of one Martian language an important part of his plot in *Out of the Silent Planet* and provides a plausible reason why that language is the Martian *lingua franca*—it is the literary and poetic language, so the scientists and craftsmen, who can express their ideas in any language, learn it. But then, to avoid introducing a new language for Venus, Lewis blandly tells us that the Martian literary language, after all, is a sort of interplanetary *lingua franca*. (The idea of a common language for unfallen creatures may or may not be plausible, but Lewis gives no hint of this when he first talks about the Martian languages.) To defend this device he builds into the story a plot element consisting of a primitive or magical theory of language (that certain sounds are innately suited to certain meanings), which he then uses to good effect in the climax of his story. This is turning one's difficulties into advantages with a vengeance!

To think that Lewis seriously believed in this "magical" theory of language would be a serious mistake, on a par with thinking that he gave primary belief to other plot devices such as the medieval theory of the planet's character and influence or the magical powers of Merlin. No one I know of has made this mistake about Lewis, but an exactly parallel mistake has been made about Tolkien. Because as part of his machinery Tolkien invents a liquid, flowing language for the Elves and a harsh dissonant language for the Orcs and other villains, he has been accused, with some degree of seriousness, of thinking the letter *l* morally preferable to the letter *k*.[1]

Aside from such devices, however, both Lewis and Tolkien have some serious points to make about language that

---

[1] Mary Ellman, "Growing Up Hobbitic", in *New American Review*, no. 2, New American Library (1968): 227; Catherine Stimpson, *J. R. R. Tolkien* (New York: Columbia University Press, 1969), p. 5. Both ignore the fact that Dwarvish as well as Orcish speech abounds in *k*.

are well worth examining. For Lewis there is almost an identification of language with rationality. The Talking Beasts of Narnia—Beavers, Owls, and Mice, for example—are larger than ordinary beasts of the same kind and may even live in houses, use tools, and have political organizations and allegiances. But their real differentia is that they are *Talking* Beasts. The evil beasts punished by Aslan in the Narnian "last judgment" lose the gift of speech and with it rationality, memory—and immortality!

A more sophisticated version of the same idea occurs in the scene where Ransom meets his first Martian creature.

> The huge, seal-like creature seated beside him became unbearably ominous. It seemed friendly; but it was very big, very black, and he knew nothing at all about it. . . . Was it really as rational as it appeared?
>
> . . . These sudden losses of confidence . . . arose when the rationality of the *hross* tempted you to think of it as a man. Then it became abominable—a man seven feet high, with a snaky body, covered, face and all, with thick black animal hair, and whiskered like a cat. But starting from the other end you had an animal with everything an animal ought to have—glossy coat, liquid eye, sweet breath and whitest teeth—and added to all these, as though Paradise had never been lost and earliest dreams were true, the charm of speech and reason.[2]

We will return to this identification of speech and rationality in due course, but let us now explore Tolkien's attitude toward language. There are no really "talking beasts" (in Lewis' sense) in Tolkien if you except Smaug the dragon, a formidable personality and not really a "beast". But each rational species— Elf, Dwarf, Ent, Man, and Hobbit, Orc, and Troll—has its

[2] C. S. Lewis, *Out of the Silent Planet* (New York: Scribner, 2003), p. 59.

own language and its own way of expressing itself. If we say that for Lewis speech is rationality, then for Tolkien speech is personality. The noble speak nobly, the evil speak evilly. This has aroused the derision of some critics who cannot rid themselves of the modern equation of sincerity with incoherence or the modern belief that there is some virtue in everyone speaking as badly as everyone else. The idea that incoherence is a necessary characteristic of ordinary speech would be equally strange to Irishmen, Iroquois, and Zulus (all nations with a tradition of oratory on great occasions or small), but the idea is prevalent in many modern cultures, especially English-speaking ones. This becomes part of the expectations of many critics when they look for realism of presentation, and, not finding this, they ignore the subtler sort of realism that is to be found in Tolkien.

Lewis' departures from pseudonaturalism in this respect are less obvious than Tolkien's, but equally real. What Stella Gibbons says of Lewis could equally be said of Tolkien, "Each being talks as such a being would." This is, of course, unrealistic in the sense that, in "real life", speech is not *always* a revelation of character. But it is such a revelation much more often than most moderns realize.

There is a red herring here that needs to be cleared away. In their children's books, where they are more limited by the form in which they have chosen to write, both Tolkien and Lewis use differences in English style to mark differences in language. Thus, for example, Lewis' Calormenes talk a stately dialect reminiscent of some English translations or imitations of Persian or Arabian authors. Now if Narnia were like our world, the Calormenes would presumably speak a different language than the Narnians; this is what Lewis wants to suggest by his use of the "dialect", at the same time avoiding complications unnecessary in a story of the sort he is writing. For similar reasons, Tolkien makes the trolls met by Bilbo in *The Hobbit* speak a sort of cockney dialect. One of his more humorless critics has austerely criticized him for this. "[Bilbo] speaks standard English but [the trolls] speak filthy rough, working-class Cockney. Recently, of course, musical groups have shown us the wit and poetry of working-class English speech."[3] I am afraid that Miss Stimpson meant that last line not as a joke, but as a serious rebuke to Tolkien, and the complex of misunderstandings it reveals would need a whole chapter to unravel.

Let me try to deal with this misunderstanding as briefly as it deserves. For certain purposes, Tolkien has pictured unpleasant characters as talking in a certain way. Presumably, the accusation being made is that by so doing he suggests that all those who talk in this way are unpleasant characters. (The parallel accusation for Lewis would be that all those who say things like "O my father and O the delight of my eyes ..." are likely to worship monstrous bird-headed gods, which is even more obviously silly.) But the false conversion is the critics' and not Tolkien's. From the relatively limited resources of English dialect, Tolkien has chosen to make the trolls speak rather like Bill Sykes. But it is only the critics who are silly enough to suggest that he means that all those who talk in this way are likely to act like Bill Sykes. (By the way, the real villain of *The Hobbit*, Smaug the dragon, speaks elegant English.)

The point is perhaps worth pursuing into the more complex relation of speech to character in the adult books. Tolkien describes the Orcs as limited in vocabulary and harsh in expression. "It is said that they had no language of their

---

[3] Stimpson, *J. R. R. Tolkien*, p. 13.

own, but took what they could of other tongues and perverted it to their own liking; yet they make only brutal jargons, scarcely sufficient for their own needs, unless it were for curses and abuse. And these creatures, being filled with malice, hating even their own kind, quickly developed as many barbarous dialects as there were groups or settlements of their race." [4] This "invented fact" has the plot advantage that Orcs of different groups must converse in Common Speech, so that Merry and Pippin in Book Three, Chapter 11, or Sam in Book Six, Chapter 1, can understand what Orcs are saying. It is also connected with the concept of the Orcs as purely evil creatures, the "anti-race" of the Elves, which we will speak of in Chapter 5 below. But the more complex and more important villains—Smaug and Saruman, for example—are masters of language (used, of course, for their own evil purposes).

> Suddenly another voice [Saruman's] spoke, low and melodious, its very sound an enchantment. Those who listened unwarily to that voice could seldom report the words that they heard; and if they did, they wondered, for little power remained in them. Mostly they remembered only that it was a delight to hear the voice speaking, all that it said seemed wise and reasonable, and desire awoke in them by swift agreement to seem wise themselves. When others spoke they seemed harsh and uncouth by contrast; and if they gainsaid the voice, anger was kindled in the hearts of those under the spell. . . . None were unmoved; none rejected its pleas and its commands without an effort of mind and will, so long as its master had control of it. [5]

[4] J. R. R. Tolkien, *The Return of the King* (New York: Ballantine Books, 2001), p. 457.

[5] J. R. R. Tolkien, *The Two Towers*, rev. ed. (New York: Ballantine Books, 2001), p. 216.

Notice that this is a misuse of language to control and enchant, propaganda to the nth degree. But the simple equation of those who speak "well" with the heroes and those who speak "badly" with the villains is obviously destroyed by the counterexamples of Smaug and Saruman, so far as Tolkien is concerned. The sense in which the villains speak "badly" is a purely moral sense and has distinguished authority: "Out of the abundance of the heart the mouth speaks" (Mt 12:34).

The clearest example of the same theme in Lewis' work is the Un-man in *Perelandra*. In tempting the Green Lady, the Un-man can use argument and imagery subtly to weave half-truths, and cloudy images. He speaks "well" in the sense of speaking subtly and effectively. "It showed plenty of subtlety and intelligence when talking to the Lady; but Ransom soon perceived that it regarded intelligence simply and solely as a weapon, which it had no more wish to employ in its off-duty hours than a soldier has to do bayonet practice when he is on leave. Thought was for it a device necessary to certain ends, but thought in itself did not interest it." [6]

Incidentally, the two passages I have quoted are an excellent example of Tolkien's and Lewis' contrasted but equally real masteries of style. Lewis' is more "modern"; the excellence of the metaphor about bayonet practice is the sort of excellence to which the modern critic is awake. But Tolkien's prose casts its own kind of spell, of which occasional archaisms like "gainsaid" are a part. Notice the frequent use of words such as "wise", "power", "heart", "enchantment" or "spell", which have ancient and complex associations for the reader. Here we find Tolkien making use in practice of

[6] C. S. Lewis, *Perelandra* (New York: Scribner, 2003), pp. 109–10.

something Lewis has discussed and defended in theory: the use of "stock responses".

For Lewis and Tolkien, it is both desirable and legitimate to make use of certain words and ideas that arouse an almost automatic response and to call on a great complex of traditional ideas. For example, to use "the sword of the king" as a metaphor for the power of the state is to make use of certain traditional attitudes and emotions. It is to remind ourselves of Solomon or Arthur, to hear echoes of St. Paul or Christ. The modern tendency is to assume that such responses *because* they are traditional are bound to be outworn, to have no profound emotional echoes. Tolkien (in much of what he wrote) and Lewis (in some of what he wrote) seem to me to provide a counterexample to this thesis for those with eyes to see. Used badly, the traditional imagery fails; used well it can still stir us. Modern imagery can equally fail; "the clubs and machine guns of the Fascist dictators" as a metaphor for state power regarded unfavorably can become a mere rhetorical cliché, arousing no particular response except boredom.

Lewis, in the first chapter of *The Abolition of Man*, argues that training of our responses to certain ideas (which to a degree means to certain words and phrases) is an indispensable part of a fully human life. Tolkien to some extent presumes responses trained in this way, to some extent offers such a training for those whose hearts are open to it. The "debunking" of Tolkien by certain critics has a great deal in common with the debunking of certain stock responses that Lewis discusses.

But certainly, if stock responses are not to be mere conditioned reflexes imposed on us for certain purposes, they must have some validity. This is the traditional idea, which Lewis defends.

Until quite modern times all teachers and even all men believed the universe to be such that certain emotional reactions on our part could be either congruous or incongruous to it—believed in fact that objects did not merely receive, but could *merit*, our approval or disapproval, our reverence or our contempt.... The little human animal will not at first have the right responses. It must be trained to feel pleasure, liking, disgust, and hatred at those things which really are pleasant, likeable, disgusting, and hateful....

. . . . . . . . . . . . . . . . . . . . . . . . . . . . . . . . . . . . . . . . . . . . . . . . . . . . . .

... Reason in man must rule the mere appetites by means of the "spirited element." [7]

Now when Lewis pictures the evil crew at Belbury and contrasts them with Ransom's companions at St. Anne's, or when Tolkien subtly contrasts and compares Elves and Orcs, the author is using literary means to exaggerate and thereby reinforce certain responses. Malice, treachery, and lying really are detestable, and in Lord Feverstone or Saruman we see them to be so. Friendship, humor, speaking well, and living well really are admirable; in Ransom or Elrond we sharpen our appreciation of them. This has caused some to accuse Tolkien and Lewis of "moral didacticism", but it is not, rightly understood, a charge either would reject—though, as Lewis said of Milton, we may sometimes be in "danger of supposing that the poet was inculcating a rule when in fact he was enamoured of a perfection".

One element of the effort to show the admirable as admirable and the detestable as detestable is making the admirable speak admirably and the detestable speak detestably. In their different ways, Lewis and Tolkien do this with great success.

[7] C. S. Lewis, *The Abolition of Man* (San Francisco: HarperCollins, 2001), pp. 14–16.

To return for a moment to the mistaken idea we discussed earlier, it does not follow from this effort that those who speak detestably are detestable. If a man's discourse drips with filthy oaths and shows a poverty of invention and sympathy, it may or may not mark a moral fault. Unfortunate background or early training may remove most or all culpability from him. And a lady who with elegance, invention, and something approaching lyricism backbites, gossips, and denigrates may be morally a hundred times worse, even if the man's language is culpable. Nor is "lower-class" language the issue; Sam speaks like a gardener and is a hero, Denethor speaks like a king and is a villain.

In the last analysis, however, the expectation that character will reveal itself in speech is a not unreasonable one. Speech, while not the only clue to character, *is* a clue to character. Those who fail to realize this are missing one part of the truth.

The use Tolkien and Lewis make of language in their fiction grows out of their professional concern with language, in interesting ways. Tolkien's field of specialization is Anglo-Saxon, and some of the things he is known for professionally are an annotated edition of the Middle English poem *Sir Gawain and the Green Knight* and a perceptive analysis of *Beowulf* and its critics.[8] The study of Anglo-Saxon itself would, I think, have some tendency to influence any imaginative person to think of roots and origins, the means by which language molds and is molded by history. The way in which modern English is built on an Anglo-Saxon

[8] J. R. R. Tolkien and E. V. Gordon, eds., *Sir Gawain and the Green Knight*, 2nd ed. (New York: Oxford University Press, 1925, 1967); J. R. R. Tolkien, "Beowulf: The Monsters and the Critics", most easily available in *An Anthology of Beowulf Criticism*, ed. Lewis E. Nicholson (Notre Dame, Ind.: University of Notre Dame Press, 1963).

foundation with Latin, French, and other borrowings, the way in which an Anglo-Saxon word (*cwik*, for example) can change and evolve over a period of time, has a tendency to remind us of how the present is based on the past and of the great gulf of history that lies behind us. Tolkien's chronologies, histories, and legends in *The Lord of the Rings* trilogy surely owe something to this habit of mind.

Furthermore, as a philologist, a man professionally concerned with language itself, Tolkien is fascinated by words and their combinations. Some of the more imaginative of us may have made up imaginary worlds, like the land of Boxen C. S. Lewis and his brother created as children.[9] We may have started with certain characters, created by ourselves or borrowed from literature (my own children took Pooh and Piglet on imaginary adventures through space), and then found ourselves creating a country and a society for them, and finally as an afterthought perhaps some place names and a few scraps of a language. By his own account, Tolkien's imagination worked the other way, to some extent, in the creation of *The Lord of the Rings* trilogy. Fascinated by imagined languages, he began to create a world for the languages to be spoken in. This reversal of the usual process is perhaps not fully understandable to those who have not themselves felt the fascination of language or the pleasures of creating a language of one's own.

The Middle English poem *Gawain* and the Anglo-Saxon epic *Beowulf* also probably played their part in influencing Tolkien's imagination. In *Sir Gawain and the Green Knight*, a monstrous green man, riding a green horse, appears at King Arthur's court at Christmas time. The king is delaying his

---

[9] See W. H. Lewis' memoir of his brother in *Letters of C. S. Lewis* (London: Collins, 1966).

feast until some remarkable incident shall have occurred. The Green Knight challenges any one of the knights at the Round Table to trade blow for blow, using a monstrous axe he carries. The king rashly accepts the challenge but is forestalled by his nephew Gawain, who takes the wager on his uncle's behalf. Gawain strikes a mighty blow and beheads the Green Knight, but the monster picks up his head and charges Gawain to seek him out in a year and a day to receive the return blow. Gawain has to search out the monster's lair, the Green Chapel, and a few days before he is due to meet the knight he arrives at a nearby castle. The lord of the castle, Bercilac, and his wife entertain Gawain courteously, but Bercilac makes a bargain with Gawain to exchange whatever each gains during Gawain's stay at the castle.

For three days Bercilac goes out to hunt, and Gawain is left at the castle with his wife. The wife attempts to seduce Gawain, who resists her advances and keeps his bargain with her husband by passing on to Bercilac the kisses Gawain has received from his wife. But on the last day the lady tempts Gawain with the gift of a magic green girdle that will prevent him from being killed. Gawain, momentarily putting life before honor, breaks his word to Bercilac by not passing on this "gain". Riding out to meet the Green Knight, Gawain receives three blows from him; the first two are feints, but the third wounds Gawain in the neck. The knight reveals himself as Bercilac in enchanted guise and tells Gawain that the two feints were for the two days when Gawain kept his word, the wound for the girdle he failed to pass on according to the terms of the bargain. Bercilac reveals that his appearance at Arthur's court was a plot by Morgan Le Fay to trouble Arthur and Guinevere. He praises Gawain and says that all is quits between them. But

Gawain knows he has failed at least partially the test set him and returns to Arthur's court a sadder but wiser man, bearing the green girdle as a reminder of his failure. When Gawain tells his tale at Arthur's court, however, the whole court assumes green girdles in courtesy and as a mark of respect for Gawain.

It is a strange and fascinating story, even in translation or summary, and the close contact with it that Tolkien had while producing his edition must have had some effect on his imagination. Nothing in *The Lord of the Rings* trilogy derives directly from it, except possibly Frodo's near failure at the last moment of his quest, when he refuses to destroy the Ring and is saved only by the last frantic attempt of Gollum to possess it. But the whole atmosphere of wonder and mystery the anonymous Gawain poet has created reminds one powerfully of Tolkien's writing.

The story of Beowulf is better known. It is essentially the tale of the encounter of Beowulf, the hero, with three monsters: Grendel, Grendel's mother, and the great dragon. The barehanded combat with Grendel, Beowulf's descent into the awful lake to meet the female monster, and the meeting with the firedrake in his old age each show different aspects of Beowulf's heroism. Tolkien has in fact borrowed an incident from the Beowulf story—the theft of a cup from the dragon's hoard, which is missed by the dragon and sets him off on a rampage that ends with his death at the hands of a hero. But the two incidents are treated quite differently by the Beowulf poet and by Tolkien. A modern translation of *Beowulf* describes the cup incident as follows:

The ancient scourge that haunts the half-light of dawn ...
[the] smooth-skinned, spiteful dragon seeks out barrows of

the dead, and flies by night, burning and encircled in fire
... He is wont to seek out what is hoarded in the earth,
and there takes up his abode beside the heathen gold, growing wise in ripeness of years, and yet for all that he is no
better off. Thus for three hundred years this scourge of the
nation guarded that immense house of treasure through his
more than human might, until this one man roused fury in
his heart. He took the gold-plated flagon to his lord.....
Thus was the hoard ransacked and the hoarded wealth carried off.....

When the serpent awoke ... he slithered along the rock,
and with ruthless rage found the footprints of his foe, for
in his stealthy cunning he had stepped too far forward and
close to the dragon's head. ... Eagerly the guardian of the
hoard searched along the ground, meaning to find the man
who had acted so cruelly towards him as he slept. Burning
with savage rage, he went circling again and again round
the whole outer wall of the barrow, but there was no one
to be found in that waste land. Yet he rejoiced at the thought
of a fight and deeds of battle, while from time to time he
turned back into the barrow to search for the rich cup; he
soon discovered that some man or other had tampered with
the gold and the lordly wealth.....

The guardian of the hoard ... sped forth, armed with
flame and fire.[10]

Here is Tolkien's view of the parallel incident:

Dragons may not have much real use for all their wealth,
but they know it to an ounce as a rule, especially after long
possession; and Smaug was no exception. He had passed
from an uneasy dream (in which a warrior, altogether insig-
nificant in size but provided with a bitter sword and great

[10] *Beowulf and Its Analogues*, trans. G. N. Garmonsway et al. (London: J. M.
Dent and Sons Ltd., 1968), pp. 60–61.

courage, figured most unpleasantly) to a doze, and from a doze to wide waking. . . . He stirred and stretched forth his neck to sniff. Then he missed the cup!

Thieves! Fire! Murder! Such a thing had not happened since first he came to the Mountain! His rage passes description—the sort of rage that is only seen when rich folk that have more than they can enjoy suddenly lose something that they have long had but have never before used or wanted. His fire belched forth, the hall smoked, he shook the mountain-roots . . . , and then coiling his length together, roaring like thunder underground, he sped from his deep lair through its great door, out into the huge passages of the mountain-palace and up towards the Front Gate.[11]

Both dragons are fire-breathing monsters who hoard gold and are infuriated at their loss. Yet the dragon in *Beowulf* is like a forest fire or a flood, a sort of natural disaster, while Smaug is a character of some complexity and subtlety.

There is some similarity of atmosphere between parts of *Beowulf* and *The Lord of the Rings* trilogy. Tolkien's Orcs and trolls owe something to Grendel and his mother, and some of the horror of the desolate mere where Grendel's mother dwells has gone into the making of Mirkwood and of the land of Mordor.

But Tolkien has not merely borrowed from the early English epics he dealt with as a scholar. He has created in our own time a work with something of the same fascination and the same mythical quality. In the making of this story, Tolkien's own experience of language and its history has played its part.

[11] J. R. R. Tolkien, *The Hobbit* (New York: Ballantine Books, 2001), pp. 215–16.

Lewis' professional preoccupation with language took a somewhat different course from Tolkien's. Primarily a scholar of medieval and Renaissance literature, Lewis was especially interested with the way in which words change their meaning and with the misunderstandings that can arise as a result of such change. In his *Studies in Words*, Lewis traces the history of a number of important words (such as "nature", "genius", "simple") over a span of hundreds of years and shows how taking such words purely in some familiar modern sense (what Lewis calls the *dangerous sense*) can seriously mislead us in our attempts to understand the writing of an earlier period.

This is a specific application of a more general thesis of Lewis': the mutual effect of thought on language and language on thought. Take the word "nature" and its equivalents in other languages (e.g., *phusis* in Greek). The word cannot bear its modern sense, as in "let's get out into the woods and enjoy Nature", until Nature can be *contrasted* with something not itself—Nature as opposed to Civilization, Nature (created things) as opposed to God.

But once invented, the concept of Nature can have important effects on our thought.

> Once you can talk about *nature* (*d.s.*) you can deify it—or "her." Hence the sense which I shall call *Great Mother Nature*; *nature* used to mean not simply all the things there are, as an aggregate or even a system, but rather some force or mind or *élan* supposed to be immanent in them. It is of course often impossible to be sure in a given instance whether the sense Great Mother Nature implied genuine personalisation (a deity believed in) or merely personification as a rhetorical figure. . . .
>
> . . . Even now I am not sure that this meaning is always used purely as a figure, to say what would equally make

sense without it. The test is to remove the figure and see how much sense remains. Of all the pantheon Great Mother Nature has, at any rate, been the hardest to kill.[12]

One of the more interesting fictional uses Lewis makes of this idea is in the chapter in *Out of the Silent Planet* where Ransom is translating for Weston, who is attempting a philosophical justification of his interplanetary imperialism. Weston's grand generalizations about life and evolution when reduced to simple language reveal their emptiness:

As soon as Ransom finished, Weston continued.

"Life is greater than any system of morality; her claims are absolute. It is not by tribal taboos and copy-book maxims that she has pursued her relentless march from the amoeba to man and from man to civilization."

"He says," began Ransom, "that living creatures are stronger than the question whether an act is bent [evil] or good—no, that cannot be right—he says it is better to be alive and bent than to be dead—no—he says, he says—I cannot say what he says, Oyarsa, in your language. But he goes on to say that the only good thing is that there should be very many creatures alive. He says there were many other animals before the first men and the later ones were better than the earlier ones; but he says the animals were not born because of what is said to the young about bent and good action by their elders. And he says these animals did not feel any pity."

"She—" began Weston.

"I'm sorry," interrupted Ransom, "but I've forgotten who She is."

"Life, of course," snapped Weston.[13]

[12] C. S. Lewis, *Studies in Words* (Cambridge, Eng.: Cambridge University Press, 1960), pp. 41–42.

[13] Lewis, *Out of the Silent Planet*, p. 135.

The personification of Life, like the personification of Nature, leads us to say things which in cold prose are ambiguous or nonsensical. When we look back at the uses of language by our two authors we can see similarities. Both use language to reveal character, both connect language and rationality. But beyond this there are differences—perhaps only differences of emphasis, but important nevertheless. Tolkien uses language to weave enchantments; his use of Elvish or Orcish words can establish a mood, can create belief in us. Lewis uses language to convince, to enlighten, as well as to make us picture strange scenes and strange beings. Both are poets, both are teachers. But in Tolkien the poet predominates, in Lewis the teacher. Both use language to change the way we look at the world, but Tolkien, we might say, works through our emotions, while Lewis works through our intellect. Both use our imaginations; as Lewis points out, "In general ... the poet's route to our emotions lies through our imaginations",[14] and this is true of Tolkien. But there is a route to the intellect through imagination, also, a route utilized both by the satirist and the teller of parables.

It may or may not be true that "a poem should not mean / But be."[15] But this notion provides the grounds for an important distinction between Tolkien and Lewis. Tolkien's Middle-earth is a superbly realized work of the imagination. If we ask "what it means", Tolkien will tell us that a secondary world is valuable in itself; its meaning is its existence. Lewis' *Perelandra* is an equally superb creation, but it is also the setting for a morality play with profound implications. If we ask why it exists, why it was created, this can be explained in terms of a lesson Lewis had to teach:

---

[14] Lewis, *Studies in Words*, p. 220.
[15] Archibald MacLeish, "Ars Poetica" (1926).

Perelandra's existence is its meaning. The approach to language in the two authors shows something of this dualty, too. For Tolkien, the philologist, language is an end in itself, an object of study, something to enjoy and play with. For Lewis, the professor of literature, language is a tool to be used, a means to express ideas and images. But we must return to the fact that these are differences in emphasis; Lewis wrote *Studies in Words*, Tolkien studied the meaning as well as the language of *Beowulf*. And both writers share a vision of the world in which Existence and Meaning, Being and Wisdom are only different names for one Reality.

# Good, Evil, and God

# 4

# Good and Evil in Lewis

In one sense, neither Lewis nor Tolkien has anything new to say about good and evil—they are both Christians, and their morality is traditional Christian morality. Those parts of Christian morality they have occasion to make use of in their fiction are limited by the nature of those works.

But beyond this there are certain emphases on parts of Christian morality, certain interpretations of Christian morality in Lewis and Tolkien (not necessarily the same ones in both), which are worth noting. To give a parallel, St. Francis' morality was the basic Catholic moral code, as it was interpreted in his time. But Francis' emphasis on universal charity and voluntary poverty arose from his own vision of what was most important in that code and from his vision of what means could most effectively serve the ends recognized by that code. The parallel is the more interesting in that Francis utilized the enthusiasm for the chivalric ideal, which he shared with many of his contemporaries, to bring to life certain Christian ideals. He spoke, for example, of Poverty as his "Lady" and of himself as her "Troubadour". If the comparison is permissible (and I think it is), this is something like Lewis' utilization of a science-fiction framework and Tolkien's use of fairy story.

Let me begin with what seems to me to be a fairly basic misunderstanding of Lewis' view of morality. By seeing that it is a misunderstanding we shall gain a better grasp of Lewis' actual view, and by understanding Lewis' interpretation of morality, we shall gain some insight into Tolkien.

The misunderstanding occurs in a study of science fiction from a theological perspective, *The Shattered Ring*, by Lois and Stephen Rose. The Roses say Lewis has the "evident purpose" of presenting "a formal 'apology' for a certain body of Christian doctrine",[1] which seems to me to show an odd idea of what a formal apology for a body of Christian doctrine would be like. But our main concern is with their characterization of Lewis' heroes and villains. About Ransom, the hero of *Out of the Silent Planet* and *Perelandra*, they say he "is treated by the author (unconsciously perhaps) as a lovable but rather dumb child".[2] Of the good characters in *That Hideous Strength* they say, "The good people are all very lovable (if at times a little weak), docile, and always polite."[3] The Roses say Lewis' conception of man is "static"[4] and elsewhere describe his good characters as passive. Lewis' Malacandrians are described in this way: "The Martians—clearly meant to embody an old but unfallen world—have no fears of death. But not in [a] fiercely life-affirming manner.... On Mars the death-fearlessness stems from resigned submission to the 'true God' Maleldil and to the nature of things; thus their lives are peaceful, unworried, and productive."[5] The consequences

---

[1] Lois and Stephen Rose, *The Shattered Ring* (Richmond, Va.: John Knox Press, 1970), p. 60.

[2] Ibid., p. 63.

[3] Ibid., p. 64.

[4] Ibid., p. 66.

[5] Ibid., p. 61.

of the averted fall on Perelandra are described by the Roses as follows: "Ransom, the Christian, preserves the natural innocence of the planet and its two inhabitants, assuring that Venus, at least, will not have to reenact the tumultuous history of earth, but will drift instead in a timeless, conflictless bliss, its inhabitants nestled against the benevolent bosom of nature."[6]

The Roses accuse Lewis of thinking that "never to have fallen is equivalent to redemption"[7] and later say that "Lewis seems to desire a *return* of man to the state of instinctive docility which he imagines Eden to be. But this can hardly be the destiny of man."[8] They contrast their understanding of Lewis' view with Dostoyevsky's "Underground Man", who says, "Shower upon [man] every earthly blessing.... Even then out of sheer ingratitude, sheer spite, man would play you some nasty trick ... simply to introduce into all this positive good sense his fatal fantastic element."[9]

The Roses continue, "Lewis' static conception denies man precisely that element of cantankerous freedom which is the essence of humanity, a freedom which is more important to man than luxury or reason or security."[10] And later, "Lewis is weak at the point of redemption precisely because his understanding of evil and of man is lacking in dynamism and complexity. He fails to see that *redemption can never be the same thing as unfallen innocence.*"[11] They find Lewis' evil characters in *That Hideous Strength* unconvincing: "It is

[6] Ibid., pp. 61–62.

[7] Ibid., p. 62.

[8] Ibid., p. 80.

[9] Fyodor Dostoyevsky, *Notes from Underground*, in *The Short Novels of Dostoyevsky* (New York: Dial Press, 1945), p. 149, cited in Rose and Rose, *Shattered Ring*, p. 65.

[10] Rose and Rose, *Shattered Ring*, p. 66.

[11] Ibid., p. 67.

difficult to take the evil they represent very seriously. They all seem to verge on utter madness and their intellectual circumlocutions tend to amount to rank stupidity. . . . [They] are just plain nasty—the kind of people children are warned against in the vague hints of grownups." [12]

Thus the Roses' reaction to Lewis—which I think is sufficiently typical of one sort of modern reaction to be worth careful analysis—may be summed up as follows: Lewis' good characters are "passive", "docile", "static", do not have the essential "dynamism" the Roses admire and demand. Lewis' "good races" are not "fiercely life affirming", they "drift in . . . conflictless bliss . . . nestled against the benevolent bosom of nature". They are characterized by "instinctive docility". The evil characters are mere caricatures, bogeymen to frighten children.

By following up these accusations we gain, I hope, a valuable insight into Lewis' real views and even some of the techniques he uses. Consider first the accusations of "passivity" and "docility". In one sense the accusation simply seems to be false. For example, Ransom's adventure in *Out of the Silent Planet* may be roughly summarized as follows:

Benighted on a walking tour, Ransom, because of a promise to a chance-met woman, forces his way into the villains' headquarters where he secures the release of the woman's half-witted son. Tricked and drugged by the villains, he almost manages to escape, but is recaptured and kidnapped to Mars by spaceship. On landing, he escapes at the first opportunity and manages to live off the land for several days. He meets and makes friends with a Martian and lives for some time in a Martian village, learning the language. With his Martian friends he goes on a hunt for a deadly

[12] Ibid., p. 64.

water-monster, which he assists in killing. When the villains catch up with him and kill one of his Martian friends, he voluntarily undertakes a dangerous journey to be judged for his part in the tragedy by the Martian "government", which he still fears and distrusts to some extent. After the "court of inquiry"—at which he uses his knowledge of the language to interpret for his kidnappers—Ransom is given the choice of staying on Mars or making a desperate dash for Earth with his former captors. He survives the dangerous journey and arrives safely home.

Such an outline gives no real idea of the excellences of *Out of the Silent Planet*, but it is plain that purely on the level of events Ransom is as "active" a hero as most. He is not a "superhero", but a believable character whose successes are well within the realm of possibility. Similar defenses could be made of some of the good characters in *That Hideous Strength*. So if the Roses' accusations of "docility", "lack of dynamism", etc., have any truth, it must be on a somewhat different level.

To see what is really bothering the Roses, let us turn to their similar accusations against the unfallen Malacandrians and the Perelandrians whose fall is averted. Lewis' actual scheme here is rather complex. Let me summarize it briefly:

The Old Worlds (Mars and by implication perhaps other such worlds) contain races who are good and happy, but not entirely independent. They are in the care of powerful spirits—angels in fact—who direct and guide them. In certain cases, these beings directly interfere to help or punish. Thus it is true in a way that the Martians are like children under guardianship.

Earth is the turning point, the first world where the "experiment" of complete independence was tried. Far from helping or guiding or directing mankind to good, the angels "assigned" to Earth are in rebellion against God. This is one factor in a situation in which man in the person of his representatives is given a choice of following God's laws freely without guardianship or of rejecting God and making himself his god. Man has failed this test (the Fall), but God, by the Incarnation and Redemption, has turned this apparent defeat into a new sort of victory. One of the consequences of this is that God now acts *through* men who are members of his Mystical Body, the Christian Church. Ransom thus bears an awesome responsibility; if he fails, as man's first parents and representatives failed, God may again have to intervene in some unforeseeable way. The "bent" (evil) chief angel of our world (Satan) must also act through a representative; but whereas Ransom is left on his own (even having partly to figure out the problem and its solution for himself), Satan's representative, formerly the scientist Weston, is now a mere puppet manipulated by Satan, his own personality superseded and almost destroyed.

Perelandra is the first of the New Worlds. By successfully passing the test that Adam and Eve failed on our world, the Green Lady and the King enter into a new relation with the angels and with nature. Far from being under the guardianship of angels, they are to give orders to them; far from "nestling on the bosom of nature", they are to take complete charge of even the natural processes of growth, change of seasons, etc. The descendants of the King and the Green Lady are eventually to take some part in the "liberation" of our world at the Second Coming of Christ, which will not be—as we tend to think of it—"the end", but the *real* beginning for man.

Lewis has used basic elements of the Christian religion (the Fall, the Redemption, the Second Coming), which he fully believes, together with mythical elements (such as the

Neoplatonic idea that the planets are moved and directed by angels) that are merely the "machinery" of the story. He is not recommending a return to the condition of the Old Worlds that are "under guardianship"; to this extent he agrees with the Roses that it is false that "never to have fallen is equivalent to redemption". But there are two ways of being "unfallen". The Malacandrians show one way: not fallen because protected from falling. But the Perelandrians show another way of being unfallen: they have faced temptation and overcome it. This is not to be sheltered or docile; as Lewis says, the evil live sheltered lives by giving in to temptation. They haven't the least idea of the difficulty of resisting a temptation for hours or days or weeks.

But we cannot go forward to the state of "successfully unfallen" Perelandra any more than we can go back to the guardianship under which Malacandra is ruled. Our state is that of fallen but redeemed man, with the consequence that if God's work is to be done at all, it must be done by *us*; not by angels, not by miraculous intervention, but by our own stumbling and flawed efforts. This is far from a call to "passivity".

One thing we must not do is use the tools of our opponents in trying to do God's work (as Christians, tragically, have so often done). As Ransom says in *That Hideous Strength*: "I am not allowed to be *too* prudent. I am not allowed to use desperate remedies until desperate diseases are really apparent. Otherwise we become just like our enemies—breaking all the rules whenever we imagine that it might possibly do some vague good to humanity in the remote future." [13]

In one of the subtler passages in *That Hideous Strength*, Lewis shows how the villains expect their opponents to try

---

[13] C. S. Lewis, *That Hideous Strength* (New York: Scribner, 2003), p. 142.

to succeed by the same means—political power, influence, money—that they themselves use. Mark Studdock, in a sense the "hero" of that book, is suspected by the villains' organization, the N.I.C.E., of being in contact with "the enemy". An officer of the N.I.C.E. "institutional police" explains why she had certain possible "contacts" followed, but not Dimble, the actual representative of Ransom's organization at St. Anne's.

> He was shadowed into Northumberland. Only three possible people left the College after him—Lancaster, Lyly, and Dimble. I put them in that order of probability. Lancaster is a Christian, and a very influential man. He's in the Lower House of Convocation. He had a lot to do with the Repton Conference. He's mixed up with several big clerical families. And he's written a lot of books. He has a real stake in their side. Lyly is rather the same type, but less of an organizer. As you will remember, he did a great deal of harm on that reactionary commission about Education last year. Both these are dangerous men. They are the sort of people who get things done—natural leaders of the other party. Dimble is quite a different type. Except that he's a Christian, there isn't really much against him. He's purely academic. I shouldn't think his name is much known, except to other scholars in his own subject. Not the kind that would make a public man. Impractical . . . he'd be too full of scruples to be much use to them. The others know a thing or two, Lancaster particularly. In fact, he's a man we could find room for on our own side if he held the right views.[14]

Notice that the evil characters essentially expect their opponents to be like themselves, for example, to be unable to use Dimble because of his "scruples". The N.I.C.E. crew

[14] Ibid., p. 234.

apparently see their opponents simply as another power-hungry group, with different vested interests, competing for power and influence. As we shall see, Tolkien also makes use of this inability of the evil forces to really understand the nature of their opponents as an important plot element in the *Ring* trilogy.

However, I think the Roses' uneasiness does have an explanation. When they say that in Lewis' view "a perfect world is based on hierarchical principles",[15] they may mean any of several things. If they mean that Lewis' view is that man ought to be subordinated to superior angelic beings, as the Malacandrians are, they are simply mistaken, as we have seen. If they mean that Lewis is not in one sense a strict egalitarian, this is true enough, but a side issue. As *That Hideous Strength* makes clear, Lewis' view is that "we must all be guarded by equal rights from one another's greed, because we are fallen . . . [but] equality is not the deepest thing".[16] Jane Studdock is offended because Ivy Maggs, her former cleaning woman, is accepted as an equal member of the company at St. Anne's. But this democracy goes with a recognition that certain persons are spiritually superior to others and a recognition that certain kinds of authority derive ultimately from God. Ransom is "Director" at St. Anne's, both because the others recognize his spiritual superiority and because the eldils have given him a certain task—a task that is "God's work"—in a very literal sense.

Subordination to angels is not Lewis' ideal, then, and subordination to better men than ourselves is something voluntary and exceptional. But if the Roses mean by a "hierarchical" view that man ought to be subordinate to *God*, then, of course,

---

[15] Rose and Rose, *Shattered Ring*, p. 64.
[16] Lewis, *That Hideous Strength*, p. 145.

this is Lewis' view and the view, one would suppose, of any Christian theist. For surely there are only three possibilities: (1) God does not exist, and thus no question of obeying Him arises; (2) God exists and is to be obeyed; or (3) God exists, but is not to be obeyed. The first of these alternatives is a typical modern view, the second is the traditional Christian view. But what is to be made of the third? If Christianity is true, then God is perfectly wise and perfectly loving. To choose His will is to choose joy for ourselves and for others; to reject His will is to reject this joy. It is certainly possible to choose something other than the will of God, but this choice, on the Christian view, is precisely what sin consists of. To admit the Christian idea of God and reject the idea of obedience to Him, is, in effect, to be a Satanist. Thus it would seem that the Roses' rejection of the "hierarchical principle" is either a rejection of Christianity or is based on one of the misunderstandings we have discussed.

But, one might ask, is it not possible to reject the will of God and still be in many ways good or admirable? The Christian answer is "in the long run, no", and this is the clue that enables us to understand Lewis' treatment of his villains. The traditional Christian view, forcefully expressed by Lewis, is that whatever excellences a creature may have are gifts from God; by cutting oneself off from God one ultimately loses *everything* good. The evil characters in *That Hideous Strength* represent the end result of this process. They have lost, almost, their basic humanity; they *are* caricatures, but as in all successful caricatures, the elements that are exaggerated are essential elements. Lewis' attitude toward them is that very few men ever actually reach such an extreme stage of separation from goodness, but it is possible for them to do so. Lewis says in "The Weight of Glory", "It is a serious thing to live in a society of possible gods and goddesses, to remember that the dullest and most uninteresting person you can talk to may one day be a creature which, if you saw it now, you would be strongly tempted to worship, or else a horror and a corruption such as you now meet, if at all, only in a nightmare." [17] In a way, *That Hideous Strength* is such a nightmare. The purpose of Wither, Frost, and Hardcastle is like that of a *memento mori*, without the inevitability; you or I *may* come to this, but need not.

There is some evidence that the Roses disagree with this whole point of view. "Such a conception of man", they say, speaking of Lewis' view, "is a bit arbitrary; it ignores the possibility that man is an indivisible unity, not to mention the insight of psychoanalysis that man's strengths and . weaknesses may be one and the same, that the strongest positive characteristics carry with them the strongest negative possibilities." [18] Like so much the Roses say, this is open to two quite different interpretations. Lewis would readily admit that "the strongest positive characteristics carry with them the strongest negative possibilities". As Lewis has George MacDonald say in *The Great Divorce*: "There's something in natural affection which will lead it on to eternal love more easily than natural appetite could be led on. But there's also something in it which makes it easier to stop at the natural level and mistake it for the heavenly. Brass is mistaken for gold more easily than clay is. And if it finally refuses conversion its corruption will be worse than the corruption of what ye call the lower passions. It's a stronger angel and therefore, when it falls, a fiercer devil." [19]

[17] C. S. Lewis, "The Weight of Glory", in *The Weight of Glory and Other Addresses* (San Francisco: HarperCollins, 2001), pp. 45–46.

[18] Rose and Rose, *Shattered Ring*, p. 63.

[19] C. S. Lewis, *The Great Divorce* (San Francisco: HarperCollins, 2001), pp. 104–5.

However, in another sense, what the Roses mean may be diametrically opposed to what Lewis means. If they are suggesting that flaws or faults in our nature may be the *source* of strengths or excellences, or might be inseparable from them, Lewis would reject this view entirely. Evil, according to Lewis, is essentially uncreative. He has Screwtape say in *The Screwtape Letters*, "To be greatly and effectively wicked a man needs some virtue. What would Attilla have been without his courage, or Shylock without self-denial as regards the flesh? But as we [i.e., Hell] cannot supply these qualities ourselves, we can only use them as supplied by the Enemy [i.e., God]—and this means leaving Him a kind of foothold in those men whom, otherwise, we have made most securely our own." [20] And as Lewis has MacDonald say toward the end of *The Great Divorce*: "Nothing, not even the best and noblest can go on as it is now. Nothing, not even what is lowest and most bestial, will not be raised again if it submits to death." [21] Thus the view that evil can be a source of any strength or excellence, or an irremovable part of any, would be totally rejected by Lewis.

The Roses cite the evidence of psychoanalysis, but all that any empirical study can show us is that good and evil are in fact mixed in man as he now exists. Man's ultimate destiny and the role of his virtues and vices in this destiny are matters for philosophy and religion.

Besides showing personal character at the extreme stage of separation from goodness, Lewis also shows a society as it becomes at such an extreme. In *The Screwtape Letters*, Lewis discusses the problems of depicting the relations of devils to each other.

---

[20] C. S. Lewis, *The Screwtape Letters* (San Francisco: HarperCollins, 2001), p. 159.

[21] Lewis, *The Great Divorce*, p. 114.

Milton has told us that "devil with devil damned, Firm concord holds." But how? Certainly not by friendship. A being which can still love is not yet a devil. Here again my symbol [Hell as "something like the bureaucracy of a police state or the offices of a thoroughly nasty business concern"] seemed to me useful. It enabled me, by earthly parallels, to picture an official society held together entirely by fear and greed.... "Dog eat dog" is the principle of the whole organisation. Everyone wishes everyone else's discrediting, demotion, and ruin; everyone is an expert in the confidential report, the pretended alliance, the stab in the back.[22]

Lewis was even more successful in the depiction of such a society in *That Hideous Strength* than he was in *The Screwtape Letters*. The way in which Mark Studdock is bamboozled by Wither, betrayed by Feverstone, snubbed by Steele, used by Cosser, bullied and blackmailed by Hardcastle, and "trained" by Frost gives a vivid picture of the way in which such a society would appear to a neophyte. The devious atmosphere of lies and double-cross is illustrated by many fine touches. For example, at a time when Studdock is locked in a cell, still being terrified and threatened by Frost and Wither, his name is being used to terrify others. The speech in which this occurs is a beautiful illustration of Wither's methods of terrorizing his subordinates.

Well, Mr. Stone, I am, on the whole, and with certain inevitable reservations, moderately satisfied with your conduct of this affair. I believe that I may be able to present it in a favourable light to those of my colleagues whose good will you have, unfortunately, not been able to retain. If you can bring it to a successful conclusion you would very much

---

[22] Lewis, *The Screwtape Letters* (New York: The Macmillan Co., 1961), pp. x, xi. This longer introduction was shortened in the current edition.

strengthen your position. If not . . . it is inexpressibly painful to me that there should be these tensions and mutual
recriminations among us. But you quite understand me, my
dear boy. If only I could persuade—say Miss Hardcastle and
Mr. Studdock—to share my appreciation of your very real
qualities, you would need to have no apprehensions about
your career or—ah—your security.[23]

In contrast, the society at St. Anne's, the headquarters of
Ransom and his companions, is one based on mutual respect
and affection, which extends even to the bear, Mr. Bultitude. Things as minor as household chores are shared.

"What is 'women's day' in the kitchen?" asked Jane of
Mother Dimble.
  "There are no servants here," said Mother Dimble, "and
we do all the work. The women do it one day and the
men the next. What? No, it's a very sensible arrangement.
The Director's idea is that men and women can't do house-
work together without quarreling. There's something in it.
Of course, it doesn't do to look at the cups too closely on
the men's day, but on the whole we get along pretty well."[24]

Dangers, too, are shared, as on the night of the hunt for
Merlin. Only MacPhee is denied a share because his lack
of Christian faith leaves him too exposed to the forces of
evil. MacPhee, incidentally, is an interesting part of the
company at St. Anne's. A nonbeliever, he is the "official
sceptic" of the establishment. His allegiance to the company is based partly on affection for Ransom, partly on
detestation for the evil at Belbury. MacPhee is partly an
affectionate caricature of Lewis' old tutor, partly a personification of nineteenth-century rationalism, which tried to
reject religion while retaining morality. But like other great

[23] Lewis, *That Hideous Strength*, p. 250.
[24] Ibid., p. 164.

Lewis characters (Reepicheep the Mouse, for example, or Puddleglum the Marsh-wiggle, or Augray the *sorn*) he is, whatever his origin, a successful result of artistic creation.

Indeed, I suspect that part of the indignation some moderns feel about Lewis—their accusations that he writes "propaganda" or, absurdly, "a formal apology for Christianity"—is that he applies one of their own techniques in reverse. The modern temper has been fed to some extent on works in which the pleasant characters represent science, progress, political leftism, and so on, and the unpleasant characters represent religion, absolute ethical values, tradition, and so on. H. G. Wells is a vintage source of this kind of technique. But in Lewis the allocations of virtue and vice are reversed. No one in his right mind would want to be part of the "society" at Belbury, and it requires very strong prejudices indeed not to be attracted by the company at St. Anne's.

But whereas people like Wells did almost seem to be saying that "progressives" are Nice People and "reactionaries" are Nasty People, Lewis is not saying that Christians are Nice People and scientists are Nasty People. He is saying that morally good people, people who *act* on the Christian principles of love and justice—even if, like MacPhee, they are honest unbelievers—are people it is good to be among; and morally evil people, whose lives are based on self-love and hatred of others—even if, like Straik, they use the language of religion—are people it is bad to be among. And this is true as a matter of experience, even if it were not almost true by definition.

Why, then, does anyone adhere to Belbury rather than St. Anne's? Because he thinks he can use Belbury to secure some aim of his own. Consider some sample motives from the Belbury crew:

*Feverstone*: "He knew that the Belbury scheme might not work, but he knew that if it didn't he would get out in time. He had a dozen lines of retreat kept open. He also had a perfectly clear conscience and had played no tricks with his mind. He had never slandered another man except to get his job, never cheated except because he wanted money, never really disliked people unless they bored him." [25]

*Wither*: "He had long since ceased to believe in knowledge itself. What had been in his far-off youth a merely aesthetic repugnance to realities that were crude or vulgar had deepened and darkened, year after year, into a fixed refusal of everything that was in any degree other than himself." [26]

Mark Studdock is nearly drawn into the orbit of Belbury by the craving Lewis has analyzed in "The Inner Ring" (collected in his *Weight of Glory*). Studdock has always longed to be an "insider", in the "inner ring" of the knowledgeable powerful who "really run things", "really know what's going on". This craving leads him from the "Progressive Element" at Bracton to the N.I.C.E. and even exerts a pull on him after his "conversion", when Frost tempts him with the vision of the ultimate "inner ring", the Satanist initiates: "For here, surely here at last . . . was the true inner circle of all, the circle whose centre was outside the human race—the ultimate secret, the supreme power, the last initiation." [27] But as an illustration of what Lewis has MacDonald say in *The Great Divorce*, Mark's association with the old tramp he is set to guard contains in a way a satisfaction of what was legitimate in Mark's desire. "Mark never noticed until years later that here, where there was no room for vanity and no more power or security than that of 'children playing in a giant's kitchen,' he had

[25] Ibid., p. 353.
[26] Ibid., p. 350.
[27] Ibid., pp. 256–57.

unawares become a member of a 'circle,' as secret and as strongly fenced against outsiders as any that he had dreamed of." [28] By the end of the book, Mark Studdock has undergone a fundamental change in his attitude, but he is still taking only the first faltering steps back to full humanity. Lewis' fully developed good characters offer a more instructive contrast to the Belbury crew.

Ransom himself is hard to come to grips with, since for much of *Out of the Silent Planet* and *Perelandra* he is simply Everyman. We see the action through his eyes, know his innermost fears and weaknesses, and find ourselves identifying with him so strongly that it is hard to give an objective estimate of him. Perhaps the outstanding impression we carry away is that Ransom is "open"—able to appreciate and love. He delights in the beauty of Mars, grows to love the *hross* and especially Hyoi, his first friend among them. After overcoming his initial fear of the *sorns*, he begins to appreciate their wisdom, their humor, even their physical beauty. On Perelandra his struggles, temptations, and victories are such as we can make our own: we hope that we would do as well as Ransom in his place, fear that we would do worse. Humility, charity, and courage are not easy characteristics to convey—we find them all in Ransom.

There are two pictures of Ransom from the "outside" in *Perelandra*, both by "Lewis", who appears as a minor character in the story. Before Ransom's trip to Perelandra, his humanity and decency are emphasized. After his return, Ransom seems "larger than life". He is "almost a new Ransom, glowing with health and rounded with muscle and seemingly ten years younger. In the old days he had been beginning to show a few grey hairs; but now the

---

[28] Ibid., p. 310.

beard which swept his chest was pure gold."[29] To Ransom, returned from Perelandra, ordinary people on Earth appear pale and sick, which indirectly emphasizes his own vigor and energy.

This transfigured Ransom prepares us for the Ransom of *That Hideous Strength*. Although a somewhat remote figure, as we have noted, he shows humor, wisdom, and sympathy in his interview with Jane Studdock. At her first sight of him he "appeared to be a boy, twenty years old". But she soon realized that "of course he was not a boy—how could she have thought so? The fresh skin on his forehead and cheeks and, above all, on his hands, had suggested the idea. But no boy could have so full a beard. And no boy could be so strong. She had expected to see an invalid. Now it was manifest that the grip of those hands would be inescapable, and imagination suggested that those arms and shoulders could support the whole house. Miss Ironwood at her side struck her as a little old woman, shrivelled and pale—a thing you could have blown away."[30]

Again, the contrast between Ransom and other "normal" persons gives us an impression of Ransom's power. Ransom's face, young but wise, with its golden beard, arouses images in Jane's mind, "the imagined Arthur of her childhood—and the imagined Solomon, too. Solomon—for the first time in many years the bright solar blend of king and lover and magician which hangs about that name stole back upon her mind. For the first time in all those years she tasted the word *King* itself with all its linked associations of battle, marriage, priesthood, mercy, and power."[31]

[29] C. S. Lewis, *Perelandra* (New York: Scribner, 2003), p. 27.
[30] Lewis, *That Hideous Strength*, p. 139.
[31] Ibid., p. 140.

But the effect of this meeting on Jane is moral, not merely physical. Her talk with him begins to make her more like Ransom. Before the meeting she travels on a small train. "Passengers got in and out of her carriage at every stop; apple-faced men, and women with elastic-side boots and imitation fruit on their hats, and schoolboys. Jane hardly noticed them: for though she was theoretically an extreme democrat, no social class save her own had yet become a reality to her in any place except the printed page." [32] After the interview, returning on the same train,

> she saw from the windows of the train the outlined beams of sunlight pouring over stubble or burnished woods and felt that they were like the notes of a trumpet. Her eyes rested on the rabbits and cows as they flitted by and she embraced them in heart with merry, holiday love. She delighted in the occasional speech of the one wizened old man who shared her compartment and saw, as never before, the beauty of his shrewd and sunny old mind, sweet as a nut and English as a chalk down. She reflected with surprise how long it was since music had played any part in her life, and resolved to listen to many chorales by Bach on the gramophone that evening. Or else—perhaps—she would read a great many Shakespeare sonnets. She rejoiced also in her hunger and thirst and decided that she would make herself buttered toast for tea—a great deal of buttered toast. [33]

For Lewis, this is no parable or symbol, but the plain truth: as we come closer to God, either in Himself or through His servants, we will grow in love and delight, in appreciation of all good things.

[32] Ibid., p. 45.
[33] Ibid., p. 149.

Perhaps the second most important of Lewis' "good" characters is Lucy, heroine of several of the Narnia books. Lucy's
character grows in the five books in which she has a role,
as she herself grows in loving and serving Aslan, the Christ-
figure of the Narnia stories. Lucy is the first of the children
to discover Narnia and has to suffer a sort of martyrdom
when at first she is not believed. Her immediate friendliness to Tumnus the Faun, her grave courtesy to all the Narnian creatures, reminds us of Alice. Even though she has
suffered from Edmund's cruelty, she is the first to plead with
Aslan to help him. She knows that Edmund should know
the sacrifice that Aslan has made for him, when Susan thinks
"it would be too awful for him" to know. She is not, of
course, perfect. For example, she snaps at Aslan when worried about Edmund's wounds. But she is growing.

Her reward is to be asked to do more. In *Prince Caspian*,
at a crucial turn in the story, only she can see Aslan and
must persuade the others to follow him on her word alone.
In *The Voyage of the Dawn Treader*, she sacrifices her water
ration to the unpleasant Eustace and undertakes to break
the spell on the Dufflepuds. And she is growing in knowledge and love of Aslan. We see this when she meets him in
*Prince Caspian*:

> "Aslan," said Lucy, "you're bigger."
> "That is because you are older, little one," answered he.
> "Not because you are?"
> "I am not. But every year you grow, you will find me
> bigger." [34]

In *The Voyage of the Dawn Treader* Lucy is dismayed to find
that she cannot return to Narnia.

---

[34] C. S. Lewis, *Prince Caspian* (New York: HarperCollins, 2000), p. 141.

"It isn't Narnia, you know," sobbed Lucy, "It's *you*. We shan't meet *you* there. And how can we live, never meeting you?"

"But you shall meet me, dear one," said Aslan.

"Are—are you there too, Sir?" said Edmund.

"I am," said Aslan. "But there I have another name. You must learn to know me by that name. This was the very reason why you were brought to Narnia, that by knowing me here for a little, you may know me better there." [35]

Even more true to life in some ways than Ransom and Lucy are the characters who change from evil to good. We have already mentioned Mark Studdock. Eustace in *The Voyage of the Dawn Treader* is reformed by the rather drastic expedient of turning him temporarily into a dragon. The objectification of his inner repulsiveness, as well as the kindness of those whom he had thought his persecutors, accomplishes a change in his character. But he has relapses in *The Silver Chair*, and even in paradise, at the end of *The Last Battle*, some of his old bumptiousness is left.

All in all, the characters whom Lewis intends us to admire are an attractive crew. Some of their characteristics, like Ransom's health and vigor after his return from Perelandra, are merely symbolic. Health, which is a physical good, is used as a symbol for moral goodness. But the traits that make these characters basically attractive are just those which attract us to people in real life—concern, respect, and affection for others, humility, courage, openness to experience, and appreciation of all good things. And for Lewis, the connection between these characteristics is clear. God's

---

[35] C. S. Lewis, *The Voyage of the Dawn Treader* (New York: HarperCollins, 2000), p. 247.

goodness is the source of all good things, leaving no room for conceit on our part.

Each good gift should remind us of the Giver and motivate us to imitate God's goodness by doing good to others. On the other hand, the pride, selfishness, and cruelty illustrated in Lewis' evil characters all arise from the fatal choice of self instead of God—the impossible attempt to be sufficient unto ourselves and to dominate others with our ideas and wishes. Lewis gives a modern version of Augustine's "two cities"—the Manor at St. Anne's, founded on love of God, and Belbury, founded on love of self.

## 5

# Good and Evil in Tolkien

Both Lewis and Tolkien, as we said in the last chapter, are Christians, and their morality is essentially Christian morality. This is so clear in Lewis that we have found critics accusing him of propaganda. It is much less clear in Tolkien, and this has tempted some critics to say that Tolkien's view of the world is "really" the modern view and not the traditional Christian view. This is so major a misunderstanding of Tolkien that the Roses' misunderstanding of Lewis pales into insignificance by comparison. The motives of this misunderstanding are revealing enough of a certain modern tendency to make them worth examining carefully.

One major critic of Tolkien who has made this mistake is Roger Sale.[1] According to Sale, Tolkien may wish it differently, but "willy nilly he belongs to our time, and the more he attempts to ignore or escape this fact the worse he becomes as a writer. . . . He is a Christian, not a skeptic, and he believes that the taproot to the past is not yet dried or withered. It

[1] Sale's thesis is set forth in a study called "England's Parnassus", first published in the *Hudson Review* and later expanded and revised as "Tolkien and Frodo Baggins" for a book of Tolkien criticism, *Tolkien and the Critics*, ed. Neil D. Isaacs and Rose A. Zimbardo (Notre Dame, Ind.: University of Notre Dame Press, 1968).

would be difficult, therefore, to expect that Tolkien would warm to the idea that his imagination is vastly superior to his theology and that his imagination is of his own time. . . . The heroism he writes of best is very modern." [2]

What does Sale mean by "modern heroism"? It "accepts the facts of modern life . . . and then simply refuses to knuckle under." [3] Again: "We see, without in the least needing to make the seeing into a formulation, what the heroism of our time is and can be: lonely, lost, scared, loving, willing, and compassionate—to bind oneself to the otherness of others by recognizing our common livingness. History may create the conditions of chaos, but man's nature is to reply to history as well as to acknowledge it." [4] Now certainly Tolkien describes such a view, but it is not *his* view; it is the view of Northern mythology. Tolkien writes in "Beowulf: The Monsters and the Critics" and in "The Homecoming of Beorhtnoth, Beorhthelm's Son" about this view. [5] It is a view Tolkien respects and in a way admires. But to confuse it with Tolkien's own view or with that expressed in *The Lord of the Rings* trilogy is a major error.

The corrective, in fact, is in the very sources where Tolkien discusses the view. In "Beowulf: The Monsters and the Critics" Tolkien writes:

> Now the heroic figures, the men of old . . . remained and still fought on until defeat. For the monsters do not depart,

[2] Ibid., pp. 283–84.

[3] Ibid., p. 284.

[4] Ibid., p. 288.

[5] J. R. R. Tolkien, "Beowulf: The Monsters and the Critics", *in An Anthology of Beowulf Criticism*, ed. Lewis E. Nicholson (Notre Dame, Ind.: University of Notre Dame Press, 1963); J. R. R. Tolkien, "The Homecoming of Beorhtnoth, Beorhthelm's Son", in *The Tolkien Reader* (New York: Ballantine Books, 2001).

whether the gods go or come. A Christian was (and is) still like his forefathers, a mortal hemmed in a hostile world. The monsters remained the enemies of mankind, the infantry of the old war, and become inevitably the enemies of the one God ... the eternal Captain of the new. Even so the vision of the war changes. For it begins to dissolve, even as the contest on the fields of Time thus takes on its largest aspect. The tragedy of the great temporal defeat remains for a while poignant, but ceases to be finally important. It is no defeat, for the end of the world is part of the design of Metod, the Arbiter who is above the mortal world. Beyond there appears a possibility of eternal victory (or eternal defeat) and the real battle is between the soul and its adversaries. So the old monsters become images of the evil spirit or spirits.[6]

Tolkien is here describing the situation of the Beowulf poet who, as modern scholarship has established, was a Christian writing at the time of Bede (ca. A.D. 675) but deliberately excluding explicit Christian elements from a tale supposed to take place at a time before Christ. The situation of the Beowulf poet is a very close parallel to Tolkien's own situation, as we will see, and he has partly learned from the Beowulf poet how to handle it.

Sale has an answer to this answer: Sale knows better than Tolkien what Tolkien "really" means. Sale knows this, he claims, because Tolkien's "imagination" is modern; he sees heroism in essentially modern terms. It may be worth spelling out why this is precisely false. The ideal Sale has in mind is roughly existentialist stoicism as we find it in Sartre and Camus. The world is chaotic and absurd; we must refuse all easy ways out—suicide, religion, other forms of

---

[6] Tolkien, "Beowulf: The Monsters and the Critics", pp. 72–73.

self-delusion—and impose our own meaning on life, with undeviating determination. This is an ideal by no means devoid of a certain "wintry grandeur" (as Lewis said of Sartre), but it is a million miles from Tolkien's vision. What Lewis said of Spenser is equally true of Tolkien. "The Existentialist feels *Angst* because he thinks that man's nature (and therefore his relation to all things) has to be created or invented, without guidance, at each moment of decision. Spenser thought that man's nature was given, discoverable, and discovered; he did not feel *Angst*. He was often sad: but not, at bottom, worried." [7]

Frodo in *The Lord of the Rings* is facing not chaos, but a definite evil, which is evil by absolute standards. "Good and ill have not changed ... nor are they one thing among Elves and Dwarves and another among Men." [8] He is not imposing his own will or his own vision, but defending a law and a vision common to Elves, Men, and Dwarves. Bilbo's finding of the Ring and his bearing of it are not chance events, but part of a great plan, prophesied in part and known to the Wise. It would be hard in some ways to find a hero more *un*like the existentialist hero.

Obviously Frodo is "lonely, lost, scared"; that is the sort of hero he is: not a Beowulf or even a Gawain, but a Jack the Giant Killer, the "youngest son", "the simple one" never expected to succeed but succeeding at last with the aid of courage, resourcefulness, luck, and powerful helpers. Not that Tolkien despises the other sort of hero; Gandalf, Aragon, Legolas, and Gimli are all variations of that traditional

[7] C. S. Lewis, *English Literature in the Sixteenth Century excluding Drama* (New York: Oxford University Press, 1954), p. 392.

[8] J. R. R. Tolkien, *The Two Towers*, rev. ed. (New York: Ballantine Books, 2001), p. 40.

type. But Tolkien's real love, and ours, is for Bilbo and Frodo, Sam, Pippin, and Merry.

Another critic who makes a mistake about Tolkien similar to Sale's is Charles Moorman. His essay, "'Now Entertain Conjecture of a Time'—The Fictive Worlds of C. S. Lewis and J. R. R. Tolkien", is to be found in another excellent collection of papers, *Shadows of Imagination*, edited by Mark R. Hillegas. Moorman also wants to say that Tolkien's vision is not Christian, but whereas Sale calls it "modern", Moorman's word is "pagan". He says that

> in spite of Tolkien's own implication in "On Fairy-Stories" that *The Lord of the Rings*, ending as it does in a "sudden joyous turn," ... possesses eucatastrophe and is hence by extension optimistic and Christian, I would maintain that it reflects the attitudes and interests of Tolkien the student of Beowulf rather than those of Tolkien the Christian. The chronicles ... are filled with accounts of never-ceasing wars against evil waged by elves, hobbits and men, and the reappearance in every age of the forces of darkness.... Though the forces of good triumph in each age their leaders pay a high cost for victory ... the scars cannot be erased.... The views of nature and civilization like those of history and the individual life advanced in *The Lord of the Rings* seem to be pagan rather than Christian in essence.[9]

This view of Moorman's seems to rest on a double misunderstanding of Christianity and of Tolkien. The "sudden joyous turn", the "eucatastrophe" of the Christian Story

[9] Charles Moorman, "'Now Entertain Conjecture of a Time'—The Fictive Worlds of C. S. Lewis and J. R. R. Tolkien", in *Shadows of Imagination*, ed. Mark R. Hillegas (Carbondale, Ill.: Southern Illinois University Press, 1966), pp. 64–65.

that Tolkien cites in "On Fairy-Stories", is the Resurrection, not the end of the world. And Christ's victory does not mean that suffering and the battle with evil are over; it means that we must each take up our cross and follow in the footsteps of Christ. The world has been saved, but we must work out that salvation, sometimes in fear and trembling.

Moorman cites the contrasting atmosphere of Lewis' Narnia stories, where the heroes and heroines seem to emerge relatively unscathed and the victory of good seems more complete. But of course, Lewis' stories were written for children and cannot contain the full weight of sorrow and sin that a story for older readers can. Furthermore, the machinery of the stories requires that, at the end of each book except the last, the children who are the heroes and heroines must return to being children in our world. And though the victory in each book seems more complete, each new adventure into Narnia is a fresh battle against evil. The victory of evil in the last book seems complete, until the "sudden joyous turn", which is the end of Narnia and the *good news* that the children are really dead in our world and can live forever with Aslan.

Furthermore, Moorman does not seem to have fully grasped Tolkien's view. He cites the fact that Frodo, wounded and sorrowful, must pass from Middle-earth. But he goes to the land of the High Elves, there to to be cured of all wounds and sorrows. Similarly, Ransom, at the end of *That Hideous Strength*, leaves Earth to return to Perelandra, for only there can his wound be healed.

In fact, Tolkien and Lewis both have a profoundly Christian view: *this* world is the vale of sorrow and struggle, and we must look for real consolation only after death or after the world ends. G. K. Chesterton expresses this view in verse.

> Here we have battle and blazing eyes,
> And chance and honour and high surprise,
> But our homes are under miraculous skies
> Where the yule tale was begun.[10]

Both Sale and Moorman genuinely admire Tolkien, and their attempt to restate his vision in their own terms arises from that admiration. But Tolkien's vision is profoundly his own and deeply Christian, and if we misunderstand this we seriously misunderstand him.

Let me now briefly describe Tolkien's world, as many hints, indirect references, and direct statements give it to us. Just as in Lewis' space trilogy the state of Earth is supposed to be the state it is in, and Lewis' secondary world "starts", so to speak, at the orbit of the moon, so for Tolkien recorded history is supposed to be much as it actually is, and Tolkien's secondary world "starts" before history begins. In both cases, there is some "interpenetration". In *That Hideous Strength*, the Arthurian legend becomes history, and in Tolkien it is suggested that Elves, Hobbits, and other creatures linger on into recorded history. But before recorded history there are certain events that Tolkien, as a Christian, holds to have actually occurred—for instance, the Fall of man. Thus, since there are Men in Tolkien's story, they must be fallen Men; the Fall is in the *past* of Tolkien's world. And, of course, the Men in the story of the Ring are obviously fallen Men.

---

[10] G. K. Chesterton, "The House of Christmas", in *The Collected Works of G. K. Chesterton*, vol. 10, *Collected Poetry*, Part 1 (San Francisco: Ignatius Press, 1994), p. 140.

What about the other races? Not being "sons of Adam", they are not necessarily fallen; they may be like Lewis' Malacandrians or Perelandrians. And, in fact, there are some analogies between Lewis' "races" and Tolkien's. Let me first give a table of my proposed correspondences, and then defend it.

| Tolkien's | correspond to | Lewis' |
|---|---|---|
| Elves (Wizards) Valar | " | Good eldils (Oyéresu) |
| Dwarves (Ents?) | " | Malacandrians |
| Orcs, trolls (Sauron) | " | "Bent" eldils (The "Bent" One") |

Elves and Orcs are unlike eldils in that eldils are purely spiritual beings. (But the function of Elves in Tolkien's story is like that of eldils in Lewis' trilogy as, for example, Tom Bombadil's function is rather like Merlin's in *That Hideous Strength*.) Elves are like eldils in being at the time of the story confirmed in goodness or badness; there is no such thing as an evil Elf or a good Orc in *The Lord of the Rings*. Ents are evidently not as confirmed in goodness like Elves. Treebeard says of his people,

> I do not understand all that goes on myself, so I cannot explain it to you. Some of us are still true Ents, and lively enough in our fashion, but many are growing sleepy, going tree-ish, as you might say. Most of the trees are just trees, of course; but many are half awake. Some are quite wide awake, and a few are, well, ah, well getting *Entish*. That is going on all the time.
>
> When that happens to a tree, you find that some have *bad* hearts. Nothing to do with their wood: I do not mean that. Why, I knew some good old willows down the Entwash, gone long ago, alas! They were quite hollow, indeed they were falling all to pieces, but as quiet and sweet-spoken as

a young leaf. And then there are some trees in the valleys under the mountains, sound as a bell, and bad right through. That sort of thing seems to spread. There used to be some very dangerous parts in this country. There are still some very black patches.[11]

However, the Ents have an "anti-race", like the Elves. Treebeard says, "Maybe you have heard of Trolls? They are mighty strong. But Trolls are only counterfeits, made by the Enemy in the Great Darkness in mockery of Ents, as Orcs were of Elves." [12] This may suggest that trolls and Orcs are actually *created* by the Enemy, but elsewhere Gandalf denies that the Enemy can create; he can only spoil and corrupt. In fact, "Nothing is evil in the beginning. Even Sauron was not so",[13] which suggests that he is, like Satan, a fallen being of great power.

Dwarves, like the Malacandrians, seem to be basically good, but there seems to be a possibility of individual falls; an evil Dwarf is not an impossibility. And Gimli the Dwarf in some way rises above his Dwarvish destiny, becoming a sort of adopted Elf.

Hobbits pose a special problem, and here I indulge in a bit of speculation that might have been entirely rejected by Tolkien himself. All that he himself says is that "it is plain indeed that ... Hobbits are relatives of ours: far nearer to us than Elves, or even than Dwarves. Of old they spoke the languages of Men, after their own fashion, and liked and disliked much the same things as Men did. But what exactly our relationship is can no longer be discovered." [14]

[11] Tolkien, *The Two Towers*, p. 83.

[12] Ibid., p. 105.

[13] J. R. R. Tolkien, *The Fellowship of the Ring*, rev. ed. (New York: Ballantine Books, 2001), p. 300.

[14] Ibid., p. 2.

However, the Hobbits are continually referred to as "Halflings", a term Tolkien explains as "half the size of a grown man". Can there also be some suggestion here of half-*breeds*? Can the Hobbits in fact be the offspring of an interbreeding of two other races? If so, which two? Not Elves and Men. The offspring of such unions appear in the story in the persons of Elrond and Arwen, and they are quite unlike Hobbits. I once thought Hobbits might be the offspring of an Elf-Dwarf cross and connected in some way with the "old quarrel" between Elves and Dwarves. Gimli falls in love with Galadriel (in a remote and chivalric way, it is true, yet she is a sort of Elvish saint or super-woman and he is not correspondingly great). What if some Dwarvish king or warrior had fallen in love with a more accessible Elf-maiden and carried her off? Might this not have led to a spreading quarrel (Helen of Troy long before Troy), and might not the offspring of such a union, perhaps intermarrying with other Dwarves, have founded a new race who found it best to vanish quietly into a remote corner of the world?

I still think this possible, from what Tolkien tells us of his world, but I am now inclined to think that a mixed ancestry of Dwarf and Man is more plausible in view of the part Hobbits play in the story. For, if Hobbits are partly human, much is explained: the fact that they have no language of their own but speak that of Men; their resemblances to both Men and Dwarves in certain respects; and, above all, the vital role they play in the process in which the Third Age—the age of many "speaking races"—comes to an end, and the Fourth Age—the age of Man—begins.

Be this as it may, the real moral focus of Tolkien's story is on the two races Hobbits and Men. They can sink to complete damnation, as the Ringwraiths have done, and as

Bilbo or Frodo might have. But they can rise to something like sanctity, as Frodo does. We have detailed pictures of moral struggle in Men (Boromir, Théoden, Denethor), in most of the Hobbit characters (especially Frodo, Sam, and Bilbo, but also Merry and Pippin), and in the Wizard Saruman, who is at least ostensibly a Man.

The constant temptation of all the characters is to give in, give up the struggle and cooperate with the Dark Lord. Against this the virtues characteristic of the heroes of the story are courage, will and endurance, and loyalty and love. We see the first sketch of this in Bilbo, hero of *The Hobbit*. At the beginning of the story he is seemingly a fussy, self-important little hobbit (not middle-aged; that is a mistake arising from applying human time-scales to longer-lived creatures). Partly by clever pressure from Gandalf, partly from injured vanity, he commits himself to an adventure with Thorin and his Dwarves. As the dangers start, he begins to find his courage, first trying to pick a troll's pocket (with disastrous results), then giving the alarm during the capture by the goblins. Lost in the flight from the goblins after Gandalf rescues the troop, Bilbo meets Gollum and outwits him in the dark, finds his magic ring, and begins to use it. In the forest he saves the Dwarves from the giant spiders, aided by a magic ring and an Elvish blade, but showing a great deal of courage and resourcefulness. He rescues the Dwarves from the Elvenking's dungeons, but the real test of his courage is when he twice faces Smaug, the great dragon, gaining the knowledge that enables Bard, the hero, to kill the villain.

At the end of the tale, however, Bilbo shows his real stature. Faced with the refusal of the Dwarves to share their wealth with the townsfolk against whom they aroused the dragon, and whose captain slew the dragon, Bilbo determines to see justice done. He gives the Arkenstone to the

Elvenking and Bard to bargain with, then goes back to face
the wrath of the Dwarves. Love of justice and love of peace
here raise Bilbo to a height not far below Frodo, the
Ring-bearer.

Frodo rises to greater heights because from the beginning he accepts the burden of the Ring purely for the
sake of others. It is no mere adventure that sends Frodo
riding out of the Shire, but a willingness to suffer so that
others may be saved—a willingness that is tested to the
last grim degree on the black plains of Mordor. Frodo is
not Christ, the Ring is not the Cross, and the salvation
his sacrifice wins is a purely secular salvation. But there
are obviously echoes of these greater realities in the fictional "passion" of Frodo. "Greater love has no man than
this, that a man lay down his life for his friends", says
Christ (Jn 15:13), and Frodo's journey is at least an illustration of this.

The growth of Frodo in courage and loyalty is clear
enough as the story develops. At the first real test, in the
den of the Barrow-wight, he is tempted to use the Ring to
save himself. "A wild thought of escape came to him. He
wondered if he put on the Ring, whether the Barrow-
wight would miss him, and he might find some way out.
He thought of himself running free over the grass, grieving
for Merry, and Sam, and Pippin, but free and alive himself." [15] He rejects the temptation and begins to grow toward
his final stature. There are other crises, and the Ring itself
betrays him several times. But he is able to resist the call of
the Ringwraiths to surrender on Weathertop and at the Ford
of Bruinen, and to make up his own mind when assailed
by the Enemy on Amon Hen.

[15] Ibid., p. 160.

Suddenly he felt the Eye. There was an eye in the Dark Tower that did not sleep. He knew that it had become aware of his gaze. A fierce eager will was there. It leaped towards him; almost like a finger he felt it, searching for him. Very soon it would nail him down, know just exactly where he was. Amon Lhaw it touched. It glanced upon Tol Brandir—he threw himself from the seat, crouching, covering his head with his grey hood.

He heard himself crying out: *Never, never!* Or was it: *Verily I come, I come to you?* He could not tell. Then as a flash from some other point of power there came to his mind another thought: *Take it off! Take it off! Fool, take it off! Take off the Ring!*

The two powers strove in him. For a moment, perfectly balanced between their piercing points, he writhed, tormented. Suddenly he was aware of himself again. Frodo, neither the Voice nor the Eye: free to choose, and with one remaining instant in which to do so. He took the Ring off his finger. He was kneeling in clear sunlight before the high seat. A black shadow seemed to pass like an arm above him; it missed Amon Hen and groped out west, and faded. Then all the sky was clean and blue and birds sang in every tree.[16]

Frodo grows even greater as he journeys on with Sam and Gollum. His gentleness to Gollum almost conquers the creature's withered heart, and his steady endurance of his burden as it grows almost overwhelming contains a moving echo of the Way of the Cross. Indeed, his nightmare journey across the blasted plains of Mordor with Sam and Gollum tends sometimes to dominate our memory of the book, so that it is easy to forget how much laughter and enchantment and delight the story contains.

[16] Ibid., p. 451.

Sam Gamgee's outstanding characteristics are his loyalty to Frodo and his love of Frodo; but Sam has his own complexities. His love of Elves and his delight in the wonders they meet along the way reveal a streak of imagination and even of poetry. His dogged endurance is hinted at even in the beginning. "I seem to see ahead, in a kind of way. I know we are going to take a very long road, into darkness; but I know I can't turn back. It isn't to see Elves now, nor dragons, nor mountains, that I want—I don't rightly know what I want: but I have something to do before the end, and it lies ahead, not in the Shire. I must see it through, sir, if you understand me." [17]

At the end, when he and Frodo have accomplished their task and seem about to die, Sam urges the exhausted Frodo to one last effort.

> "I am glad that you are here with me," said Frodo. "Here at the end of all things, Sam."
>
> "Yes, I am with you, Master," said Sam, laying Frodo's wounded hand gently to his breast. "And you're with me. And the journey's finished. But after coming all that way I don't want to give up yet. It's not like me, somehow, if you understand."
>
> "Maybe not, Sam," said Frodo; "but it's like things are in the world. Hopes fail. And end comes. We have only a little time to wait now. We are lost in ruin and downfall, and there is no escape."
>
> "Well, Master, we could at least go further from this dangerous place here, from this Crack of Doom, if that's its name. Now couldn't we? Come, Mr. Frodo, let's go down the path at any rate!"

[17] Ibid., p. 97.

"Very well, Sam. If you wish to go, I'll come," said Frodo; and they rose and went slowly down the winding road.[18]

Merry and Pippin at first show mainly their loyalty to Frodo. "'It all depends on what you want,' put in Merry. 'You can trust us to stick to you through thick and thin—to the bitter end. And you can trust us to keep any secret of yours—closer than you keep it yourself. But you cannot trust us to let you face trouble alone, and go off without a word. We are your friends, Frodo. Anyway: there it is. We know most of what Gandalf has told you. We know a good deal about the Ring. We are horribly afraid—but we are coming with you; or following you like hounds.'"[19] But as time goes on they begin to reveal other qualities. Their cheerfulness persists in the face of danger and hardship; their frankness and friendliness win them the friendship of the formidable Treebeard. Merry's affection for King Théoden of the Rohirrim along with Pippin's quixotic offer of fealty to Denethor show a generosity only hinted at earlier. To some extent the various qualities that make us so fond of Bilbo in *The Hobbit* are distributed among the hobbits in *The Lord of the Rings* trilogy, and Merry and Pippin have Bilbo's endearing perkiness and cheerfulness. Their very weaknesses make them more "human"— bring them nearer to us.

Gandalf can be a remote and enigmatic character, but his humor and his gruffness (a bark that is usually worse than his bite, at least for his friends) make him a memorable

---

[18] J. R. R. Tolkien, *The Return of the King* (New York: Ballantine Books, 2001), p. 244.

[19] Tolkien, *Fellowship of the Ring*, p. 244. (One major failing of the movie *The Lord of the Rings* is how justice is not done to Merry and Pippin.)

character and even one who inspires affection. Frodo composes his first poem when he believes Gandalf is dead. One of the lines is "swift in anger, quick to laugh", and even after Gandalf's apotheosis, his temper and his humor survive.

In a way, Gandalf is more "human" than Aragorn, more understandable and familiar to us than Gimli the Dwarf or Legolas the Elf. Gimli's astonished love for Galadriel humanizes him a bit. Legolas remains the most remote of the Fellowship, as Tolkien intends. But all three—Aragorn, Gimli, and Legolas—are intended by Tolkien to be somewhat remote. They are heroes or supermen. They do not lose their dignity, even when they momentarily lose their courage, as Legolas does at the sight of the Balrog and Gimli does on the Paths of the Dead.

It is not the heroes, but the very limited and fallible hobbits who are the real focus of the story. Perhaps Tolkien had learned from the early English poets that though Beowulf is a formidable character, the fallible Gawain is a more living one. Even Gandalf and Galadriel have the possibility of failing; they are both tempted by the power of the Ring, but are able to resist the temptation.

It may be well here to clear up a minor misunderstanding about the Ring itself. It has been blithely identified with power by both friendly and unfriendly critics. Mary Ellman accused Tolkien's characters of being afraid of power, and even some of his admirers talk merely about the "dangers of power". But, of course, the Ring has not merely neutral power, but Satanic power: the Dark Lord "has put a great part of his own power into it", and this is why its destruction does more than deprive Sauron of *more* power—it destroys him. When Gandalf and Galadriel refuse the Ring, it is not because "power corrupts"; they are, apart from Sauron, the most powerful persons in the story. Rather, they reject it because using the Ring to do good would be attempting to use Satan's power to do good, and this will inevitably defeat the good purpose and turn it to evil.

Saruman tries to tempt Gandalf with the power of the Ring and the plea that the end justifies the means:

"Listen, Gandalf, my old friend and helper!" he said, coming near and speaking now in a softer voice. "I said *we*, for *we* it may be, if you will join with me. A new Power is rising. Against it the old allies and policies will not avail us at all. There is no hope left in Elves or dying Númenor. This then is one choice before you, before us. We may join with that Power. It would be wise, Gandalf. There is hope that way. Its victory is at hand; and there will be rich reward for those that aided it. As the Power grows, its proved friends will also grow; and the Wise, such as you and I, may with patience come at last to direct its courses, to control it. We can bide our time, we can keep our thoughts in our hearts, deploring maybe evils done by the way, but approving the high and ultimate purpose: Knowledge, Rule, Order; all the things that we have so far striven in vain to accomplish, hindered rather than helped by our weak or idle friends. There need not be, there would not be, any real change in our designs, only in our means." [20]

Both in the case of Saruman and in the case of Gollum, there is a sense that there may be a real possibility of their redemption. When Gandalf pleads with Saruman after his defeat, Saruman wavers for a moment. Just before Gollum betrays Frodo, he almost gives in to love for him. Each being in the story (except Orcs) is good or evil by his own choice, and that choice is a genuinely free one, though powerful

---

[20] Tolkien, *Fellowship of the Ring*, p. 291.

forces from inside and out attempt to influence it. As Gandalf says of Gollum:

> "Even Gollum was not wholly ruined. He had proved tougher than even one of the Wise would have guessed—as a hobbit might. There was a little corner of his mind that was still his own, and light came through it, as through a chink in the dark: light out of the past. It was actually pleasant, I think, to hear a kindly voice again, bringing up memories of wind, and trees, and sun on the grass, and such forgotten things.
>
> "But that, of course, would only make the evil part of him angrier in the end—unless it could be conquered. Unless it could be cured." Gandalf sighed "Alas! there is little hope of that for him. Yet not no hope. No, not though he possessed the Ring so long, almost as far back as he can remember. For it was long since he had worn it much: in the black darkness it was seldom needed. Certainly he had never 'faded'. He is thin and tough still. But the thing was eating up his mind, of course, and the torment had become almost unbearable." [21]

Remember the salient points we found in Lewis' discussion of good and evil, the responsibility of each person to do God's work, the danger of using evil means—this is Tolkien's message as well as Lewis'. The apparent absence of explicit religion in Tolkien will be discussed in the next chapter, but Tolkien's moral message seems to be the same as Lewis'.

The character of evil is also alike in Tolkien and Lewis. In Tolkien's stories, just as in Lewis', one prominent characteristic of the evil characters is their inability to trust each other or cooperate with each other effectively. We get the

[21] Ibid., p. 60.

first sketch of this in *The Hobbit*, where the first evil creatures encountered, the trolls, are defeated because of their
quarreling with each other. At several crucial points in *The
Lord of the Rings* trilogy the hobbits are able to take advantage of the quarrels of Orcs with other Orcs (Merry and
Pippin's escape from the Uruk-hai, Sam and Frodo's escape
from Cirith Ungol). On a somewhat higher level, Saruman's rivalry with Sauron weakens both sides in the uneasy
alliance, providing another advantage for the Fellowship of
the Ring. And, as we have mentioned already, Sauron's inability to picture his adversaries as anything but rivals for his
power is a key element in his final defeat. As Gandalf says
before the last battle: "Sauron knows ... that this precious
thing which he lost has been found again ... [and that]
there are some among us with strength enough to wield it.
... It can be used only by one master alone, not by many;
and he will look for a time of strife, ere one of the great
among us makes himself master and puts down the others.... We must march out to meet him at once. We must
make ourselves the bait.... He will take that bait, in hope
and in greed, for he will think that in such rashness he sees
the pride of the new Ringlord." [22]

And Gandalf says earlier, "Let folly be our cloak, a veil
before the eyes of the Enemy! For he is very wise, and
weighs all things to a nicety in the scales of his malice. But
the only measure that he knows is desire, desire for power;
and so he judges all hearts. Into his heart the thought will
not enter that any will refuse it, that having the Ring we
may seek to destroy it. If we seek this, we shall put him out
of reckoning." [23]

[22] Tolkien, *Return of the King*, p. 160.
[23] Tolkien, *Fellowship of the Ring*, p. 302.

The Fellowship of the Ring is, indeed, beyond Sauron's comprehension. The great hero and captain, Aragorn, turns aside from his great destiny to become the guide and protector of a young hobbit who has hardly drawn a sword in anger. The Elf, Legolas, and the Dwarf, Gimli, overcome the estrangement of their races and become fast friends. All three turn aside from seemingly more important matters to pursue the Uruk-hai day after day in hope of rescuing Merry and Pippin. Even Boromir, nearly overcome by his desire for the Ring, repents and dies sacrificing his life trying to save the younger hobbits. Ironically, this is a "useless" sacrifice, since the Orcs have orders to take hobbits alive. But it is Boromir's *amende honorable* and, we are made to feel, his salvation. All of this loyalty, sacrifice, subordination of higher to lower, would be totally incomprehensible to Sauron, as Tolkien makes us see.

In fact, as both Lewis and Tolkien show us, there is a fatal contradiction on the side of evil. No one in his right mind would want to be one of Sauron's slaves. But one might, in certain moods, want to be Sauron or, failing this, one of his satraps. Yet only the highest throne is really secure; there is only one position really worth having, even at the most cynical estimate. Thus all but one on the side of darkness are doomed to frustration. In the company of the good, however, there is a complicated "dance" of subordination; for example, Aragorn delights to honor Frodo and Frodo delights to honor him, and both delight to honor Sam. The mystery of evil is that it rejects joy for an ambition that is in its nature unattainable.

6

# Religion in Tolkien

Many critics find no religious element at all in Tolkien's Middle-earth. But perhaps it is wise to make clear what we mean by the much-abused term "religion". I take it that the usual elements of religion are belief in a Being or Beings greater than man and worthy of worship, and a belief in some sort of life after death. Are these two elements present in Tolkien? There is a problem here for Tolkien, the Christian writing of a pre-Christian era, a problem that is illuminated by his comments on the Beowulf poet, who has essentially the same problem.

> He cast his time into the long-ago, because already the long-ago had a special poetical attraction. He knew much about old days and though his knowledge ... was rich and poetical rather than accurate with the accuracy of modern archaeology (such as that is), one thing he knew clearly: those days were heathen—heathen, noble, and hopeless.

This chapter was written before the posthumous publication of J. R. R. Tolkien's *Silmarillion* in 1977. An epilogue has been added to the end of this chapter discussing how *The Silmarillion* adds to our understanding of the religious element in Tolkien's work.

> But if the specifically Christian was suppressed, so also were the old gods. Partly because they had not really existed, and had been always, in the Christian view, only delusions or lies fabricated by the evil one, the *gastbona*, to whom the hopeless turned especially in times of need. Partly because their old names (certainly not forgotten) had been potent, and were connected in memory still, not only with mythology or such fairy-tale matter as we find, say, in *Gylfaginning*, but with active heathendom, religion not actually essential to the theme.[1]

This is Tolkien's problem in a nutshell. If he shows his people at worship, for instance, whom is he to show them worshipping? A man of Tolkien's activity of mind could invent fifty pantheons, with appropriate myths and rituals. But this would be to show his heroes worshipping false gods. Is he to make them monotheists then? But how is he to make their monotheism plausible? None of his races have a philosophical bent, like the Greeks. Is he to give them a special revelation, like the Hebrews? But if so, how is this to connect with the Judeo-Christian revelation? Wisely enough, Tolkien does not show his characters at worship.

And yet he does not entirely avoid the idea of superior beings, of worship. Hints here and there through the manuscript are expanded in the Appendices. There are the Valar, the "Guardians of the World", and behind them the figure of "the One". The Valar are not unlike more remote eldils, from the little we hear of them. But at one point this background religion comes into the foreground. If any group in Middle-earth is to be close to God or the gods, it should be the Elves, and among these the High Elves.

---

[1] J. R. R. Tolkien, "Beowulf: The Monsters and the Critics", in *An Anthology of Beowulf Criticism*, ed. Lewis E. Nicholson (Notre Dame, Ind.: University of Notre Dame Press, 1963), pp. 71–72.

For in Tolkien's imaginary history the High Elves are those who have dwelt in the Blessed Realm, the Undying Lands, and have then returned to Middle-earth to live for a while before returning via the Grey Havens. They are the wisest, best, and most powerful of all the races in Middle-earth, and all of the greatest Elf figures in legend and song, as well as in the main story, are of the High-elven kindred.

Now look at the early part of Frodo's adventures, when he has left Bag End, but not yet the Shire. He and his companions fall in with a group of Elves, who are singing this song:

> Snow-white! Snow-white! O Lady clear!
>> O Queen beyond the Western Seas!
> O Light to us that wander here
>> Amid the world of woven trees!
>
> Gilthoniel! O Elbereth!
>> Clear are thy eyes and bright thy breath!
> Snow-white! Snow-white! We sing to thee
>> In a far land beyond the Sea.
>
> O stars that in the Sunless Year
>> With shining hands by her were sown,
> In windy fields now bright and clear
>> We see your silver blossom blown!
>
> O Elbereth! Gilthoniel!
>> We still remember, we who dwell
> In this far land beneath the trees,
>> Thy starlight on the Western Seas.

The song ended. "These are High-Elves! They spoke the name of Elbereth!" said Frodo in amazement.[2]

---

[2] J. R. R. Tolkien, *The Fellowship of the Ring*, rev. ed. (New York: Ballantine Books, 2001), pp. 88–89.

Elbereth is "Queen beyond the Western Seas"; we shall explore the significance of this in a moment. But if the "stars ... with shining hands by her were sown", she is evidently something like a goddess, even if the language is partly metaphorical. "O Light to us that wander here" recalls certain Roman Catholic hymns to the Blessed Virgin. And indeed, Elbereth seems to play a part very similar to that of Mary in Catholic worship.

Later on, when the Fellowship of the Ring are leaving Lothlórien, the great Elf-queen Galadriel sings a song. It is given in "Elvish" with a translation attached.

> "Ah! like gold fall the leaves in the wind, long years numberless as the wings of trees! The years have passed like swift draughts of the sweet mead in lofty halls beyond the West, beneath the blue vaults of Varda wherein the stars tremble in the song of her voice, holy and queenly. Who now shall refill the cup for me? For now the Kindler, Varda, the Queen of the Stars, from Mount Everwhite has uplifted her hands like clouds, and all paths are drowned deep in shadow; and out of a grey country darkness lies on the foaming waves between us, and mist covers the jewels of Calacirya for ever. Now lost, lost to those from the East is Valimar! Farewell! Maybe thou shalt find Valimar. Maybe even thou shalt find it. Farewell!" Varda is the name of that Lady whom the Elves in these lands of exile name Elbereth.[3]

Here again, the terms used of Varda are appropriate only to a goddess or a saint. Gildor also says to the hobbits, "May Elbereth protect you",[4] which makes sense only if Elbereth is supposed to have the power to know what is happening

[3] Ibid., p. 424.
[4] Ibid., p. 94.

to the companions and the power to help them. Such expressions as "May God protect you", "May Mary protect you", "May St. Patrick protect you" make sense, but if we substitute merely historical or legendary figures we get nonsense: "May George Washington protect you", "May Uncle Sam protect you."

Elbereth is invoked by the hobbits at every moment of crisis—for instance, at the first attack of the Black Riders, when Frodo puts himself in great peril by putting on the Ring. "The third [figure] . . . sprang forward and bore down on Frodo. At that moment Frodo threw himself forward on the ground, and he heard himself crying aloud: *O Elbereth! Gilthoniel!* At the same time he struck at the feet of his enemy." [5] He calls on Elbereth again at the Ringwraiths' next attack.[6] Again, when Sam rescues Frodo from the tower of Cirith Ungol, he must leave him to hunt for disguises for them: "Now you draw up the ladder, if you can, Mr. Frodo; and don't you let it down till you hear me call the pass-word. *Elbereth* I'll call. What the Elves say. No orc would say that." [7] Just before this, Sam, in his fight with Shelob, has called on Elbereth.

In fact, as we look through the whole trilogy, with our minds alerted to the importance of Elbereth's name, we are surprised at the number of times it is mentioned. At many moments of crisis there is some mention of invocation of Elbereth, especially by the Elves (Gildor, Galadriel), but also by Sam and Frodo. Men and Dwarves do not call on her, nor does Gandalf, although he mentions her name with respect. It seems that Elbereth is primarily the Lady of the

[5] Ibid., p. 221.
[6] Ibid., p. 242.
[7] J. R. R. Tolkien, *The Return of the King* (New York: Ballantine Books, 2001), p. 199.

Elves and secondarily the patroness or protector of Elf-friends like Sam and Frodo. By them she is invoked in danger, and songs are sung in her praise. This is far from any formal worship, of course, but we have found a bright Being invoked by the highest race of creatures—as we might expect—and called on by the heroes of the story at the moments of greatest crisis—as we might expect.

Outside of the trilogy itself there is one more source of information—the notes, mainly linguistic, that Tolkien contributed to *The Road Goes Ever On*, a song cycle based on Tolkien's poetry with music by Donald Swann. In discussing the Elvish words of the song "O Elbereth Gilthoniel", mentioned above, Tolkien draws a parallel with Sam's invocation of Elbereth before his battle with Shelob. Amid the linguistic details, he makes this point in passing: "As a 'divine' or 'angelic' person Varda/Elbereth could be said to be 'looking afar from heaven' (as in Sam's invocation); hence the use of a present participle. She was often thought of, or depicted, as standing on a great height looking towards Middle-earth, with eyes that penetrated the shadows, and listening for the cries for aid of Elves (and Men) in peril or grief. Frodo (vol. I, p. 208) and Sam both invoke her in moments of extreme peril. The Elves sing hymns to her. (These and other references to religion in *The Lord of the Rings* are frequently overlooked.)" [8] This comment in passing by Tolkien seems to confirm all that we have guessed from the trilogy itself. Elbereth is "divine" or "angelic"; the songs the Elves sing to her are called specifically "hymns". She can hear and answer "cries for aid". She hears the cries primarily of Elves, and Men are mentioned parenthetically

---

[8] Donald Swann and J. R. R. Tolkien, *The Road Goes Ever On: A Song Cycle* (New York: Ballantine Books, 1967), p. 65.

as also crying to her. I think this is the clearest statement that Tolkien has given about religion in *The Lord of the Rings* trilogy, and characteristically it is an oblique reference in a series of remarks on Elvish philology.

In view of the difficulties we have considered above, these hints are perhaps all Tolkien can be expected to give us. I think, by the way, that there are elements of personality and personal history involved in Tolkien's failure to say much about God. Tolkien was a more reticent man than Lewis, by all accounts, and less inclined to speak much of the things closest to his heart. Also, Tolkien, practically a cradle Catholic, was less inclined to talk about religion than Lewis, the convert to Christianity.

About life after death there is an interesting situation in Tolkien's world. The Elves are immortal and, when they leave Middle-earth, go to live "beyond the Western Seas in Elvenhome or Eressëa". This is a place to which one *can* physically voyage and yet also somehow otherworldly: "in Eressëa, in Elvenhome that no man can discover".[9] It is not the same as the Uttermost West: "the seed of that tree before came from Eressëa, and before that out of the Uttermost West".[10] Numenor, Tolkien's version of Atlantis, was "the westernmost of all Mortal lands ... [from it] the farsighted could descry the white tower of the Haven of the Eldar in Eressëa".[11] Later in the same paragraph: "But one command had been laid upon the Númenoreans, the 'Ban of the Valar'; they were forbidden to sail west out of sight of their own shores or attempt to set foot on the Undying Lands. For though a long span of life had been granted to

[9] Tolkien, *Return of the King*, p. 242.
[10] Tolkien, *Fellowship of the Ring*, p. 274.
[11] Tolkien, *Return of the King*, p. 344.

them [the Númenoreans] . . . they must remain mortal, since
the Valar were not permitted to take from them the Gift of
Men (or the Doom of Men, as it was afterwards called)." [12]
When they break this prohibition and "set foot upon the
shores of Aman the Blessed, the Valar laid down their Guardianship and called upon the One, and the world was changed.
Númenor was thrown down and swallowed in the Sea, and
the Undying Lands were removed for ever from the circles
of the world." [13]

Here we have the elements of the background religion
we mentioned before: the Valar, who like eldils give orders
to mortals and punish the breaking of their rules; the One
behind the Valar. (Elbereth, one presumes, is one of the
Valar.) Eressëa is evidently an earthly paradise, where all
who dwell have unending life. Unending but not, I think,
eternal. There is a suggestion that at the end of this world
Eressëa, too, will end, and the Elves go on to some heavenly destiny. Meanwhile, they live in Eressëa.

We can reconstruct the geography of Tolkien's imagined
world in this fashion. The Uttermost West is the dwelling
of the godlike Valar, who give commands to Men and even
to Elves, although these commands are not always obeyed.
East of the Uttermost West is Eressëa, the dwelling-place
of the Elves. East of this was "the great Isle of Elenna, westernmost of all Mortal lands [where] they founded the realm
of Númenor". [14] But Elenna has sunk into the sea, leaving
no land, apparently, between Middle-earth and Eressëa. Does
all this imply a flat earth? Númenor sank into the sea and
eventually "the Undying Lands were removed for ever from

[12] Ibid.
[13] Ibid., p. 346.
[14] Ibid., p. 344.

the circles of the world." Thus, even if Middle-earth is iden-
tified with Europe, the fact that one can sail west from
Europe without encountering either Atlantis or the Blessed
Realm does not contradict Tolkien's imagined history.

Of course, the idea that gods or angels could have a local
habitation, a literal "land" or "realm" and not a metaphorical one, is strange to modern minds. But it fits very well
into the mythical atmosphere of Tolkien's world.

Nor does this imaginary history necessarily contradict
Tolkien's Christianity. That men once shared the earth
with other rational beings, that they were all under the
rule and guardianship of some sort of Supernatural Being,
that they faced the servants of the Evil One in physical
battles—none of this contradicts anything in Christian belief,
any more than the similar situation on Lewis' Malacandra
does.

The Wizards or *Istari*, such as Gandalf and Saruman, may
indeed be physical manifestations or embodiments of the
mysterious Valar. They are described as follows:

> When maybe a thousand years had passed, and the first
> shadow had fallen on Greenwood the Great, the *Istari* or
> Wizards appeared in Middle-earth. It was afterwards said
> that they came out of the Far West and were messengers
> sent to contest the power of Sauron, and to unite all those
> who had the will to resist him; but they were forbidden to
> match his power with power, or to seek to dominate Elves
> or Men by force and fear.
>
> They came therefore in the shape of Men, though they
> were never young and aged only slowly, and they had many
> powers of mind and hand. They revealed their true names
> to few, but used such names as were given to them. The
> two highest of this order (of whom it is said there were
> five) were called by the Eldar Curunír, "the Man of Skill",

and Mithrandir, "the Grey Pilgrim", but by Men in the North Saruman and Gandalf. Curunír journeyed often into the East, but dwelt at last in Isengard. Mithrandir was closest in friendship with the Eldar, and wandered mostly in the West and never made for himself any lasting abode.[15]

In response to a question, Tolkien has said that Gandalf is "an angel".[16] Using the terms of Tolkien's own mythology, this suggests that Gandalf is one of the valar, the Guardians. Is this true of all Wizards? Then Saruman is similarly one of the "angels", but a fallen one. Perhaps even Sauron and his more remote predecessor in evil, Morgoth the Enemy,[17] are Guardians who have betrayed their guardianship.

Again the notes to *The Road Goes Ever On* give us some help. In explaining an Elvish word that means "veil", Tolkien remarks that

> The simple word *fana* acquired a special sense. Owing to the close association of the High-Elves with the *Valar* it was applied to the "veils" or "raiment" in which the Valar presented themselves to physical eyes. These were the bodies in which they were self-incarnated. They usually took the shape of the bodies of Elves (and Men). The *Valar* assumed these forms when, after their demiurgic labours, they came and dwelt in *Arda*, "the realm." They did so because of their love and desire for the Children of God (*Erus[-]en*), for whom they were to prepare the "realm." The future forms of elves and men had been revealed to them, though they had no part in their design or making, and the precise time of their appearance was not known. In

[15] Ibid., p. 403.

[16] Edmund Fuller, "The Lord of the Hobbits: J. R. R. Tolkien", in *Tolkien and the Critics*, ed. Neil D. Isaacs and Rose A. Zimbardo (Notre Dame, Ind.: University of Notre Dame Press, 1968), p. 35.

[17] Tolkien, *Return of the King*, p. 342.

these *fanar* they later presented themselves to the Elves (though they could also assume other wholly "inhuman" shapes, which were seldom seen by Elves or Men). [They] appeared as persons of majestic (not gigantic) stature, vested in robes expressing their individual natures and functions. The High-Elves said that these forms were always to some degree radiant, as if suffused with a light from within.[18]

This links up with our previous speculations and suggests others. Is even the Balrog, for example, perhaps a fallen Valar, imprisoned in an "inhuman" form? Gandalf speaks to it as if they shared some secret knowledge: " 'You cannot pass', he said. . . . 'I am a servant of the Secret Fire, wielder of the flame of Anor. You cannot pass. The dark fire will not avail you, flame of Udûn. Go back to the Shadow!' " [19] And if the Balrog is not a being of the same degree of power as Gandalf, how can it nearly destroy him?

Gandalf is described as dying and coming to life again. In the Chronology of Appendix B we have the entries:

January 23    Gandalf pursues the Balrog to the peak of Zirakzigil.

January 25    He casts down the Balrog, and passes away. His body lies on the peak.

February 14    . . . Gandalf returns to life. . . .[20]

At his first reappearance to his friends, Gandalf is almost transfigured.

He laid his hand on Gimli's head, and the Dwarf looked up and laughed suddenly. "Gandalf!" he said. "But you are all in white!"

[18] Swann and Tolkien, *Road Goes Ever On*, p. 66.
[19] Tolkien, *Fellowship of the Ring*, p. 370.
[20] Tolkien, *Return of the King*, p. 412.

"Yes, I am in white now," said Gandalf. "Indeed I *am* Saruman, one might almost say, Saruman as he should have been. But come now, tell me of yourselves! I have passed through fire and deep water, since we parted. I have forgotten much that I thought I knew, and learned again much that I had forgotten. I can see many things far off, but many things that are close at hand I cannot see. Tell me of yourselves!" [21]

This suggests that the fight with the Balrog has destroyed Gandalf's connection with the *fana*, the physical envelope in which he is "self-incarnate", and he must restore his connection with it, thereby giving his *fana* new attributes. Perhaps in the interim he returned to some form of non-corporal life. Then he is recognized by his companions: "'Gandalf,' the old man repeated, as if recalling from old memory a long disused word. 'Yes, that was the name. I was Gandalf.'" [22] His "body" has apparently lain on Zirakzigil for three weeks (January 25 to February 14); I am not sure of the significance of this, though the three weeks perhaps remind us of the three days during which Christ was in the tomb.

It is interesting to compare Tolkien's "angelology" with Lewis'. The statement that angelic beings can assume either human or inhuman forms suggests the scene in *Perelandra* where the eldils assume human forms to honor the King and the Green Lady, after experimenting with various inhuman manifestations. The fact that the Oyéresu of Perelandra and Malacandra are "feminine (not female)" and "masculine (not male)" suggests the genders of Tolkien's

---

[21] J. R. R. Tolkien, *The Two Towers*, rev. ed. (New York: Ballantine Books, 2001), p. 116.
[22] Ibid.

Valar. Elbereth is said to be in some sense the "spouse" of Manwe, the Elder King, chief of the Valar.[23] The "demiurgic work" of the Valar reminds us of Lewis' use of the Neoplatonic idea of angels as the "ruling Intelligences" of heavenly bodies. But it is made quite clear that angels do not "design or make" the forms of Men or Elves. Both Lewis and Tolkien believe angels are real beings, but their fictional angels borrow details from philosophical speculation and from myth.

The parallels between Gandalf's "resurrection" and that of Christ are obvious, so obvious it may be worthwhile to say something again about Tolkien's attitude toward allegory. In the introduction to the Ballantine edition of the trilogy he says,

> As for any inner meaning or "message", it has in the intention of the author none. It is neither allegorical nor topical.... I cordially dislike allegory in all its manifestations, and always have done so since I grew old and wary enough to detect its presence. I much prefer history, true or feigned, with its varied applicability to the thought and experience of readers. I think that many confuse "applicability" with "allegory"; but the one resides in the freedom of the reader, and the other in the purposed domination of the author.
>
> An author cannot of course remain wholly unaffected by his experience, but the ways in which a story-germ uses the soil of experience are extremely complex, and attempts to define the process are at best guesses from evidence that is inadequate and ambiguous.[24]

Thus Tolkien, by his own account, is not writing what we called strict allegory. Nor, I contend, is he writing what I

[23] Swann and Tolkien, *Road Goes Ever On*, p. 66.
[24] Tolkien, *Fellowship of the Ring*, p. xi.

have called "loose allegory"; he is not attempting to tell us that "life is like this." Rather, he is telling us a story, which can be enjoyed purely in its own right. Like all good stories, it has echoes of others, including that greatest of all stories—which Tolkien believes is a true story—the life of Christ.

Gandalf and Frodo are not allegorical masks for Christ, as in a strict allegory, nor symbols for some aspect of human condition, as in a loose allegory. They are people in their own right. But because they are almost real people they can, as real people can, express Christ in their own way.

It is part of the Roman Catholic idea of the saints that each mirrors Christ in an individual way, expressing facets of the infinite Personality, which could not all be expressed in one finite life, no matter how great. The historical Christ, for example, was not a philosopher, nor a king; but St. Thomas Aquinas and St. Louis of France show us something of what He might have been like if He had been. Thus Gandalf and Frodo, while being very real and very individual, also have something to tell us about Christ.

In this, Tolkien is, I might say, contrasted with Lewis as Catholic to Protestant. In Lewis, there are Maleldil and the eldils, and there is Aslan in the Narnia stories. But in Lewis' Protestant Christian imagination there is no human or quasi-human mediator between God and man. On the other hand, in Tolkien's Catholic Christian imagination we have Elbereth, whom it would not surprise us to find addressed as "our Lady", and we have Elves and Wizards who are like the wonderworking saints of medieval legend. In Frodo we see the imitation of Christ on a more human level.

Both tendencies, in fiction and also in real life, have their dangers. Lewis says, in *The Allegory of Love*, "When Catholicism goes bad it becomes the world-old, world-wide

*religio* of amulets and holy places and priestcraft: Protestantism, in its corresponding decay, becomes a vague mist of
ethical platitudes. Catholicism is accused of being much too
like all the other religions; Protestantism of being insuffi-
ciently like a religion at all. Hence Plato, with his transcen-
dent Forms, is the doctor of Protestants; Aristotle, with his
immanent Forms, the doctor of Catholics." [25]

In fiction Tolkien's "saints" are in some danger of degen-
erating into "superman" figures, and the closeness of our
confrontation with Aslan and Maleldil in Lewis is sometimes almost embarrassing. But both men avoid the dangers, by and large. Gandalf, even after his apotheosis, does
not become all-powerful: he is still in danger from the Black
Riders. And by making Aslan a lion, Lewis can have him
say and do things that in a human figure would be embarrassing. Again, the eldils contrast with and highlight the
impression we get of Maleldil. The Elves, though good and
powerful, are not perfect any more than Gandalf is. They
are not really very interested in Men or Hobbits—they go
their own way: "The Elves have their own labours and their
own sorrows, and they are little concerned with the ways
of hobbits, or of any other creatures upon earth. Our paths
cross theirs seldom, by chance or purpose. In this meeting
there may be more than chance; but the purpose is not
clear to me, and I fear to say too much." [26] Also, they are
limited in at least some ways: for instance, they can be killed,
in battle or by accident.

In the story of Aragorn and his Elf-bride Arwen—which
is told in an Appendix—Arwen, who chooses to live and

---

[25] C. S. Lewis, *The Allegory of Love* (New York: Oxford University Press,
1925), p. 323.
[26] Tolkien, *Fellowship of the Ring*, p. 94.

die as a mortal to share the fate of her husband, is described as the *only* Elf truly to die. Since great numbers of Elves are apparently slain in various battles in *The Hobbit* and *The Lord of the Rings* trilogy, this would seem to imply that these somehow did *not* really die. Some sort of translation "beyond the Western Sea" for Elves who "die" in Middle-earth would account for this apparent inconsistency. Certainly the Elves have no fear of death; and when Legolas goes with Aragorn on the Paths of the Dead "there was not a heart among them that did not quail, unless it were the heart of Legolas of the Elves, for whom the ghosts of Men have no terror." [27] At the attack on the four at the ford near Rivendell, Frodo sees Glorfindel the Elf-lord as a shining white figure. Gandalf tells him later, "You saw him for a moment as he is upon the other side." [28] Evidently the Elves are not wholly of this world even when they dwell in Middle-earth.

What of Hobbits? As far as I can see, Tolkien gives no answer at all to this except in the cases of Frodo and Sam, both of whom join the Elves in their earthly paradise as a reward for their struggles. There is some suggestion of a sort of limbo for Dwarves in *The Hobbit*; when Thorin is dying he says, "I go now to the halls of waiting to sit beside my fathers, until the world is renewed." [29]

In Catholic theological speculation, the good men who lived before the time of Christ waited in "the Limbo of the Fathers" for the redemptive death of Christ, after which they could enter heaven. Nothing Tolkien says either suggests or denies that this is the case, except some hints in the case of the marriages between Men and Elf-maids. By

---

[27] Tolkien, *Return of the King*, p. 48.
[28] Tolkien, *Fellowship of the Ring*, p. 249.
[29] J. R. R. Tolkien, *The Hobbit* (New York: Ballantine Books, 2001), p. 288.

choosing to marry Aragorn, Arwen is evidently to choose the lot of a mortal and *thus* to be separated from her Elvish kindred—"a bitter parting beyond the end of the world".[30]

Thus we have the following situation: the fate of Elves is immortality in Eressëa; the fate of Dwarves to "go to the halls of waiting ... until the world is renewed"; and the fate of Men and Hobbits is left uncertain except that death is called "the gift of the One to Men".[31]

So much for *explicitly* religious elements. But the whole framework of *The Lord of the Rings* trilogy is that of a struggle between good and evil on a cosmic scale, with everyone having to choose one side or another. Furthermore, there is a plan behind what happens; Frodo was *meant* to find the Ring.[32] As Patricia Meyer Spacks says in an essay collected in the Isaacs and Zimbardo volume:

A theological scheme is implied though not directly stated in *The Lord of the Rings*, and it is of primary importance to ... the work. The fact of freedom of the will implies a structured universe, a universe like the Christian one in that only through submission to the Good can true freedom be attained—willing acceptance of evil involves necessary loss of freedom; a universe like the Christian one, further, in that it includes the possibility of Grace.... If the trilogy, as has been said, deals with a "pre-religious" age, an age in which worship was confined to adherence to a special ethos, the fact remains that the author includes in it all the necessary materials for religion.[33]

[30] Tolkien, *Return of the King*, p. 374.
[31] Ibid., p. 378.
[32] Tolkien, *Fellowship of the Ring*, p. 41.
[33] Patricia Meyer Spacks, "Power and Meaning in *The Lord of the Rings*", in *Tolkien and the Critics*, pp. 86, 89–90.

A little of Tolkien's feelings about religion comes out in one of his short pieces, "Leaf by Niggle" (reprinted in *The Tolkien Reader*), the nearest thing to allegory that Tolkien has written. "There was once a little man called Niggle, who had a long journey to make. He did not want to go, indeed the whole idea was distasteful to him; but he could not get out of it. He knew he would have to start some time, but he did not hurry with his preparations."[34]

The first stage in the journey is a "hospital" where Niggle works hard and lives a restricted life. He then goes on to a country place that is like the landscape of a great picture that Niggle, a painter, had been working on before his journey. Finally he travels on to "walk ever further and further towards the Mountains, always uphill".[35]

The journey, of course, is death; the preparations, those preparations for death that we all neglect. The period of treatment that Niggle undergoes at the "hospital" is something like the Catholic idea of Purgatory; the journey into the Mountains is "exploration into God" (in Christopher Fry's fine phrase). But there are some very idiosyncratic elements in this afterlife as pictured by Tolkien. First, part of the effect of the "hospital treatment" on Niggle is a seemingly prosaic change. "He could take up a task the moment one bell rang, and lay it aside promptly the moment the next one went, all tidy and ready to be continued at the right time. He got through quite a lot in a day, now; he finished small things neatly. He had no 'time of his own' (except alone in his bed-cell), and yet he was becoming master of his time; he began to know just what he could

---

[34] J. R. R. Tolkien, "Leaf by Niggle", in *Tree and Leaf* in *The Tolkien Reader* (New York: Ballantine Books, 2001), p. 100.
[35] Ibid., p. 118.

do with it. There was no sense of rush. He was quieter inside now, and at resting-time he could really rest." [36] But it is this change that enables him to finish the work of art that he had left unfinished on earth. In doing this he has the help of Parish, whom he had somewhat grudgingly helped when both were alive. Only after completing this work can he go on to the Mountains.

One critic has suggested that "Leaf by Niggle" was written at that period when Tolkien had despaired of finishing *The Lord of the Rings* trilogy. Niggle's unfinished picture may then be a symbol of Tolkien's unfinished work. (The interruptions of the work required by charity and duty would then give some hint of why that work was so long unfinished.) But after completion of the "picture" and Niggle's departure, the "picture"—really now a sort of little subworld—is used as a sort of preparation area for others who are learning to be strong enough to journey on into the Mountains. "'It is proving very useful indeed,' said the Second Voice. 'As a holiday, and a refreshment. It is splendid for convalescence; and not only for that, for many it is the best introduction to the Mountains. It works wonders in some cases. I am sending more and more there. They seldom have to come back.'" [37] This, I think, gives a very good idea of how Tolkien sees his work, "rest and refreshment", "convalescence" from the modern view of the world but also "for many . . . the best introduction to the Mountains". But since an introduction is not the thing itself, we also see perhaps why the religious element in *The Lord of the Rings* trilogy, while present, is muted and in the background.

[36] Ibid., p. 109.
[37] Ibid., p. 120.

## Epilogue to Chapter 6: *The Silmarillion*

Since this book was first written, several books have been published that cast further light on Tolkien's ideas and on his fiction. Most important of these is the posthumous collection of Tolkien's writings published under the title *The Silmarillion*,[38] although it contains besides the *Silmarillion* proper several other independent works. The authorized biography of Tolkien by Humphrey Carpenter has also appeared[39] as well as several other books casting light on Tolkien's work and thought. In this epilogue, I will briefly relate *The Silmarillion* to what has been said in this book about Tolkien, drawing occasionally on information given to us by Carpenter and other writers about Tolkien.

The collection titled *The Silmarillion* was edited by Christopher Tolkien, J. R. R. Tolkien's son, from the manuscripts left behind by his father. As both Christopher Tolkien and Humphrey Carpenter tell us, there were a number of different versions of each of the works contained in *The Silmarillion*, and one of the reasons that J. R. R. Tolkien himself did not publish the work before his death was his reluctance or inability to choose between different versions of the story. We must, therefore, be cautious of accepting the versions chosen by Christopher Tolkien as representing Tolkien's settled views on some difficult points. But the general trend of the stories casts considerable light on some of the issues I discussed in this book.

First the basically religious character of Tolkien's thought is much clearer in *The Silmarillion* than in the works published earlier. The first book contained in *The Silmarillion* is

[38] J. R. R. Tolkien, *The Silmarillion* (Boston: Houghton Mifflin, 1977).
[39] Humphrey Carpenter, *Tolkien* (Boston: Houghton Mifflin, 1977).

*Ainulindalë*, The Music of the Ainur. It is basically a creation myth. God, who is referred to as Eru or, more often Ilúvatar, creates first angelic, nonmaterial beings referred to generally as the Ainur; they were with him before anything else was made. Ilúvatar reveals to the Ainur his plan for the creation of the material universe, Arda, and the eventual creation in Arda of the two races of beings with material bodies: first Elves, then Men. This revelation of Ilúvatar is presented in the form of a Great Music with three major themes.

Except for the mythological presentation of God's revelation as the Great Music, we have here theological ideas familiar to us from the Bible and from Milton's *Paradise Lost*: angels are created before the material universe; God reveals to them something of his plans. But we now have an element original to Tolkien. The themes of creation are laid down by Ilúvatar, but the Ainur are invited to "show forth [their] powers in adorning this theme . . . with [their] own thoughts and devices".⁴⁰ In other words, some elements of the created universe are not directly invented by God, but are "variations" of God's creation themes by the angels. (In the next book, the *Valaquenta*, we find that the creation of the race of Dwarves is such a "variation" by one of the Ainur.)

One result, however, of this freedom to create variations on Ilúvatar's themes given to the Ainur is that the greatest of the Ainur, Melkor, attempts to introduce variations inconsistent with the themes, creating discord. But out of this discord Ilúvatar creates greater harmony; in fact, the second and third themes are Ilúvatar's response to Melkor's discords. Here again familiar theological ideas are given

⁴⁰ Tolkien, *Ainulindalë*, in *The Silmarillion*, p. 3.

mythological expression: Lucifer, greatest of the angels, is envious of God's power and attempts to make himself a rival of God, but his rebellion is used for good purposes by God's wisdom and power. These ideas and the freedom of the Ainur to make variations on Ilúvatar's themes and Melkor's misuse of this freedom in an effort to spoil Ilúvatar's plans are an underlying motif of all the books in *The Silmarillion*.

After Ilúvatar has revealed the coming creation of the world to the Ainur, he causes the world he has revealed to come into existence. He sends some of the Ainur into this world to prepare it for Elves and Men, the "Children of Ilúvatar". The Ainur find the world unshaped and dark; it is for them to carry out its shaping and lighting according to the vision shown them in the Great Music. Melkor, who covets this new creation as his realm, and its foreshadowed inhabitants as his servants, continually tries to wrest the shaping to his own purposes.

The work of the angelic Ainur as "subcreators" of the world was already a major departure from traditional Judeo-Christian theology: we now get a further departure. The Ainur themselves take on material form, modeled on the form of the to-be-created Elves and Men they have seen in the Great Music. On entering into the world and taking these forms they become the Valar, the Powers of the World, and are sometimes referred to as "gods". The Valar are not bound to these material forms but can take them off and put them on as we do clothing, but just as Men are normally clothed, the Valar are normally embodied. The *Ainulindalë* ends with this embodiment of the Valar and the beginning of conflicts between Melkor and the Valar over the control of Arda, the world; as the Valar form the work, he tries to destroy or distort these forms. Because of Melkor's interference, the Valar are not able to completely carry out either Ilúvatar's original design for the world or their own permitted variations of that design. This is the third major departure from traditional Judeo-Christian theology: the idea that the actual physical form of the universe has been interfered with and spoiled by the Enemy of God.

The story continues in the *Valaquenta*, the "account of the Valar". In it we find that besides the Valar themselves, who are only the greatest of the Ainur who Ilúvatar has sent into the world, there are lesser self-embodied spirits, the Maiar. The Valar themselves are fourteen spirits, seven of whom take male form, seven female form. Like the Greek gods whom, perhaps surprisingly, they resemble rather more than they do the Norse gods, the Valar have divided responsibilities: Manwë rules the sky, Ulmo the sea, and Aule the earth. Varda, who is called Elbereth by the Elves, is Manwë's consort, and Yavanna, who loves growing things, is the consort of Aule. Of the major Valar, Ulmo has no consort, nor does Nienna, a female Vala (singular of Valar) who seems to be especially associated with compassion and healing. Again, the notion of angelic beings as male and female and as paired off in something like marriage is a departure from Judeo-Christian angelology, although there are some hints of it in some byways of Judaic theology.

Of Melkor we are told that he is the only Vala to turn away from Ilúvatar, but he corrupts many of the Maiar, some before his evil is apparent but some at a later time—again a departure from traditional angelology in which all of the fallen angels turn against God at the same time. (The Balrogs are identified as fallen Maiar, as I conjectured.)

Before going on to the *Silmarillion* proper, which is called the *Quenta Silmarillion* or "The History of the Silmarils", let us ask ourselves whether the creation myth of the Ainulindalë and the transmutation of the angels into something

like pagan gods alters our picture of Tolkien as basically a
Christian writer. To answer this question, we must ask ourselves what Tolkien was trying to do in these stories. They
are certainly not attempts to rewrite the Genesis account
or even to interpret it; that is, Tolkien does not propose
them as subjects for primary belief either for himself or
for us. What they are is an attempt to create myth as a
kind of literature, commanding secondary, not primary
belief. The Christian artists of the Renaissance used pagan
mythology in their painting and sculpture not because they
believed in pagan mythology, but because it offered them
artistically interesting themes. Tolkien, who enjoyed myth
as a literary experience, was moved to try his own hand at
myth-making.

When we look at *The Silmarillion* as a whole we find that
it fits perfectly the description of myth given by C. S. Lewis
that we discussed in Chapter 2 above. The stories of *The
Silmarillion* depend "hardly at all on such usual narrative
attractions as suspense or surprise.... Human sympathy is
at a minimum.... The experience may be sad or joyful but
it is always grave ... not only grave but awe-inspiring." [41]
And as Lewis says of myth in general there is a numinous
element in *The Silmarillion*: "It is as if something of great
moment had been communicated to us." [42]

The creation of a private mythology may seem an eccentric kind of literary creation, but I can see no reason to
rule it out as illegitimate. There seems no reason why those
who enjoy myth as Tolkien and Lewis did cannot create
their own myths for enjoyment. That this was Tolkien's own

[41] C. S. Lewis, *An Experiment in Criticism* (Cambridge, Eng.: Cambridge
University Press, 1961), p. 44.
[42] Ibid.

view of what he was doing we have the evidence of some private papers quoted in Carpenter.[43]

Of the ideas we have mentioned that depart from traditional Judeo-Christian views I would judge that Tolkien took with some degree of seriousness the idea that created beings have or can have some part in the making of the universe, since it is an idea he mentions at the end of the essay "On Fairy-Stories"; the Christian may "dare to guess that ... he may actually assist in the exfoliation and the multiple enrichment of creation".[44] The idea that Satan may have to some extent "spoiled" the physical universe he may or may not have taken seriously; it has been offered by competent theologians as a possible explanation of some "natural evils". (There is a hint of it in C. S. Lewis' *Problem of Pain*, which we know that Lewis read to the Inklings.) The idea that angels have taken on fairly permanently bodily forms and that these forms are male and female have been held seriously by some theologians (Milton may have been influenced by one such theologian as Lewis tells us in *A Preface to Paradise Lost*). But I doubt if Tolkien entertained these ideas with any degree of primary belief; they are the mythological trappings, the "supposals" of his story.

When we arrive at the *Silmarillion* proper, the *Quenta Silmarillion*, we again begin with an account of "the beginning of days", a myth not of the creation but of the mythical prehistory of the world. These first several chapters play somewhat the same role that an account of Theseus might play in the history of Athens or the story of Romulus and

[43] Carpenter, *Tolkien*, pp. 89–90.
[44] J. R. R. Tolkien, "On Fairy-Stories", in *Tree and Leaf*, in *Tolkien Reader*, p. 89.

Remus in a history of Rome; they are feigned myth whereas the rest of the *Quenta Silmarillion* is feigned history with mythological elements. The material given in these early chapters confirms several guesses made in this book and modifies some of my other conjectures. It is true, as I suggested on page 111 above, that Elves do not truly die. Tolkien tells us that when an Elf is killed his spirit goes to the "Halls of Mandos", and the Elf may eventually return to Arda in embodied form (though no instance of this is given). The suggestions that the Uttermost West is the home of the Valar, that Eressëa is an island to the east of it where Elves lived, and that Númenor was on an island somewhat to the east of Eressëa are confirmed, but must be somewhat modified; a number of the Elves live on Valinor, the island in the Uttermost West, and Eressëa is a smaller island in a bay on the east side of Valinor where only some of the Elves live.

In the version of the *Quenta Silmarillion* that Christopher Tolkien has given us the world was indeed flat before the action of Eru in removing Valinor and Eressëa from "the circles of the world", but there are a few hints that there are variant versions in which this is not so. But Tolkien does not hesitate to be unashamedly mythological and unscientific in his account; in his story the stars are created long after the creation of Earth, and the sun and moon are created last of all. For some time the world has no lights in the sky and then for a while the light of the stars (which are created by Varda: thus the lines quoted on page 107 above are *not* metaphorical).

The light of the lands of the world before the raising of the sun and moon is provided at first by two "lamps" set on high pillars; when Melkor destroys these, the Valar light the Land of Aman, which is Valinor, the Uttermost West, with two radiant trees, leaving the rest of the world in twi-light under the light of the stars created by Varda. Eventu-ally Melkor destroys these trees too, but before this several key events have occurred. The Elves have been created and awake in "Middle-earth", the central part of the flat world imagined by Tolkien. Eventually they are called by the Valar to the West to live in the light of the Two Trees under the protection of the Valar. Some kindreds of the Elves, the Vanyar and Noldor, come all the way to Valinor; some of the Teleri come later and more reluctantly. Not all of the Teleri come all the way, and those that do dwell at first on Eressëa rather than on Valinor. Some Elves, the Avari, refuse to leave Middle-earth at all.

The reluctance of some Elves and the refusal of others is due to lies and rumors spread by Melkor, who continually acts to spoil the plans of the Valar and turn Elves and Men away from Ilúvatar. Even after the Vanyar and Noldor are established in Valinor, and the Teleri begin to come from Eressëa to Valinor, Melkor continues his subtle plots. One of the greatest of the Noldor, Fëanor, creates three marvel-ous jewels, the Silmarils, which have some of the light of the Two Trees in them. After subtly poisoning the attitude of the Noldor to the Valar, Melkor strikes physically, killing the Two Trees, and steals the Silmarils. Influenced by his love of his creations and the lies of Melkor, Fëanor leads a great many of the Noldor back to Middle-earth, swearing vengeance on Melkor and seeking independence from the Valar. To get the ships of the Teleri, who have become great seafarers, Fëanor leads the first war of Elf with Elf; the van-guard of his group become killers of their own race, and even those who do not take part in the attack become guilty of complicity by continuing with Fëanor (some of the group repent and turn back).

This and subsequent incidents force us to revise my ear-lier idea that the Elves are a wholly good race; under the influence of Melkor they can kill, covet, and steal, but as opposed to Men who are a fallen race it is individual Elves, always under some influence from Melkor, who sin, and their sin does not affect other Elves unless those Elves vol-untarily make themselves part of the sin of the others. In Adam all Men fell, but by Fëanor only some Elves are led astray.

As the story of the Silmarils unfolds, the battle between good and evil moves to a more physical level. Melkor attacks the "immigrant" Elves and those who have stayed in Middle-earth with Balrogs, dragons, and hordes of Orcs. We learn that Orcs are the descendants of corrupted Elves, explain-ing the horror with which they are regarded by Elves and confirming that evil powers can only corrupt, not create.

After causing all sorts of trouble and sorrow, two of the Silmarils are destroyed; the other is returned to the Valar and becomes the Evening Star. These later parts of the *Quenta Silmarillion* are more "realistic"; there are battles, chases, the building of strongholds and their betrayal, stories of happy and unhappy love. But underlying everything is the unend-ing battle between good and evil; Melkor is eventually cap-tured and exiled into the Outer Dark, but his lieutenant, Sauron, takes up the battle on the side of evil.

The remaining books of *The Silmarillion* are the *Akallabêth*—Tolkien's version of the Atlantis legend—and a brief account *Of the Rings of Power and the Third Age*. These books expand material already in the Appendices of *The Lord of the Rings* and contain few surprises for those who have studied those Appendices. Like *The Lord of the Rings*, *The Silmarillion* ends with genealogies and indices of names and contains fascinating and evocative maps.

In general, *The Silmarillion* deepens but does not change our assessment of J. R. R. Tolkien. As might be expected, the work as a whole is so logical and well-knit that many guesses made on the basis of hints in the earlier work are confirmed in this book. Much is revealed, but much is held back. We can guess that the *Istari*, the Wizards, are Maiar, but this is not clearly stated. The "Secret Fire" or "Hidden Fire" mentioned in some important contexts is unexplained; Tolkien told Clyde Kilby that the term refers to the Holy Spirit.[45] Tolkien keeps some of his reticences.

In particular there is no hint or mention, despite their deep importance to Tolkien, of Christ or Christianity. If *The Silmarillion* seems to end on a somewhat dark and despairing note, it is because Tolkien has not allowed himself to introduce any hint of the true Hope of the world. Partly this is his personal reticence, partly it is his artistic purpose: the reasons for this silence are analogous to those discussed. But the Christian hope is in Tolkien's own heart and is hidden in the heart of his work. As he said in "On Fairy-Stories", "This story is supreme and it is true. . . . God is the Lord of angels, and of men—and of elves."[46]

[45] Clyde Kilby, *Tolkien and the Silmarillion* (Wheaton, Ill.: Harold Shaw Publisher, 1976), p. 59.

[46] Tolkien, "On Fairy-Stories", p. 89.

# 7

# Religion in Lewis

In view of many misunderstandings, perhaps the first thing to notice about religion in Lewis' imaginative works is that there is much less of it than some people seem to suppose. When we remember that the Roses call Lewis' space trilogy "a formal 'apology' for ... Christianity", it comes as something of a shock to find that of the 160 pages of *Out of the Silent Planet* in the paperback edition, only twenty-seven contain anything that might be called a religious reference. The first four or five are casual indications that Ransom is a believer; he contemplates suicide and, since he is "a pious man", hopes he will be forgiven if forced to it. At the landing of the spaceship he "licked his dry lips and prayed for the end"; when he hopes to escape, "he prayed, and felt his knife." Waking after his first night on Mars, "he ... applied himself vigorously to his devotions and his toilet." There is a mention of "Paradise" when he finds the "talking beast", his first Martian. (You will see I am trying to count all possible references.) He finds that the Martians are mono-theists who use the name Maleldil for God. After this there are a dozen or so references to Maleldil in connec-tion with crops, the way man is constituted, death, and so on. When Ransom meets the eldils, the evil ruling eldil of our world is more or less identified with Satan, and the Oyarsa of Mars evinces curiosity about God's dealings with Earth including, presumably, the Incarnation. (Earth is "blockaded", and no direct information reaches the eldils.) In the concluding chapter, it is said that the dangers represented by the forces behind Weston are "not temporal, but eternal". Some of these references are important to the plot; none are vital. It would be possible, in fact, to remove all of these references without destroying the story or perhaps without even seriously damaging it. But the point is that these scattered references, important to the plot or not, are seen by the Roses as "a formal 'apology' for . . . Christianity".

There are two reasons for this, I think. One is that the Roses expect to find Lewis an "allegorical" writer and therefore find allegory where it is not really present as, for example, in the different occupations of the three Martian races. The second, the question of "hierarchy", we have already discussed. The Martians and Ransom agree that man should obey God. The Martians also assume that rational animals will be subject to eldils—which, as we have seen, is not true on Earth or Venus.

But Lewis did not write strict or even loose allegory, except for his early work, *The Pilgrim's Regress*. All of his stories rest on what may be called a "supposal" or, as Lewis sometimes called it, a "feigning". Suppose (or feign) that a man reached another planet and found unfallen races. . . . Suppose that the story of the fall of man were played out again on a different world, but this time we feign a man of our own world is present. . . . Suppose there is another world, of Talking Beasts and Dwarves and Fauns, and in that world we feign Christ is a great lion, the King of the Beasts. The story often consists of supposing or feigning these things and *then* going on to explore the consequences of this supposal. As Lewis says in a letter:

> By an allegory I mean a composition (whether pictorial or literary) in which immaterial realities are represented by feigned physical objects; e.g. a pictured Cupid allegorically represents erotic love (which in reality is an experience, not an object occupying a given area of space) or, in Bunyan, a giant represents Despair.
>
> If Aslan represented the immaterial Deity in the same way in which Giant Despair represents Despair, he would be an allegorical figure. In reality however he is an invention giving an imaginary answer to the question, "What might Christ become like, if there really were a world like Narnia and He chose to be incarnate and die and rise again in *that* world as He actually has done in ours?" This is not allegory at all. So in *Perelandra*. This also works out a *supposition*. ("Suppose, even now, in some other planet there were a first couple undergoing the same that Adam and Eve underwent here, but successfully.")
>
> Allegory and such supposals differ because they mix the real and the unreal in different ways. Bunyan's picture of Giant Despair does not start from supposal at all. It is not a supposition but a *fact* that despair can capture and imprison a human soul. What is unreal (fictional) is the giant, the castle, and the dungeon. The Incarnation of Christ in another world is mere supposal; but *granted* the supposition, He would really have been a physical object in that world as He was in Palestine and His death on the Stone Table would have been a physical event no less than his death on Calvary. Similarly, if the angels (who I believe to be real beings in the actual universe) have that relation to the Pagan gods which they are assumed to have in Perelandra, they might *really* manifest themselves in real form as they did to

Ransom. Again, Ransom (to some extent) plays the role of Christ not because he allegorically represents Him (as Cupid represents falling in love) but because in reality every real Christian is really called upon in some measure to *enact* Christ. Of course Ransom does this rather more spectacularly than most. But that does not mean that he does it allegorically. It only means that fiction (at any rate my kind of fiction) chooses extreme cases.[1]

Note that what Lewis is doing is not like most illustrative fantasy, where the real interest is in certain aspects of human nature or the human condition, which are merely isolated and exaggerated by the supposal. Rather, Lewis is interested in these supposals partly for their own sake and partly because they provide a restatement in new terms of ideas Lewis held to be true on other grounds. The restatement in terms of fantasy enables us to see them with fresh eyes— remember Tolkien's idea of Recovery—but is also interesting in itself. To take a not-altogether-fanciful parallel, a young man in love might try to imagine his beloved as she might have been if she had been born in another age or in another world. These imaginings might help him understand her better or appreciate her more, but it might also simply be a way of delighting in her "infinite variety".

Lewis was, I think, genuinely enamored of certain basic Christian ideas. He stated them clearly and gracefully in his radio talks, which have been collected in *Mere Christianity*,[2] and defended them in his various apologetic works. But those who think Lewis intended his fictional works as *arguments* for Christianity obviously have little idea of what argument is. Lewis did, and he gave very good arguments when

---

[1] *Letters of C. S. Lewis*, ed. W. H. Lewis (London: Collins, 1966), p. 283.
[2] C. S. Lewis, *Mere Christianity* (San Francisco: HarperCollins, 2001).

it was his business to argue. Of course, one may propagandize for a view in literature in a variety of ways, but the attempt to rule out any attempt in literature to create sympathy or understanding for a given view would rule out at least half of admittedly great literature.

Just as the explicitly theological elements in *Out of the Silent Planet* may in theory be left out without destroying the story, so *That Hideous Strength* may be read purely as a thrilling combat between good and evil forces—without adverting to the fact that the evil forces are quite literally diabolical; the powerful beings on the side of good, literally angels; and the good side, literally God's side. The reader of science fiction will remember many stories of conflict almost equally cosmic.

*Perelandra* is more explicitly theological, for the framework of the story is the temptation of a new Eve and a possible, and only barely averted, new Fall—not of man but of the manlike race inhabiting Venus. Thus it has certain resemblances to *Paradise Lost*, and, indeed, the parallels are interesting ones. In Milton's work, Satan is in many ways the chief character. Lewis, among others, has argued against the often-encountered idea that Milton's Satan is intended to be a sympathetic character, or that he succeeds in any way in being an admirable or heroic character. Be this as it may, Lewis' Tempter in *Perelandra* avoids any possibility of admiration by any sane mind, or at least so one would think. It is one of the most chilling representations of sheer evil in literature. Here is the description of Ransom's reaction when he realized that the body of Weston had become a mere vehicle for Satan or one of his cohorts:

And now, forcing its way up into consciousness, thrusting aside every mental habit and every longing not to believe, came the conviction that this, in fact, was not a man: that Weston's body was kept, walking and undecaying, in Perelandra by some wholly different kind of life, and that Weston himself was gone.

It looked at Ransom in silence and at last began to smile. We have all often spoken—Ransom himself had often spoken—of a devilish smile. Now he realised that he had never taken the words seriously. The smile was not bitter, nor raging, nor, in an ordinary sense, sinister; it was not even mocking. It seemed to summon Ransom, with horrible naïveté of welcome, into the world of its own pleasures, as if all men were at one in those pleasures, as if they were the most natural thing in the world and no dispute could ever have occurred about them. It was not furtive, nor ashamed, it had nothing of the conspirator in it. It did not defy goodness, it ignored it to the point of annihilation. Ransom perceived that he had never before seen anything but half-hearted and uneasy attempts at evil. This creature was whole-hearted. The extremity of its evil had passed beyond all struggle into some state which bore a horrible similarity to innocence. It was beyond vice as the Lady was beyond virtue.[3]

The sight of the Un-man's face is so terrible that Ransom faints. When he comes to himself he remembers an old belief that the mere sight of the devil was one of the greatest torments of hell. The Un-man does not again show himself as so terrible, but we see him tormenting Ransom and torturing some of the Perelandrian animals.

Terrible as the Un-man is, he is also clearly seen as despicable. "No imagined horror could have surpassed the sense which grew within him as the slow hours passed, that this creature was, by all human standards, inside out—its heart

---

[3] C. S. Lewis, *Perelandra* (New York: Scribner, 2003), p. 95.

on the surface and its shallowness at the heart. On the surface, great designs and an antagonism to Heaven which involved the fate of worlds: but deep within, when every veil had been pierced, was there, after all, nothing but a black puerility, an aimless empty spitefulness content to sate itself with the tiniest cruelties, as love does not disdain the smallest kindness?" [4]

Eventually Ransom must fight physically with the Un-man to prevent him from wearing down the Green Lady's resistance by "third-degree" tactics. Ransom's reactions during the fight vary from terror to pity to what one might almost call "holy hatred".

> An experience that perhaps no good man can ever have in our world came over him—a torrent of perfectly unmixed and lawful hatred. The energy of hating, never before felt without some guilt, without some dim knowledge that he was failing fully to distinguish the sinner from the sin, rose into his arms and legs till he felt that they were pillars of burning blood. What was before him appeared no longer a creature of corrupted will. It was corruption itself to which will was attached only as an instrument. Ages ago it had been a Person: but the ruins of personality now survived in it only as weapons at the disposal of a furious self-exiled negation. [5]

There are interesting parallels here to Tolkien's Elves, who seem to have a similar complete aversion to the Orcs and their master, the Dark Lord. Even the name of the Orcs in Elvish speech is *yrch*, which sounds almost like a gagging or spitting sound.

The Perelandrian Eve, the Green Lady, may be compared in various ways with Galadriel and the other feminine

[4] Ibid., p. 106.
[5] Ibid., p. 135.

figures in *The Lord of the Rings* trilogy. She is less remote and mysterious than they, but she is undoubtedly a great lady, though as the first woman of her race she is naïve and childish in some ways. In fact, Lewis assumed an extraordinarily difficult task in attempting to draw such a character. He discussed some of the problems in a letter (dated November 9, 1941) to a friend who was one of the group of Anglican nuns to whom *Perelandra* is dedicated: "I've got Ransom to Venus and through his first conversation with the 'Eve' of that world: a difficult chapter. I hadn't realized till I came to write it all the Ave-Eva business. I may have embarked on the impossible. This woman has got to combine characteristics which the Fall has put poles apart—she's got to be some ways like a Pagan goddess and in other ways like the Blessed Virgin. But if one can get even a fraction of it into words, it is worth doing." [6]

It is interesting to compare Lewis' story of an averted Fall with his comments on Milton's *Paradise Lost*. Part of Lewis' aim in his *Preface to Paradise Lost* is to defend Milton against charges that he departed from Christian orthodoxy and introduced theological novelties of his own in the Fall story. In reply to this, Lewis argues that "Milton's version of the Fall story is substantially that of St. Augustine, which is that of the Church as a whole." [7] The following summary of this version (paraphrased from Lewis' account) casts interesting light on the Perelandra story:

God created all things good; what we call bad things are good things perverted. Good can exist without evil, but

---

[6] *Letters of C. S. Lewis*, p. 361.

[7] C. S. Lewis, *A Preface to Paradise Lost* (New York: Oxford University Press, 1942), p. 66.

not evil without good. Though God has made all creatures good He knows that some will voluntarily make themselves bad, and He also knows the good use He will then make of their badness. Whoever tries to rebel against God produces the result opposite to his intention. Those who will not become God's sons become His tools. The Fall consisted in disobedience. The fruit was not bad or harmful except insofar as it was forbidden, and the only point of forbidding it was to instill obedience. While the Fall *consisted in* disobedience, it *resulted* from pride. Hence Satan approaches Eve through her pride: first by flattery and second by urging her selfhood to direct revolt against being subject at all. Finally, the great moral of the story of the Fall is "that Obedience to the will of God makes men happy and that Disobedience makes them miserable".[8]

In *Perelandra*, Lewis uses this full battery of ideas, but the other half of the moral is applied. In Milton's story, disobedience makes men miserable, in Lewis', obedience makes the Perelandrians happy. The Green Lady has a real possibility of choice.

> It was suddenly borne in upon him that her purity and peace were not, as they had seemed, things settled and inevitable like the purity and peace of an animal—that they were alive and therefore breakable, a balance maintained by a mind and therefore, at least in theory, able to be lost. There is no reason why a man on a smooth road should lose his balance on a bicycle; but he could. There was no reason why she should step out of her happiness into the psychology of our own race; but neither was there any wall between to prevent her doing so. The sense of precariousness terrified him: but when she looked at him again he

[8] See ibid., pp. 66–71.

changed that word to Adventure, and then all words died out of his mind.[9]

The Un-man attempts to persuade her to break the prohibition against spending the night on the Fixed Land. Like the apple in Milton's version of the Genesis story, this is a test of obedience, but it is also symbolic of the nature of the temptation the Un-man holds out. The Green Lady and the King have lived from moment to moment, accepting the will of God. Since their world is a paradise, with no threats to them and with many unexpected delights, they can live to the full command of Christ to "do not be anxious about tomorrow" (Mt 6:34). The Un-man tempts the Lady to leave this state of perfect trust in God and take command of her own future. As Ransom sees, this temptation is dangerous because it embodies a half-truth. The Green Lady and the King *must* grow and mature, must begin to make their own choices. But if they begin by ignoring the one prohibition that has been laid on them, begin by disobeying the will of God, they will lose freedom, not gain it. In the same way, a young person faced with his first real responsibility may choose apparent freedom by escaping or evading the responsibility, or choose real maturity and real freedom by accepting the responsibility. False freedom chooses the easier way and remains immature; real freedom chooses the harder way and grows.

The Un-man's temptation of the Green Lady is more subtle than Satan's temptation of Eve. The Un-man gives her a false, overdramatic picture of herself as a tragic heroine, sacrificing herself for the King. Rather than directly tempting her to disobedience, he subtly suggests that God

[9] Lewis, *Perelandra*, p. 59.

really *wants* her to disobey and thus grow and mature. But because the Lady is able to resist, the Un-man's actions bring about just the opposite of what he had planned. He wanted slavery and misery for Perelandra; he brings about their freedom and happiness. Like Satan, the Un-man becomes God's tool.

The closing scenes of *Perelandra* show the King and the Green Lady (now called the Queen) preparing to take up their destiny as rulers of their planet and parents of their race. When that race has grown and matured, they will gain angelic powers and even play a part in freeing our own demon-occupied and dominated planet. Thus the whole Miltonic or Augustinian version of the story of the Fall can be found in *Perelandra*, but given a new direction, for this is the story of a success, not of a failure.

And yet, with all the theological dimensions of *Perelandra*, how much of it is still simply exciting adventure on a vividly imagined world! When we compare Lewis' descriptions of *Perelandra* with the average science-fiction adventure on new worlds, we are amazed at his inventiveness and descriptive power. The mere conception of the floating islands would be enough for a novel to many writers of science fiction. When we think of the singing beast, the caves of crystal in which Ransom recovers from his wounds, the mountain he climbs after his recovery, with its brilliantly imagined flora and fauna, we realize how seldom in stories of other worlds we have ever seen any conceptions that are really new in the way Lewis' are. And they are not only new, but beautiful in a way which, as Stella Gibbons bears witness, can create an actual longing to see and enjoy such scenes.

In the main, then, Lewis' theological framework is the orthodox Christian picture of the Fall. But, in addition,

Lewis *adds* imaginative elements to the background of Christianity. In the space trilogy, the angels of traditional Christian theology become beings of a "supermaterial" rather than a "nonmaterial" sort. Their "envelopes" or "photosomes" could, in principle, be detected scientifically. In *Perelandra*, we have a development of the role of eldils. Whereas in *Out of the Silent Planet* they are mainly the rulers of the "rational animals" of Mars, in *Perelandra* there is already the suggestion that they are the "guiding intelligences" of planets, as in certain medieval theories. In *That Hideous Strength*, "eldilology" is further developed to bring in the medieval theory of the planets and their influence. But, of course, these imaginative details are not matters of primary belief. We will discuss some aspects of their function in the next chapter, but part of the reason for them is simply literary. Milton described heavenly wars in concrete terms (sometimes with incongruous effect, e.g., the cannon of the heavenly army). Dante gave detailed descriptions of the geography of hell. If we are to write about nonmaterial realities in literature, one way (and a way used by the greatest writers) is to give concrete imagery for the imagination to work on, while the intellect separates meaning from imagery.

But aside from these invented details, certain emphases and interpretations mark Lewis' dealings with Christian beliefs, as they marked his dealings with Christian morality. Consider, for example, Lewis' story of the averted Fall in *Perelandra*. How is the Lady tempted; what are the arguments of the Tempter? The basic appeal is the same as that in Genesis: "You will be like God" (Gen 3:5). But the Un-man tempts the Lady with two techniques. First, he attempts to convince her that disobeying a clear prohibition of God is somehow "really" doing what God wants done; that the "growing up", the full maturity of the creature, which God desires for it, can be achieved by disobedience of God's command. Second, he tries to convince the Lady that she must sacrifice herself for the sake of her husband, the King; bring him a gift that, although he does not desire it and would reject it if he had a choice, is somehow "good" for him.

Thus the idea of being like a god is made concrete in two ways. Man is to be a god *to himself*, by deciding what is good for him without regard to the will of God; and man is to be a god *to others*, by deciding what is good for them without regard to their own choices or preferences and, again, without regard to God's will for them. Some knowledge of the world, combined with a little reflection, will show that perhaps ninety percent of the harm done in the world by "good" people arises from one or the other of these temptations.

Consider the second temptation. Inquisitors, totalitarian governments, authoritarian parents, domineering spouses are obvious examples. But so are social workers, reformers of all sorts, and (getting close to home) teachers. The leftist who decides that the middle class needs a violent lesson and the rightist who decides the leftist needs a forcible bath and haircut are both often prey to this temptation in a particularly virulent form.

The first temptation is, outside of Christianity, usually not recognized as a temptation at all. This is to be expected. More troubling is the fact that it is increasingly not recognized as a temptation within Christianity.

In *That Hideous Strength*, we find some of the same themes, together with others. The N.I.C.E. plays on both temptations to secure support: the idea that "man must take charge of his destiny", that to secure uncertain future goods we must do things now that are obviously evil; and also the idea that great numbers of people are going to be "done good to", whether they like it or not (e.g., Ivy's husband and the villagers of Cure Hardy).

In all of Lewis' imaginative works, one of the great themes is that to choose God is to choose joy, and to choose anything else, no matter how apparently noble or delightful or wonderful, is ultimately to choose frustration, nothingness, sorrow. Certainly, joyous Christians are nothing new; one thinks of Chesterton, Traherne, Ignatius of Antioch. But they are not especially common in our age (only Robert Farrar Capon comes to mind of living writers). And at any rate, Lewis' emphasis on joy has its own special notes. A quotation from Denis de Rougemont that Lewis uses a number of times in different contexts—"Love ceases to be a demon only when it ceases to be a god"—gives his general attitude to all good things. His attitude is not that "you must cease enjoying that and obey God" (although, of course, this may need to be said at certain times), but, rather, "Obey God or you will soon cease to enjoy that, or anything else." He has George MacDonald say in *The Great Divorce*, "Some mortals misunderstand. They say of some temporal suffering 'No future bliss can make up for it' not knowing that Heaven, once attained, will work backwards and turn even that agony into a glory. And of some sinful pleasure they say 'Let me but have *this* and I'll take the consequences,' little dreaming how damnation will spread backwards and contaminate the pleasure of the sin." [10]

This could, of course, be parodied as "be good and you will be happy", but what Lewis says is more complex than this. To paraphrase things he says on a number of occasions, his message is more like this: "Make a serious and

---

[10] C. S. Lewis, *The Great Divorce* (San Francisco: HarperCollins, 2001), p. 69.

constant effort to obey God and you will have struggle and pain, but also moments of joy and peace, and you will be on the right road to happiness. Choose anything other than God's will and however great the pleasure at the beginning you will be on the road to fear, anger, hatred, despair and sorrow."

Lewis' most complex attempt to deal with religious issues in fictional form is *Till We Have Faces*. Besides themes already discussed in connection with other works, *Till We Have Faces* contains insights into the problem of the suffering of the innocent, or apparently innocent. Orual writes her book as a complaint against the gods. What has she done to deserve the treachery of her sister Redival, the triple loss of her sister Istra?—first as a sacrifice to the god of the Grey Mountain; then, when Istra has beyond all expectation survived exposure on the mountain, to apparent madness; and finally to the god of the mountain, first as husband and later as avenger of the betrayal Orual forces her to.

But as Orual writes, and as she goes on living after the completion of the first book of her story, she gradually begins to learn some of the answers to her complaints. She sees how the behavior of Redival is partly due to Orual's turning from Redival to Istra; how her fiercely possessive love of Istra has turned into something monstrous, needing the removal of its object for any hope of cure; how her sufferings have aided Istra and Istra's sufferings have aided Orual. Here things that Lewis argues for in *The Problem of Pain*[11] are given fictional life. But above all, *Till We Have Faces* shows how pain makes us grow, mature, become "real". As Orual says at the end of her second book: "When the time comes to you at which you will be forced at last to utter

[11] C. S. Lewis, *The Problem of Pain* (San Francisco: HarperCollins, 2001).

the speech which has lain at the center of your soul for years, which you have, all that time, idiot-like, been saying over and over, you'll not talk of the joy of words. I saw well why the gods do not speak to us openly or let us answer. Till that word can be dug out of us, why should they hear the babble that we think we mean? How can they meet us face to face till we have faces?" [12]

In sum, then, Lewis' imaginative works reveal a mind that thinks naturally in Christian terms and can give these terms new imaginative life. Those who agree with Lewis will be grateful for seeing ideas they share expressed in a vivid, imaginative form. But even those who disagree most with Lewis should be grateful to him for giving them a glimpse not only into a Christian mind but also into a Christian imagination.

---

[12] C. S. Lewis, *Till We Have Faces* (San Diego: Harcourt, 2003), p. 294.

# CONCLUSIONS

8

# The Baptism of the Imagination

The imaginative fiction of Lewis and Tolkien has various effects on those who read it. Here I will somewhat arbitrarily divide the total effect into parts and discuss each in turn. The first effect for many is that attributed by the Second Voice in "Leaf by Niggle" to Niggle's completed work—"a holiday and a refreshment". In Lewis' Narnia story, *The Voyage of the Dawn Treader*, Lucy encounters in a book of spells a spell "for the refreshment of the spirit".

> And what Lucy found herself reading was more like a story than a spell. It went on for three pages and before she had read to the bottom of the page she had forgotten that she was reading at all. She was living in the story as if it were real, and all the pictures were real too. When she had got to the third page and come to the end, she said, "That is the loveliest story I've ever read or ever shall read in my whole life. Oh, I wish I could have gone on reading it for ten years.... Oh dear, it's all fading away again.... How can I have forgotten? It was about a cup and a sword and a tree and a green hill, I know that much. But I can't remember, and what *shall* I do?" And she never could remember; and ever since that day what Lucy means by a good story is

a story which reminds her of the forgotten story in the
Magician's Book.[1]

Many of us in reading the fantasies of Tolkien and Lewis
have had an experience not unlike that of Lucy.

The next effect ascribed by the Second Voice to Niggle's work is that "it's splendid for convalescence." In relation to Tolkien's work, the convalescence is, especially from
the modern view of the world, pointless, absurd, and futile.
Because Tolkien's world is not specifically Christian, it can
serve as a halfway house for those struggling out of the
grayness of the modern view. For Tolkien's view is a world
of purpose, a world where there is a real struggle between
good and evil, a hope and danger that go beyond the
personal. As Lewis says in a review of *The Lord of the
Rings* trilogy:

> The value of the myth is that it takes all the things we
> know and restores to them the rich significance which has
> been hidden by "the veil of familiarity." The child enjoys
> his cold meat, otherwise dull to him, by pretending it is
> buffalo, just killed with his own bow and arrow. And the
> child is wise. The real meat comes back to him more
> savory for having been dipped in a story; you might say
> that only then is it real meat. If you are tired of the real
> landscape, look at it in a mirror. By putting bread, gold,
> horse, apple, or the very roads into a myth, we do not
> retreat from reality: we rediscover it. As long as the story
> lingers in our mind, the real things are more themselves.
> This book applies the treatment not only to bread or apple,
> but to good and evil, to our endless perils, our anguish,
> and our joys. By dipping them in myth we see them more

[1] C.S. Lewis, *The Voyage of the Dawn Treader* (New York: HarperCollins,
2000), p. 157.

clearly. I do not think he could have done it any other way.[2]

Tolkien himself says the same thing in these words: "By the forging of Gram cold iron was revealed; by the making of Pegasus horses were ennobled; in the Trees of the Sun and Moon root and stock, flower and fruit are manifested in glory."[3] Thus it is not only the refreshment of holiday we get while actually reading the story that is important, but the new eyes we bring back to familiar scenes. (The same, of course, is true of any good holiday.)

Lewis can have this effect, too, for those who have no phobia against his basically Christian outlook. (And increasingly, people lack such a phobia by lacking any real knowledge of Christianity.) But for the Christian, Lewis can also have the effect of purging the imagination of inadequate images associated with his beliefs. Thus Lewis' eldils cleanse our imaginations of misleading associations of angels with vapid-looking ladies in pastel bathrobes, or chubby infants with wings. Yet Lewis does not intend to replace one false image of angels with another. No doubt it is an advantage to replace a bad image with a better one, but the point is to be able to get beyond the images—insofar as this can be done, that is. Lewis says in *Letters to Malcolm,*

> Talk of meeting [God] is, no doubt, anthropomorphic; as if God and I could be face to face, like two fellow-creatures, when in reality He is above me and within me and below me and all about me. That is why it has to be balanced by

[2] C. S. Lewis, "The Dethronement of Power", in *Tolkien and the Critics*, ed. Neil D. Isaacs and Rose A. Zimbardo (Notre Dame, Ind.: University of Notre Dame Press, 1968), pp. 15–16.

[3] J. R. R. Tolkien, "On Fairy-Stories", in *Tree and Leaf*, in *The Tolkien Reader* (New York: Ballantine Books, 2001), p. 75.

all sorts of metaphysical and theological abstractions. But never, here or anywhere else, let us think that while anthropomorphic images are a concession to our weakness, the abstractions are the literal truth. Both are equally concessions; each singly misleading, and the two together mutually corrective. Unless you sit to it very lightly, continually murmuring, "Not thus, not thus, neither is this Thou", the abstraction is fatal. It will make the life of lives inanimate and the love of loves impersonal. The naif image is mischievous chiefly in so far as it holds unbelievers back from conversion. It does believers, even at its crudest, no harm. What soul ever perished for believing that God the Father really has a beard?[4]

Again, when Lewis makes Christ appear as a magnificent golden lion in the Narnia stories, this helps to get rid of certain silly or puerile ideas of Christ. (Jane Studdock in *That Hideous Strength* remembers "pictures of Christ, apparently seven feet tall, with the face of a consumptive girl".) But certainly the idea of Christ as a golden lion is not intended to inspire primary belief. Remember that Aslan does not allegorically "stand for" Christ, he *is* Christ as Christ is feigned to be in that world.

An analogy may be useful here. Lewis, in *The Discarded Image*, describes in great detail the medieval world view. This world view "had a serious defect—it was not true". But the point is that there are many world views, and our own present world view may be no truer. Lewis says, "I hope no one will think I am recommending a return to the Medieval Model. I am only suggesting considerations that may induce us to regard all Models in the right way,

[4] C.S. Lewis, *Letters to Malcolm, Chiefly on Prayer* (San Diego: Harcourt, 2002), p. 21.

respecting each and idolizing none.... No Model is a cat-
alogue of ultimate realities, and none is a mere fantasy." [5]
What Lewis says about "Models", or world views, may be
said with equal truth about the images and associations that
surround our ideas of God or Christ or angels. Even the
much-derided image of God as an old man with a white
beard attempts to convey ideas of venerability, authority,
dignity. (In fact, it fails with many moderns partly because
we no longer associate dignity, authority, and venerability
with age.) Even the pictures of Christ that so repelled Jane
Studdock were attempts to convey the mercy and patience
that are really present in the gospel picture of Christ.

It might be thought that if all images are to some extent
misleading, we should do without images. But this has a
curious effect. If we try to think of a purely spiritual being—
God, an angel, a disembodied soul—we rightly leave out
the ideas of size, shape, weight, color, and so on. But the
effect of removing these ideas and putting *nothing* in their
place is to leave ourselves with the idea of something thin,
gaseous, ghostly. This is not true of everyone, of course;
some minds are less dependent on images. But I suspect
that even some very able philosophers have been subconsciously influenced by this idea of spirit as something thin
and gaseous. The difficulty so many philosophers have felt
about the ability of mind to affect body may, I think, be
traced partly to the fact that subconsciously the problem
has seemed to be "how can this insubstantial, gassy stuff
affect this solid, massive material?" The medieval theory of
"animal spirits" that Lewis discusses in *The Discarded Image*[6]

[5] C. S. Lewis, *The Discarded Image* (Cambridge, Eng.: Cambridge University Press, 1964), p. 222.
[6] Ibid., pp. 167–69.

is good, indirect evidence of this: animal spirits are an insubstantial sort of matter that can be affected by mind and that in turn can affect body.

Lewis counteracted this danger of thinking that spirit is insubstantial and gaseous by giving us a counterimage, that of spirit as supersolid. The eldils in *Out of the Silent Planet* and *Perelandra* are described as being more solid and real than material beings. "What we call firm things—flesh and earth—seem to [the eldil] thinner, and harder to see, than our light, and more like clouds, and nearly nothing. To us an *eldil* is a thin, half-real body that can go through walls and rocks: to himself he goes through them because he is solid and firm and they are like cloud." [7]

This idea is used again in *The Great Divorce*, where the spirits of the blessed in heaven are "Solid People" compared with whom the visitors from hell are thin and ghostly. The result of journeying further into heaven is to grow more and more solid. Lewis also uses the idea of size: "All Hell is smaller than one of your earthly worlds; but it is smaller than one atom of *this* world, the Real World. Look at your butterfly. If it swallowed all Hell, Hell would not be big enough to do it any harm or to have any taste." [8]

By such devices and others, Lewis has managed, at least for some, to make the detestable quality of hell and the desirableness of heaven imaginatively real. Even the hints, which are all we receive in *Screwtape Letters* or *The Great Divorce* about the nature of heaven, get from many of us an imaginative and emotional response out of all proportion to their brevity; and the final chapters of *The Last Battle*, in which the heroes and heroines of the Narnia books go

---

[7] C. S. Lewis, *Out of the Silent Planet* (New York: Scribner, 2003), p. 95.
[8] C. S. Lewis, *The Great Divorce* (San Francisco: HarperCollins, 2001), p. 138.

"further up and further in" into Aslan's country, are to my mind one of the best suggestions of heaven in literature. But the great joy of that country is to be with Aslan, and the essential lovableness of Aslan is something that builds up all through The Chronicles of Narnia.

I am not entirely sure how Lewis has accomplished the feat of making a Christ-figure both convincing and lovable, but he has, succeeding where Milton and others as great have failed. I suspect that part of the secret is Lewis' own quiet goodness and devotion to Christ. But from the purely literary and philosophical point of view we can see some of the techniques Lewis used to build up a picture of Aslan. Lewis has put Aslan "on stage" sparingly. Of the approximately 1,300 pages in the seven Narnia books, Aslan appears on well less than a third, and his appearance is generally either the climax of the story or some turning point in it. His presence is something special, a great occasion, not everyday life—not yet, at any rate.

The writer did not make the mistake—which would be a very natural one in a children's book—of making Aslan too meek and mild: he is an imposing, even sometimes terrifying, figure. As Lewis says in The Lion, the Witch and the Wardrobe: "People who have not been in Narnia sometimes think that a thing cannot be good and terrible at the same time. If the children had ever thought so, they were cured of it now. For when they tried to look at Aslan's face they just caught a glimpse of the golden mane and the great, royal, solemn, overwhelming eyes; and then they found they couldn't look at him and went all trembly." [9] When any of the children attempt to lie to Aslan or be less than honest

[9] C. S. Lewis, The Lion, the Witch and the Wardrobe (New York: HarperCollins, 2000), p. 126.

with themselves or him, his growl is terrible. And his strength and power are always in the background: "The Lion shook his mane and clapped his paws together ('Terrible paws,' thought Lucy, 'if he didn't know how to velvet them!')." [10]

Lewis has made it clear that to be with Aslan is joy, but also that Aslan is capable of sorrow and of being hurt and appreciates his human friends. After Aslan has returned from death, Lewis vividly portrays his joy and power.

> "Oh, children," said the Lion, "I feel my strength coming back to me. Oh, children, catch me if you can!" He stood for a second, his eyes very bright, his limbs quivering, lashing himself with his tail. Then he made a leap high over their heads and landed on the other side of the Table. Laughing, though she didn't know why, Lucy scrambled over to it to reach him. Aslan leaped again. A mad chase began. Round and round the hilltop he led them, now hopelessly out of their reach, now letting them almost catch his tail, now diving between them, now tossing them in the air with his huge and beautifully velveted paws and catching them again, and now stopping unexpectedly so that all three of them rolled over together in a happy laughing heap of fur and arms and legs. It was such a romp as no one has ever had except in Narnia; and whether it was more like playing with a thunderstorm or playing with a kitten Lucy could never make up her mind. And the funny thing was that when all three finally lay together panting in the sun the girls no longer felt in the least tired or hungry or thirsty. [11]

Aslan never magically solves the children's problems. They must fight and struggle and plan, and finally Aslan will give them help against problems they cannot overcome

[10] Ibid., p. 129.
[11] Ibid., pp. 163–64.

themselves. For example, he kills the Witch and turns the victims she has turned to stone back into flesh. But Peter and Edmund must fight the Witch's army, and Lucy must use the medicine she got from Father Christmas to cure ordinary wounds. Lewis shows Aslan as unpredictable, not to be used for the purposes of others: "Mr. Beaver had warned them, 'He'll be coming and going,' he had said. 'One day you'll see him and another you won't. He doesn't like being tied down—and of course he has other countries to attend to. It's quite all right. He'll often drop in. Only you mustn't press him. He's wild, you know. Not like a *tame* lion.' " [12]

One minor but very telling point is that Lewis always shows Aslan as behaving in a "lionlike" way; he is never just "a man dressed in a lion skin". Pauline Baynes' illustrations for the Narnia books, with one or two unfortunate exceptions, carry out this idea. The point here is a rather subtle one. I think what Lewis had in mind was this: just as Christ was really man, not just a puppet or mask of God, so if Christ should become incarnate as a great talking lion, He would subject himself to that condition and work within it.

This gives some hint of Lewis' technique—not imitation or allegory, but what he has called, in a very interesting essay, "Transposition".[13] Just as a musical piece written for the piano may sound quite different when transposed for the violin and may reveal new aspects and new beauties, so Christ's life "transposed" to the world of Narnia and the body of a great lion shows us something new about that

[12] Ibid., pp. 181–82.

[13] "Transposition" is collected in C. S. Lewis, *The Weight of Glory and Other Addresses* (San Francisco: HarperCollins, 2001), pp. 91–115.

life. Thus, for example, the fact that Aslan is a lion enables Lewis to express the joy and glory of the Resurrection as a physical "romp".

Aslan in his actions and language reveals his affection for those who are his friends. His praise is an accolade, and his tenderness and love are clear. Yet friendship with Aslan is not easy and must be chosen and struggled for, Lewis shows. Lucy, Aslan's greatest friend, is asked to perform the hardest tasks. ("That's how I treat my friends", said Christ to St. Teresa in a vision. "Yes, Lord," she said, "that's why you have so few.")

Susan, who has often hesitated and faltered in following Aslan, at last becomes a "dropout".

> "Sir," said Tirian, when he had greeted all these. "If I have read the chronicles aright, there should be another. Has not your Majesty two sisters? Where is Queen Susan?"
>
> "My sister Susan," answered Peter shortly and gravely, "is no longer a friend of Narnia."
>
> "Yes," said Eustace, "and whenever you've tried to get her to come and talk about Narnia or do anything about Narnia, she says 'What wonderful memories you have! Fancy you're still thinking about all those funny games we used to play when we were children.'"
>
> "Oh Susan!" said Jill, "she's interested in nothing now-a-days except nylons and lipsticks and invitations. She always was a jolly sight too keen on being grown-up."
>
> "Grown-up, indeed," said the Lady Polly. "I wish she *would* grow up. She wasted all her school time wanting to be the age she is now, and she'll waste all of the rest of her life trying to stay that age. Her whole idea is to race on to the silliest time of one's life as quick as she can and then stop there as long as she can." [14]

[14] C. S. Lewis, *The Last Battle* (New York: HarperCollins, 2000), p. 154.

It is always easier to say "May we come with you—wherever you're going?" than to follow all the way to the end. Susan is not necessarily lost completely, but how much she has lost!

And so may we lose much. If Lewis has achieved the end he attempted, then the picture of Aslan should be a valuable corrective to some faults the average Christian is all too prone to. If we presume too much on Christ's tenderness, we may remember Aslan's growl. If we find ourselves too much at ease in Zion, we should remember the "He's wild, you know. Not like a *tame* lion." But if our picture of Christ grows too stern or gray, we should remember the joy, the wild romp.

All these aspects of Aslan are present in the picture of Christ as we have it in the gospels. His presence is a great occasion, "but you do not always have me" (Jn 12:8). He can be terrible, as when He drove the moneychangers from the temple. To be with Him is joy: "Lord, it is well that we are here!" (Mt 17:4). He sorrows and wants our companionship: "Could you not watch one hour?" (Mk 14:37). His joy is in us after the Resurrection: "Did not our hearts burn within us ... ?" (Mk 24:32). He asks us to bear burdens: "He who does not take his cross and follow me is not worthy of me" (Mt 10:38). He is not "tame" even to his friends: "Get behind me, Satan! ... for you are not on the side of God, but of men" (Mt 16:23). He is truly man, "one who in every respect has been tempted as we are, yet without sin" (Heb 4:15). He is tender to us: "Fear not, little flock" (Lk 12:32). And we must take care to remain His friends: "Every one who acknowledges me before men, I also will acknowledge before my Father who is in heaven; but whoever denies me before men, I also will deny before my Father who is in heaven" (Mt 10:32–33).

Of course, the gospel picture is far richer than Lewis'. Richer but more confusing, harder to grasp in one piece.

Aslan is only an echo or an image of Christ, but such echoes and images help us to see the Original in a truer light.

Thus, for those who believe in the realities Lewis is expressing in new terms, he has done an especially valuable service. But even for the enemies of that vision of the world or the champions of rival visions, Lewis has surely done a service. For unless we understand what an opponent loves and why he loves it, we have not made a real start in understanding that opponent. And for understanding this, a poet may be at times more useful than a philosopher.

This leads us to the final characteristic the Second Voice attributed to Niggle's work: "for many it is the best introduction to the Mountains". Here we need to make a distinction. An introduction, as we have said, is necessarily not the thing introduced. The quotation that heads the last chapter of *Surprised by Joy*, Lewis' account of his conversion to Christianity, is from St. Augustine: "For it is one thing to see the land of peace from the wooded ridge . . . and another to tread the road that leads to it" (St. Augustine, *Confessions*, 7, 21). But to continue the metaphor, unless we see that land from afar and learn to love it, we are not likely to take the road. The reading of works like Tolkien's and Lewis' awakens a certain appetite in us, but it does not satisfy that appetite. It may be that that appetite will never be satisfied, but must be eternally frustrated. It may be, as Lewis and Tolkien believe, that it can be satisfied, that "the Gospels contain a fairy-story, or a story of a larger kind which embraces all the essence of fairy-stories. . . . But this story has entered History and the primary world." [15] The tellers of tales can hardly help us to decide this question. We must turn to philosophy and to history and look at

[15] Tolkien, "On Fairy-Stories", pp. 88–89.

hard and complex questions: Could this happen? What would it mean if it did? *Has* this happened?

This is why we have rejected so strongly the Roses' idea of Lewis' fiction as a "formal 'apology' for ... Christianity". An apology, especially a "formal" one, must appeal to reason, not merely to imagination or emotion. Lewis never confused the two appeals, and we would be wise not to.

Where the subcreator *can* help us is in arousing our interest, engaging our desire. What Tolkien says of the Christian Story, that "there is no tale ever told that men would rather find was true", is simply untrue for many moderns. Because their temper of mind is so widely separated from the world of Christianity, because they are ignorant of it, or worse, because they have distorted ideas of it, the Christian Story simply "turns off" many moderns.

Tolkien combats this disinterest indirectly, Lewis more directly. The Roses, for example, attacked Lewis' "hierarchical" view of the universe and, indeed, it is a view for which the modern mind has scant sympathy. Lewis, in *The Discarded Image*, says that just as "hardly any battery of new facts could have persuaded a Greek that the universe had an attribute so repugnant to him as infinity, hardly any such battery could persuade a modern that it is hierarchical." [16] But Tolkien, by giving us figures of authority who really command our respect (Gandalf, Aragorn, Elrond, Frodo himself), undermines this modern prejudice. Of course, some critics hate hierarchy more than they like Tolkien, and Tolkien has been taken to task for the hierarchical aspects of his world. But others, I suspect, have begun to learn from Tolkien the meaning of such terms as *dignity*, *venerability*, and *authority* (the same terms, remember, that some of the older images of God tried to convey).

[16] Lewis, *Discarded Image*, p. 222.

One of Tolkien's most successful efforts of this kind (I do not know whether such efforts were undertaken consciously or simply arise from the whole cast of Tolkien's mind) is the understanding that the figure of Frodo gives us. The idea that A's suffering may benefit not only A himself, but also B, is one of the most basic in Christianity, underlying not only ordinary Christian life, but also the mystery of redemption. Charles Williams, a friend of both Lewis and Tolkien, celebrated this doctrine and gave it his own peculiar angle in what he called the doctrine of "co-inherence". But Tolkien has given it concrete form in the person of Frodo. Frodo, as we have said, is not a figure of Christ—he is too limited, too imperfect, for that. But he is what every Christian should be, an imitator of Christ, one who carries out or imitates in his limited and imperfect way the redemptive suffering of Christ. The often-quoted words of Frodo to Sam, "It must often be so: when things are in danger: some one has to give them up, lose them, so that others may keep them",[17] are words that apply to soldiers who die for their countries, to martyrs who die for civil rights, but preeminently they apply to Christ. That someone else must pay the price for what I enjoy, that I must accept this sacrifice with love and make it in my turn for yet others, is, says Williams, one of the basic laws of the universe. Seeing Frodo, we learn to understand this.

Seeing Frodo, but also seeing Orual; seeing Ransom on Perelandra, Aslan in Narnia. Lewis has dealt with the theme, too, and more explicitly. I do not know how many have taken the route from Tolkien to Lewis to Christianity, but it seems to me to be a possible route for the imagination to lead and the intellect to follow on. Yet, whether one goes

[17] J. R. R. Tolkien, *The Return of the King* (New York: Ballantine Books, 2001), p. 338.

on from Tolkien to Lewis, or goes on at all from Tolkien, I suspect the reading of Tolkien for many has had the same effect that the reading of George MacDonald's *Phantastes* had on the young Lewis. "It was as if I had been carried sleeping across a frontier, or as if I had died in the old country and came alive in the new. For in one sense, the new country was exactly like the old.... But in another sense all was changed. I did not know (and was long in learning) the name of the new quality, the bright shadow that rested on the travels of Anodos. I do now. It was Holiness." [18]

The more specific and demanding effect of Lewis' writing on a mind open to conviction may be represented by this quotation from Chad Walsh: "In *Perelandra* I found my imagination being baptised. At the time I was slowly thinking, feeling and fumbling my way towards the Christian faith, and had reached a point where I was more than half convinced that it was true. This conviction, however, was a thing more of the mind than of the imagination and heart. In *Perelandra* I got the taste and smell of Christian truth. My senses as well as my soul here baptised. It was as though an intellectual abstraction or speculation had become flesh and dwelt in its solid bodily glory among us." [19]

So while for some the words of Lewis and Tolkien may be only a "holiday and refreshment" in a meaningless world, for others "it's splendid for convalescence" from the view that the world is meaningless. And for those ready for the journey their work can be "the best introduction to the Mountains", to that great enterprise of "exploration into God" to which Lewis and Tolkien invite us.

---

[18] C. S. Lewis, *Surprised by Joy* (New York: Harcourt, 2002), p. 179.
[19] Chad Walsh, "Impact on America", in *Light on C. S. Lewis*, ed. Jocelyn Gibb et al. (New York: Harcourt, Brace and World, 1966), p. 107.

# 9

# The Christian Intellect

There are a number of ways of arriving at truth, and almost all of them are inappropriate to imaginative writing. Mathematics arrives at proof by calculation and by deductive proof, which are obviously unsuited to works of the imagination. But the appeal of science to observation and experiment or of history to documentary evidence is equally inappropriate to imaginative writing, for such writing makes no claim to empirical truth—the "facts" of imaginative writing are fictional. Argument—by which philosophy establishes truth—can, however, occur in imaginative writing, because an argument in real life, in a work of fantasy, or in a dream, can in each case be judged simply on its merits as an argument. Thus it is possible that a work of imagination could contain arguments worth considering.

In fact, we will find certain arguments are embodied in the imaginative works of Lewis. But to do full justice to the argumentative backing for the ideas embodied in the fictional works of Lewis and Tolkien, we will have to look briefly at some of Lewis' nonfictional works, in which he defends the position he shares with Tolkien.

In general, when we defend a metaphysical theory, we try to establish certain things: first, that the theory makes sense;

second, that there are no decisive arguments against the theory; and, finally, that there are strong arguments in favor of the theory. Of course, a religion is more than just a metaphysical theory, but the higher religions at least embody, or consist partly of, such a theory. Thus, in arguing for the truth of the religious and ethical views he shares with Tolkien, Lewis can be regarded as arguing for the truth of the metaphysical theory embodied in Christianity. In this necessarily somewhat brief treatment, we will have to confine ourselves to the essentials of this view, and we will regard these essentials as (1) the creation of the universe by God; (2) the redemption of mankind by Christ; and (3) the salvation of individual souls.

A view may be challenged as not making sense in various ways. It may be self-contradictory, so vague or ambiguous as to be meaningless, or it may fail to meet some reasonable standards of meaningfulness that apply to any utterance. Lewis was not greatly concerned with or involved with the kind of technical points that have occupied some philosophers about alleged inconsistencies or contradictions in the Christian view (for example the so-called "paradoxes of omnipotence"), although he says something about them in *The Problem of Pain*. Insofar as he was concerned with the whole question of whether Christianity makes sense, Lewis dealt with it by trying to define traditional Christian beliefs as clearly and cogently as he could. His book *Mere Christianity*, a compilation of talks originally given on the radio, is one of his best efforts in this direction; but essays printed in other collections deal even more successfully with specific points.[1] As to the sort of challenge to Christianity

---

[1] For example, "On Obstinacy in Belief", in *The World's Last Night and Other Essays* (San Diego: Harcourt, 2002), which deals with misunderstandings about religious belief.

that argues that by certain standards of meaningfulness religious statements are nonsensical, it usually turns out that the theories of meaningfulness are themselves controversial and embody a rival metaphysical view. At any rate, Lewis was very little concerned with such controversies.

About more direct attacks on religious belief, Lewis had a great deal to say. A modern writer on philosophy of religion has summed up the major modern objections to religion as falling under four main heads: (1) psychological objection, based on the theory that religion is based on wish-fulfillment; (2) a "scientific" objection based on the idea that there can be no adequate evidence for the miracles that seem to be an integral part of the Christian Story; (3) a philosophical objection based on the unverifiability of religious statements; and (4) a moral objection based on the problem of evil in a world created by a good God.[2]

The first of these objections Lewis answered in a number of places in his apologetic works, and the argument occurs in recognizable forms in some of his imaginative works also. The basic argument is that belief in God, Redemption, or salvation cannot be explained as "wishful thinking", because everyone has wishes on both sides of the matter. That there should be a God who is completely superior to us, who makes demands on us and has plans for us, who holds us responsible for our actions and may punish us is far from being the desire of many of us, or of any of us in some moods.

When he comes to deal with the possibility of miracles, Lewis' basic arguments take the form of a dilemma. He shows that Hume's famous argument against the possibility of miracles begs the question, for Hume is assuming what

[2] Sten H. Stenson, *Sense and Nonsense in Religion* (New York: Abingdon Press, 1969), pp. 4–5.

he is supposed to be proving, that natural laws cannot be suspended. To say that "uniform experience" shows that natural laws are never broken is simply to assume that miracles have never occurred, which is supposedly the point at issue. But it also raises a deeper issue. Experience can never prove the uniformity of nature, since all arguments from experience assume the uniformity of nature, as Hume himself saw. Thus we have what is called "Hume's Problem of Induction": How are any arguments from experience to be justified? There are difficulties about justifying them a priori, and if we justify arguments from experience by arguing from experience, we seem to be arguing in a circle. Lewis poses the following dilemma: "Theology says to you in effect, 'Admit God and with Him the risk of a few miracles, and I in return will ratify your faith in uniformity as regards the overwhelming majority of events.' The philosophy which forbids you to make uniformity absolute is also the philosophy which offers you solid grounds for believing it to be general.... The alternative is really much worse. Try to make Nature absolute and you find that her uniformity is not even probable. By claiming too much, you get nothing. You get the deadlock, as in Hume." [3]

Thus, unless there is another way out of Hume's dilemma (and philosophers have been unable to agree on any alternative), the theist has a reason for believing in arguments from experience, and the nontheist does not. So, far from there being an incompatibility between theism and scientific reasoning, scientific reasoning essentially depends on a theistic philosophy. (That this is historically true, Whitehead, among others, has argued.)

[3] C. S. Lewis, *Miracles: A Preliminary Study* (San Francisco: HarperCollins, 2001), pp. 169–70.

Stenson's third point, that religious claims are "meaningless" because unverifiable, is one about which Lewis has nothing special to say. It is perhaps for this reason that Austin Farrer thought Lewis had "dropped out" of the contemporary philosophical debate and could not usefully be recommended to the *philosophically* puzzled undergraduate. Yet I wonder if Lewis was not wise. The verifiability criterion of meaning is now admitted, even by its early defenders, to be impossible to state in a way that does not make it so weak as to admit all sorts of statements that the early positivists wished to exclude as "meaningless", or so strong as to eliminate perfectly acceptable scientific theories. Indeed, the theory—which demands that every "meaningful" statement be either logically true or false, or else provable as true or false by the methods of science—seems to be self-refuting, for the theory itself seems neither to be logically true nor provable to be true by the methods of science. Thus Lewis, who wrote for the common reader rather than for the professional philosopher, was perhaps under no obligation to enter the somewhat technical discussions about verifiability that agitated philosophical circles during the time he was writing. What he chose to do instead was of more lasting value.

The problem of evil is perhaps the most important difficulty about belief in God for both philosophers and non-philosophers. Within professional philosophy, the most successful counterattacks on those who have posed this problem have been the argument that moral evil is due to man's free will (the "Free-Will Defense"), and the argument that physical evil (pain and suffering) is explainable as a means of bringing about certain states of character that could not exist without pain and suffering (the "Soul-Making Theodicy").

John Hick's book *Evil and the God of Love*[4] is perhaps the best exposition of this view by a professional philosopher. But Lewis' *Problem of Pain* had given essentially this sort of argument many years before Hick wrote. Lewis' brief book is "popular" in a way in which Hick's book does not attempt to be, but the essentials of the argument are there.

Austin Farrer summarizes Lewis' argument in this way:

> The very constitution of the world opens the possibility of pain. Our own perversity has seized upon it; we have tormented one another, we have poisoned ourselves. Nevertheless, God's "permission" of evil so multiplied is not simply to be accounted for by his respecting our free will. He takes the harms we mutually inflict and overrules them for our good.
>
> The primary function of mental pain, says Lewis, is to force our misdirectedness on our attention. But just as it belongs to our fallen state to be blind to holiness until we suffer the consequences of sin, and blind to a higher good until natural satisfactions are snatched from us; so equally it belongs to our state that we cannot achieve disinterestedness until it costs us pain. Sympathy is made real by the sharing of distress, and martyrdom is the typical expression of devotion to God.
>
> Such is the central answer Lewis gives to the problem he has undertaken to discuss; and it is difficult to deny that it is the distinctively Christian answer. Many other wise things can be said about the endurance of pain, but it is less evident that they arise out of the Christian revelation.[5]

We recognize that some of these points have been made fictionally in *Till We Have Faces*. Is not Orual blind to the

---

[4] John Hick, *Evil and the God of Love* (New York: Harper and Row, 1966).

[5] Austin Farrer, "The Christian Apologist", in *Light on C. S. Lewis*, ed. Jocelyn Gibb et al. (New York: Harcourt, Brace and World, 1966), p. 38.

selfish possessiveness of her love for Istra, her neglect of Redival, her battening on Bardia—until the loss of Istra, the separation of Redival, and the death of Bardia bring them home to her? Does not Orual's suffering with and for Istra bring her to a state where the god can say to her, "You, too, are Psyche"?

So much for defense of the Christian metaphysical view against attack. Some philosophers might be content to allow the *possibility* of Christian belief, to show that such a belief is not irrational. But Lewis goes further than this; he gives arguments to show that the Christian metaphysical view is not only possible, but true. One of the most original of these occurs in *Miracles*: it has the form that logicians call "disjunctive syllogism". Two alternatives are posed; one is eliminated leaving the other as the only possibility. Lewis argues that either theism is true—that is, God exists—or naturalism, the view that all events are due to mere chance or natural necessity, is true. But naturalism is self-refuting, for if naturalism is true our thoughts are determined by nonrational causes. But no thought determined by non-rational causes is valid, thus naturalism is self-refuting. So only theism remains.

Lewis himself puts the argument in this way:

> To understand that logic must be valid is to see at once that this thing we all know, this thought, this mind, cannot in fact be really alien to the nature of the universe. Or, putting it the other way round, the nature of the universe cannot be really alien to Reason. We find that matter always obeys the same laws which our logic obeys. When logic says a thing must be so, Nature always agrees. No one can suppose that this can be due to a happy coincidence. A great many people think that it is due to the fact that Nature produced the mind. But on the assumption that Nature is herself mindless this

provides no explanation. To be the result of a series of mindless events is one thing: to be a kind of plan or true account
of the laws according to which those mindless events happened is quite another.... But if the validity of knowledge
cannot be explained in that way, and if perpetual happy coinci-
dence throughout the whole of recorded time is out of the
question, then surely we must seek the real explanation elsewhere.... Unless all that we take to be knowledge is an illusion, we must hold that in thinking we are not reading
rationality into an irrational universe but responding to a rationality with which the universe has been saturated.[6]

Of course, one might try to show that there is some third
alternative between theism and naturalism or try to show
that naturalism is not self-refuting. But on the face of it,
Lewis has given a powerful argument for theism. To say
that this argument is open to objection, and those objections to answers, is simply to say that it is a philosophical
argument. As Austin Farrer says, "Philosophy is an ever-
shifting, never-ending, public discussion." [7]

Lewis also gives, in several places, a version of the moral
argument for the existence of God. For example, in *Mere
Christianity* he argues that people, when they have moral
disagreements, do in fact appeal to common standards of
justice. Without such, in fact, standard *arguments* about moral
matters cannot occur.

Everyone has heard people quarrelling.... They say things
like this: "How'd you like it if any one did the same to
you?" ... "Leave him alone, he isn't doing you any harm"
... "Come on, you promised." ...

[6] C. S. Lewis, "De Futilitate", collected in *Christian Reflections*, ed. Walter
Hooper (Grand Rapids: Wm. B. Eerdmans Publishing, 1967), pp. 64–65.
[7] Farrer, "The Christian Apologist", p. 31.

Now what interests me about such remarks is that the man who makes them is not merely saying that the other man's behaviour does not happen to please him. He is appealing to some sort of standard of behaviour which he expects the other man to know about. And the other man very seldom replies, "To hell with your standard." Nearly always he tries to make out what he has been doing does not really go against the standard, or that if it does there is some special excuse.... It looks, in fact, very much as if both parties had in mind some kind of Law or Rule of fair play and decent behaviour or morality or whatever you like to call it, about which they really agreed. And they have. If they had not, they might, of course, fight like animals, but they could not *quarrel* in the human sense of the word. Quarrelling means trying to show that the other man is in the wrong. And there would be no sense in trying to do that unless you and he had some sort of agreement as to what Right and Wrong are.[8]

Lewis answers various objections to the view that there is such a universal moral law and refers to his book *The Abolition of Man*,[9] in which he shows that cultures widely separated in space and time have had essentially the same moral code. Lewis concludes the following:

It seems, then, we are forced to believe in a real Right and Wrong. People may sometimes be mistaken about them, just as people sometimes get their sums wrong; but they are not a matter of mere taste and opinion any more than the multiplication table. Now if we are agreed about that, I go on to my next point, which is this: None of us are really keeping the Law of Nature.... These then are the two points I wanted to make. First, that human beings all over the

---

[8] C. S. Lewis, *Mere Christianity* (San Francisco: HarperCollins, 2001), pp. 3–4.
[9] C. S. Lewis, *The Abolition of Man* (San Francisco: HarperCollins, 2001).

earth have this curious idea that they ought to believe in a certain way and cannot really get rid of it. Secondly, that they do not in fact behave in that way. They know the Law of Nature; they break it. These two facts are the foundations of all clear thinking about ourselves and the universe we live in.[10]

Author Lewis then argues that a materialistic view of the universe offers no explanation of the moral law and our failures to keep it, and the religious view does. The argument is basically an inductive one: here is a fact about the universe—the moral law and our failure to live up to it. Here are competing hypotheses about the universe: the nonreligious view and the religious view. The religious view accounts for the facts, the nonreligious view does not. Therefore, by the ordinary standards of inductive reasoning we ought to accept the view that is able to explain the facts—the religious view.

It would be *possible* to argue that the religious view does not explain the facts, but such an argument seems to have little chance of success. It would be possible to deny the facts or argue that they can be explained on purely naturalistic grounds, but we then either deny the existence of the moral law or explain it away. And if we do either, we run up against a serious difficulty. If we want to condemn anything on moral grounds—war, racism, exploitation—we are thereby admitting the existence of a moral law, as Lewis has argued. Thus the price we pay for rejecting the religious view is the inability to condemn anything morally. If "that's wrong" means no more than "I don't like that", the man we are condemning can simply reply, "I do like it."

[10] Lewis, *Mere Christianity*, pp. 7–8.

Ordinary people and philosophers have been inconsistent on this point in rather different ways. Ordinary people may be relativists in theory, but try to use the language of moral condemnation when they are really involved or indignant. Philosophers, while often denying in theory the existence of a moral law, appeal to our ordinary judgments of right and wrong to support or criticize philosophical theories about morality. But if A can justify or support B, A must be prior to B.

We may note that the argument depends on the principle "if objective right and wrong exist, God exists", which is simply the contrapositive of the principle often appealed to by existentialists and others, "If God does not exist, objective right and wrong do not exist." Sartre argues, "No God, therefore no right and wrong"; Lewis argues, "Right and wrong, therefore God." But their major premises are equivalent.

Now neither of the two arguments we have examined is conclusive in the sense that it compels assent. But each argument shows a price we must pay for rejecting theism. The first argument shows that we must either accept the existence of God or deny the validity of human reasoning. The second argument shows that we must either accept the existence of God or deny the validity of any moral judgment. Many people can thus be accused of inconsistency: they try to reject God but at the same time retain reason or morality. But if someone simply denies the validity of reasoning and of moral judgment, then there is no appeal we can make to him—no rational appeal, since he denies reason, and no practical appeal, for he denies morality. Of course, there may be some way out of the dilemmas that Lewis' arguments pose, but he has given us a powerful *prima facie* case.

Another often-encountered argument for religion is the argument from religious experience. Sometimes this argument focuses on mystical experiences that are completely outside the lot of most of us, and it has been argued that someone else's experience, no matter how convincing to him, can never be a sufficient reason for *us*. But Lewis argues from a religious experience he feels all of us have had in some form or other. It is an experience of longing, of a desire for joy that in itself is a joy beyond all other joys. This experience is the theme of Lewis' autobiographical *Surprised by Joy* and his autobiographical allegory *The Pilgrim's Regress*. The evidential value of this sort of longing he succinctly expresses in *Mere Christianity*:

> Most people, if they had really learned to look into their own hearts, would know that they do want, and want acutely, something that cannot be had in this world....
>
> ... If I find in myself a desire which no experience in this world can satisfy, the most probable explanation is that I was made for another world. If none of my earthly pleasures satisfy it, that does not prove that the universe is a fraud. Probably earthly pleasures were never meant to satisfy it, but only to arouse it, to suggest the real thing. If that is so, I must take care, on the one hand, never to despise, or be unthankful for, these earthly blessings, and on the other, never to mistake them for the something else of which they are only a kind of copy, or echo, or mirage. I must keep alive in myself the desire for my true country, which I shall not find till after death; I must never let it get snowed under or turned aside; I must make it the main object of life to press on to that other country and to help others to do the same.[11]

[11] Ibid., pp. 135, 136–37.

As with the previous two arguments, we can reject Lewis' conclusion, at a price. Just as the first argument showed that to reject God is to reject reason, and the second showed that to reject God is to reject morality, so this third argument shows that to reject God is to reject our hope of real happiness. Unless Lewis is wrong, the result of all three rejections will be, indeed, a grim and meaningless world.

About the other essentials of the Christian world view, redemption and salvation, of course no purely philosophical argument can be conclusive. For we must also examine certain historical evidence about the life of Christ and the history of Christianity. Lewis attacked on two fronts here. As an expert in the history of literature he attacked certain excesses of modern biblical criticism on purely professional grounds. He also argued that, given the record we have of Christ's life, we must conclude either that He was God or that He was a lunatic or an evil man. As Lewis says:

> I am trying here to prevent anyone saying the really foolish thing that people often say about Him: "I'm ready to accept Jesus as a great moral teacher, but I don't accept His claim to be God." That is the one thing we must not say. A man who was merely a man and said the sort of things Jesus said would not be a great moral teacher. He would either be a lunatic—on a level with the man who says he is a poached egg—or else he would be the Devil of Hell. You must take your choice. Either this man was, and is, the Son of God: or else a madman or something worse. You can shut Him up for a fool, you can spit at Him and kill Him as a demon; or you can fall at His feet and call Him Lord and God. But let us not come out with any patronising nonsense about His being a great

human teacher. He has not left that open to us. He did not intend to.[12]

There is an echo of this argument in *The Lion, the Witch and the Wardrobe*, when Lucy claims to have stepped through the wardrobe into Narnia and the others do not yet believe her. They appeal to Professor Kirk. " 'Logic!' said the Professor half to himself. 'Why don't they teach logic at these schools? There are only three possibilities. Either your sister is telling lies, or she is mad, or she is telling the truth. You know she doesn't tell lies and it is obvious that she is not mad. For the moment then, and unless any further evidence turns up, we must assume she is telling the truth.' " [13]

Finally we should take note of an interesting piece of argument that occurs as part of the action in *The Silver Chair*. Eustace and Jill have broken the enchantment on Prince Rilian, and the Witch is trying to get all three back under her spell. Lewis has some excellent fun here showing that the same sort of argument that has been used by some to explain away the idea of God and heaven and so on can be used by the Witch to deny the reality of anything outside her own underground kingdom. But our main concern is with the speech Puddleglum the Marsh-wiggle makes in reply to the Witch's blandishments. (He has just put his foot into the fire to destroy the effect of a hypnotic powder the Witch is burning.)

> The pain itself made Puddleglum's head for a moment perfectly clear and he knew exactly what he really thought. There is nothing like a good shock of pain for dissolving certain kinds of magic.

[12] Ibid., p. 52.
[13] C. S. Lewis, *The Lion, the Witch and the Wardrobe* (New York: Harper-Collins, 2000), p. 48.

"One word, Ma'am," he said, coming back from the fire; limping, because of the pain. "One word. All you've been saying is quite right, I shouldn't wonder. I'm a chap who always liked to know the worst and then put the best face I can on it. So I won't deny any of what you said. But there's one thing more to be said, even so. Suppose we *have* only dreamed, or made up, all those things—trees and grass and sun and moon and stars and Aslan himself. Suppose we have. Then all I can say is that, in that case, the made-up things seem a good deal more important than the real ones. Suppose this black pit of a kingdom of yours *is* the only world. Well, it strikes me as a pretty poor one. And that's a funny thing, when you come to think of it. We're just babies making up a game, if you're right. But four babies playing a game can make a play-world which licks your real world hollow. That's why I'm going to stand by the play-world. I'm on Aslan's side even if there isn't any Aslan to lead it. I'm going to live as like a Narnian as I can even if there isn't any Narnia. So, thanking you kindly for our supper, if these two gentlemen and the young lady are ready, we're leaving your court at once and setting out in the dark to spend our lives looking for Overland. Not that our lives will be very long, I should think; but that's small loss if the world's as dull a place as you say." [14]

And this, I think, would be Lewis' final answer to any attack on Christianity in the name of modern viewpoint: he knows perfectly well that Christianity is true, just as the children and the Marsh-wiggle know perfectly well that trees and sun and grass exist. But if, *per impossible*, Christianity was false, it would still be a *bigger* view of the universe than that of the materialist. If it were a dream, it would be man's greatest dream. As Tolkien says, "It has pre-eminently the

---

[14] C. S. Lewis, *The Silver Chair* (New York: HarperCollins, 2000), pp. 181–82.

'inner consistency of reality.' There is no tale ever told that men would rather find was true." [15] And just as Puddleglum would be "on Aslan's side even if there isn't any Aslan to lead it [and] . . . live as like a Narnian as [he] can even if there isn't any Narnia", so Lewis and Tolkien would, I think, want to be on Christ's side even if there isn't any Christ to lead it, be citizens of the kingdom of God even if there isn't any kingdom of God.

Indeed, Lewis says in *Letters to Malcolm*, "Even now, even if—let's make an impossible supposition—His voice, unmistakably His, said to me, 'They have misled you. I can do nothing of that sort for you. My long story . . . is nearly over. I die, children. The story is ending,'—would that be the moment for changing sides? Would not you and I take the Viking way: 'The Giants and Trolls win. Let us die on the right side, with Father Odin.' " [16] Tolkien, I am sure, would agree. The view of Northern mythology is false; the monsters will not defeat the gods. But if they did, then, as Lewis says in *Poems*,

> the weary gods . . .
Will limp to their stations for the last defence. Make it your
    hope
To be counted worthy on that day to stand beside them
For the end of man is to partake of their defeat and die
This second, final death in good company. The stupid, strong
Unteachable monsters are certain to be victorious at last
And every man of decent blood is on the losing side. [17]

---

[15] J. R. R. Tolkien, "On Fairy-Stories", in *Tree and Leaf*, in *The Tolkien Reader* (New York: Ballantine Books, 2001), p. 89.

[16] C. S. Lewis, *Letters to Malcolm, Chiefly on Prayer* (San Diego: Harcourt, 2002), p. 174.

[17] C. S. Lewis, *Poems*, ed. Walter Hooper (San Diego: Harcourt, 2002), p. 4.

In summary, then, everything points to the reality of God: reason, morality, the deepest desires of our hearts. The usual objections to belief in God can be answered. Belief is reasonable. But it is also a total commitment of the whole person; better to die with God than live without God.

# 10

# The Continuing Battle

"All this is very well," it might be said, "but what relevance do Lewis and Tolkien have to the problems we face today?" Now partly this demand for relevance is itself a mistake in the eyes of Lewis and Tolkien; the greatest problems we face are "eternal not temporal". But the objection can be answered, at least partially, on its own terms.

Consider, for example, our modern problems of racial tensions. One effect of entering secondary worlds with a number of nonhuman "speaking races" must surely be to make us see that differences in color or culture among human races are fairly trivial differences. People from other cultures or (sometimes) of other races are different from ourselves, but why not rejoice in and enjoy such differences, as Sam the hobbit enjoys Elves or as Lewis' Malacandrian races enjoy each other?

The *sorns* in *Out of the Silent Planet* find certain things Ransom tells them about Earth interesting. "Two things about our world particularly stuck in their minds. One was the extraordinary degree to which problems of lifting and carrying things absorbed our energy. The other was the fact that we had only one kind of *hnau* [rational being]:

they thought this must have far-reaching effects in the narrowing of sympathies and even of thought. 'Your thought must be at the mercy of your blood,' said the old *sorn*. 'For you cannot compare it with thought that floats on a different blood.' " [1] But though we lack differences of the sort Ransom found on Mars we can perhaps to some extent compare our thoughts with those that "float on a different blood".

Notice that in Tolkien openness and interest in other races are not characteristic of Hobbits as such. The Shire hobbits are a closed-minded and provincial lot, suspicious even of hobbits who live beyond the Brandywine River or in Bree, to say nothing of Elves, Dwarves, and Wizards. (The Bree hobbits reciprocate by calling the Shire hobbits "outsiders".) It is only Bilbo, Frodo, Sam, Merry, and Pippin who in various degrees are interested in other creatures. And how richly they are rewarded! To put it at its lowest, they have much more *fun*, one would think, than the average hobbit.

Similarly, those in our world who close themselves into their own culture are shutting themselves off from a great deal of enjoyment, if nothing worse. And this fault is not confined to the white "middle American"; some Black, Chicano, and other ethnic groups seem to feel they can appreciate their own cultural heritage only by despising that of others. The truth is that real appreciation for any one race or culture helps you gain real appreciation of all others. Sam and Frodo and the others could appreciate the hobbit virtues after wandering with Elves and Dwarves. Ransom returned from Venus and Mars to preside over the peaceful and joyous community at St. Anne's.

---

[1] C. S. Lewis, *Out of the Silent Planet* (New York: Scribner, 2003), pp. 102–3.

In our increasingly hard and hateful times, it is becoming difficult to *appreciate*. But it is well worth the effort.

Ecology is another major issue of our times. Lewis' vision of man's original destiny can be seen on Perelandra, where the King and the Queen (or Green Lady) are to rule their planet as God's stewards, enhancing not destroying their environment, helping and guiding the animals instead of abusing them. Tolkien shows us the reverse side of the coin: the Dark Lord blasts and destroys the natural surroundings in and near Mordor; and when Saruman begins to become like the Enemy, he begins to lay waste the area near his tower and destroys trees. In contrast, Legolas delights in the ancient forest of Fangorn, and Gimli is in ecstasy at the beauty of the great caverns below Hornburg.

Students who enjoy Tolkien are awake to this aspect of his work. A construction project on my campus once destroyed some grass and trees near the library building, perhaps a necessary but certainly regrettable preliminary to expansion of the library. On the board fence surrounding the project, a number of slogans were painted. One near the entrance said simply, "The Gates of Mordor". Unfair, perhaps, but Tolkien—who was moved to write "Leaf by Niggle" when a tree near his home was cut down—would have understood.

Another "relevant" aspect of Lewis and Tolkien is their insistence on personal responsibility, on doing what we can (and often more than we want to) in whatever situation we face. Frodo with the Ring and Ransom on Perelandra are obvious examples. The theme of responsibility (and growth through accepting responsibility) is a constant theme in Tolkien and Lewis. Bilbo in *The Hobbit*, Niggle in "Leaf by Niggle", Lucy, Peter, Jill, and Eustace in the Narnia stories all demonstrate the theme. Our own particular responsibility may look quite undramatic, quite unlike the Ring or a quest set by Aslan, but sticking determinedly to a task is a virtue Lewis and Tolkien have managed to make more exciting than most other authors I can think of.

Another aspect of the sort of heroism celebrated by Lewis and Tolkien is that it is preeminently a heroism for hard times and seemingly hopeless situations. Now I would not willingly discourage the fainthearted, but any hope based on the idea that the problems of our country or our world are likely to be solved without heroism and sacrifice (or even, perhaps, with them) is bound to be disappointed. And a sojourn in the secondary worlds of Tolkien or Lewis is no bad preparation for facing grim situations and fighting for seemingly hopeless causes. As Gimli the Dwarf says of the land of the Rohirrim: "There is good rock here. This country has tough bones." [2]

We have seen that Lewis and Tolkien both emphasize the danger of using evil means for even the best ends. As our situation grows more and more grave, this is a temptation to which we are particularly susceptible. The radical who destroys and burns to make a better world or the conservative who uses repression in defense of freedom and order is increasingly characteristic of our time. And increasingly it is becoming difficult for those who use such means to see anything wrong with using them. The purity of their goals and the urgency of their situation increasingly blind them to what they are doing to themselves and others. We live more and more in Mordor, and whichever side wins in any of our tangled controversies, the prospects for ease or peace or freedom are increasingly dim.

[2] J. R. R. Tolkien, *The Two Towers*, rev. ed. (New York: Ballantine Books, 2001), p. 161.

The insistence on responsibility in Tolkien and Lewis, the reminders that bad means contaminate the ends they are used for, may seem to be contradicted by the fact that some in the "youth culture" appear to couple an enjoyment of Tolkien, or even of Lewis, with irresponsibility, retreat into the world of drugs, retreat from reality. I think this can be partly accounted for by simple despair. As Lewis says of his life at one point, when his love of fantasy and romance in literature was coupled with a materialistic philosophy, "Nearly everything I loved I thought to be imaginary." This, it seems to me, is the situation of many moderns. They lack Tolkien's and Lewis' belief in realities beyond this world, or the strength that would enable them "to live like a Narnian even if there isn't any Narnia".

Now there is no easy solution for this problem. If the facts about the universe are really such as to warrant despair, then no rhetoric or persuasion is likely to convince some people not to despair. Some people of Stoic temperament will feel pride in demonstrating an "unconquerable soul", but many will simply try to escape or forget in whatever way offers itself. If the universe *is* absurd and futile, then drugs, suicide, an immersion in sex or violence are no more appropriate or inappropriate as responses to it than Stoic courage. If there is no basic right and wrong then why should we be impressed by the existentialists' talk of "inauthenticity", for if nothing is wrong, how can it be wrong to be inauthentic?

Again, while many who think the universe absurd and futile have demonstrated nobility and compassion, if any choice is as good as any other, then nobility and compassion are no better as choices than degradation and exploitation of others. The idea that we can retain the essentials of the Christian moral code while rejecting the beliefs justifying that code is an error of the Victorian age that by now should be thoroughly discredited.

We have also disproved, simply by experience, the idea that mere material affluence or a certain kind of social order or any rearrangement of that sort will prove a remedy for man's condition.

John Wain is more clear-sighted than most moderns when he says,

> Naturally I think that human life is tragic. No shallow optimism, no easy faith that humanity will be happy when this or that piece of social engineering has been completed or when we have finished our conquest of Nature. What difference would it have made if my wife and I had met each other on Jupiter instead of Earth? The longest journeys are made within the self. The solitude that can exist within the human mind is more absolute than the emptiness of interstellar space. That is why I care nothing for technology, nothing for science. With all their improvements, they can never touch anything but the surface of human life. The same problems face every man and they always begin again. There are many ways of making life more tolerable, but none of ridding it of its basically tragic quality.[3]

Wain himself finds his vocation as an artist. His desire to create gives purpose to his life. But for those who lack such a purpose, or some parallel to it (Wain recognizes that for some, science is what his art is to him), the outlook that Wain offers can lead easily to despair.

It is true that, with the optimism and idealism of youth, many young people still hope to bring happiness to

[3] John Wain, *Sprightly Running: Part of an Autobiography* (New York: St. Martin's Press, 1963), p. 262.

themselves and everyone by some revolutionary transformation of society. But this is simply another "piece of social engineering", and as Wain recognizes, such changes are no solution to the problems of the human condition.

The alternative that Tolkien and Lewis offer is the Christian alternative. But surely, many will say, it has been tried and found to be no solution. But Tolkien and Lewis would agree with Chesterton that "Christianity has not been tried and found wanting. It has been found difficult and not tried."

But *what* has not been tried? Obviously the world can go very badly, indeed, in places or at times where everyone is nominally a Christian. What *would* make a difference would be a real effort by enough people to make a Christian society and to live a Christian life. But to many of us "a Christian society" or "a Christian life" has very little meaning. Lewis and Tolkien can help us.

Lewis has a brief chapter on "Social Morality" in *Mere Christianity*. He emphasizes that the foundation of any good society is the Golden Rule, "Do as you would be done by." Apart from this,

> Christianity has not, and does not profess to have, a detailed political programme for applying "Do as you would be done by" to a particular society at a particular moment.... It was never intended to replace or supersede the ordinary human arts and sciences: it is rather a director which will set them all to the right jobs, and a source of energy which will give them all new life, if only they will put themselves at its disposal.... [S]ome Christians—those who happen to have the right talents—should be economists and statesmen ... and their whole efforts in politics and economics should be directed to putting "Do as you would be done by" into action.... The application of Christian principles, say, to

trade unionism or education, must come from Christian trade unionists and Christian schoolmasters.[4]

Here we have again the note so frequently heard in Lewis and Tolkien: the call to personal responsibility. But what would a Christian society be like? Lewis gives us an idea.

> The New Testament, without going into details, gives us a pretty clear hint of what a fully Christian society would be like. Perhaps it gives us more that we can take. It tells us that there are to be no passengers or parasites: if man does not work, he ought not to eat. Every one is to work with his own hands, and what is more, every one's work is to produce something good.... On the other hand, it is always insisting on obedience—obedience (and outward marks of respect) from all of us to properly appointed magistrates, from children to parents, and (I am afraid this is going to be very unpopular) from wives to husbands. Thirdly, it is to be a cheerful society: full of singing and rejoicing, and regarding worry or anxiety as wrong. Courtesy is one of the Christian virtues.[5]

In *The Lord of the Rings* trilogy, we have a sort of illustration of such a society in the Fellowship of the Ring. Aragorn is respected, not only for his royal blood, but for his great knowledge and experience and his long struggle against the Enemy. Gandalf is valued not only for his power but also for his wisdom. These two are the leaders of the party and are respected as such. But their wisdom and experience are at the service of Frodo, the Ring-bearer, and they like and respect Sam, Merry, and Pippin. Legolas and Gimli

---

[4] C. S. Lewis, *Mere Christianity* (San Francisco: HarperCollins, 2001), pp. 82–83.
[5] Ibid., p. 84.

put their formidable talents fully into the search for Merry and Pippin and are delighted to find them safe.

Similarly, as we have seen, the society at St. Anne's is one where respect, affection, and joy are found together. There is no "swank"; Ivy Maggs is not just *treated* as a full member of the Company as a pretense; she *is* a full member. But Ransom is undoubtedly in charge, and his orders are carried out.

This, by the way, may be one reason why idealistic attempts at community, including many contemporary communes, have come to a bad end. There are expressions of love and unity, and a good deal of talk about freedom. But without responsibility ("Every one is to work ...") and respect for each other and for some kind of authority, "love" and "freedom" can come to mean exploitation and freeloading.

Notice, however, that both the Fellowship and the company at St. Anne's have some aspects of a commune. Perhaps a hint that could be taken from them is that each is devoted to a purpose: they got together not merely for the sake of getting together, but to accomplish something worth doing. Groups of civil rights workers in Mississippi, groups of pro-lifers, and peace marchers (as well as soldiers and civilians fighting in wars they believe to be just) report experiences of deep community, and this may be part of the reason.

But lacking a Christian society and lacking opportunities for such specialized communities (as many of us do), there are still many things we can do individually to make society better, including sharing our goods with others. Thus social morality leads us back again to individual responsibility: Christian society can be built only by living a Christian life.

In trying to understand the Christian life, a good place to begin is with that curious trio who struggles over the marshes and mountains to Mordor in Tolkien's *Lord of the Rings* trilogy—Frodo, Sam, and Gollum. One of Christ's least popular commandments has always been that which tells us to "love your enemies, do good to those who hate you" (Lk 6:27). But in Frodo's treatment of Sméagol, the hobbit who has become Gollum, the monster, we see this commandment at work in a situation we can believe in. Again, Christ's words "Whoever would be great among you must be your servant" (Mt 20:26) are exemplified in Sam, whose service to Frodo increases his stature to that of a hero and ruler.

Frodo himself, carrying the burden of the Ring, exemplifies the man who "takes up his cross", who remains faithfully despite terrible suffering. Love and forgiveness, humility and service, faithfulness and endurance: these are not all of the Christian virtues, but they are some of the most important.

The solution that Tolkien and Lewis offer to our human problems is difficult. If the universe is meaningless, we may do anything we like; no response is more appropriate than another, and there is no holding to account, no responsibility. Man is on his own, and if he makes a mess of things he will simply die, and that is the end of the story. But if Tolkien and Lewis are right, man has an ultimate and inescapable responsibility. As Lewis says,

> There are no *ordinary* people. You have never talked to a mere mortal. Nations, cultures, arts, civilisations—these are mortal, and their life is to ours as the life of a gnat. But it is immortals whom we joke with, work with, marry, snub, and exploit—immortal horrors or everlasting splendours. This does not mean that we are to be perpetually solemn. We must play. But our merriment must be of that kind (and it is, in fact, the merriest kind) which exists between people

who have, from the outset, taken each other seriously—no flippancy, no superiority, no presumption. And our charity must be a real and costly love, with deep feeling for the sins in spite of which we love the sinner—no mere tolerance or indulgence which parodies love as flippancy parodies merriment.[6]

This is indeed to bear the *weight* of glory. But the weight we are asked to bear *is* glorious. The Christian world view of Lewis and Tolkien may be false, and if so we must reject it. But as Tolkien tells us, "To reject it leads either to sadness or wrath."[7]

There is a good deal of sadness and wrath in the modern world. Lewis and Tolkien have tried at least to show us "a more excellent way".

---

[6] C. S. Lewis, "The Weight of Glory", in *The Weight of Glory and Other Addresses* (San Francisco: HarperCollins, 2001), p. 46.

[7] J. R. R. Tolkien, "On Fairy-Stories", in *The Tolkien Review* (New York: Ballantine Books, 2001), p. 89.

# APPENDICES

# Forerunners and Friends

I begin this discussion of those who have influenced Lewis and Tolkien by raising a question about the importance of influences. Why should we care that A influenced B or that B got a certain idea or image from A? Surely the point is the truth or beauty of the idea or image, not its origin. It seems to me that there are two bad reasons and two good reasons for being concerned with influences.

The two bad reasons are, first, an overconcern with originality and, second, a misapplication of the evolutionary idea. Overconcern with originality leads us to make an absurd fuss over who was "really" the first to use an idea or image. For example, pedants are fond of pointing out that Winston Churchill was not the first to use the phrase "iron curtain". But unless Churchill had used it in a famous speech, the phrase would never have gained currency. Or to take a case closer to home, an obscure seventeenth-century writer used the idea of letters from a devil for political purposes. But this does not take away the genuine originality of *The Screwtape Letters*. In fact, the "who was first" syndrome like the "which is biggest, tallest, longest" syndrome is simply an idiosyncrasy of our time.

The second bad reason—the misapplication of the evolutionary idea—supposes that there is something like an evolutionary development in ideas, that the better is always later and always develops from the earlier. But if this is true at all, it is true in a very qualified way. What we more often find is a much more complex situation, as any history of philosophy or literature will show. The best may come first, to be followed by misunderstandings or weak imitations. The latter may develop from the earlier or in defiance of it, or by a happy misunderstanding of an earlier view, or in many other ways. Thus, if we expect to find a steady straight-line development, we will be baffled.

But this brings us to the first good reason for studying influences. Sometimes but not always, the study of those who have influenced, or even those who have been influenced by, an author will help us to understand things we might not otherwise understand about that author. Where the author is obscure or difficult to understand because of distance in time or difference in culture, then such help may be very valuable. I think, however, that Tolkien and Lewis are in most cases understandable enough without such aid.

The second good reason is simply that such information is interesting. If I admire B, I may be very interested in finding that he admired A. This may or may not lead me to admire A, but it might nevertheless be a fascinating piece of information. Thus, for example, I find it interesting although not particularly useful or illuminating to know that Thornton Wilder's novel about Caesar, *The Ides of March*, was almost certainly influenced by Edith Hamilton's *The Roman Way*. Such interest is perhaps akin to the interest we feel in gossip, but may be no worse for that.

With these preliminaries, let us investigate what authors have influenced Tolkien and Lewis, and in what ways. Two authors frequently mentioned are William Morris and George MacDonald. Lewis has put his debt to both authors on record. He edited a collection of excerpts from Mac-Donald, *George MacDonald: An Anthology*, and used Mac-Donald as a figure in *The Great Divorce*. Lewis' admiration for Morris is recorded in an essay, "William Morris", collected in *The Literary Essays of C. S. Lewis*. Tolkien speaks with admiration of MacDonald in his essay "On Fairy-Stories", but does not mention Morris. Interestingly enough, there are a number of parallels between Morris' work and Tolkien's. Morris, like Tolkien, created a secondary world of knights and swords, wizards and magic. It was set in a vaguely medieval world, but Morris' Middle Ages were a never-never land with little relation to the real medieval period. Morris was also subjected to criticisms rather like the criticisms of Tolkien we discussed in Chapter 2 above, and Lewis' defense of Morris could stand equally as a defense of Tolkien.

> The question about Morris' style is not whether it is an artificial language—all endurable language in longer works must be that—but whether it is a good one. And it is here that sheer ignorance begins to play its part. I cannot help suspecting that most of the detractors when they talk of Morris' style are really thinking of his printing: they expect the florid and the crowded, and imagine something like Sidney's *Arcadia*. In fact, however, this style consistently departs from that of modern prose in the direction of simplicity. Except for a few archaic words—and since the appearance of the S.O.E.D. it is a pleasure to be sent to the dictionary—it is incomparably easier and clearer than any "natural" style could possibly be, and the "dull finish," the careful avoidance of rhetoric, gloss, and decoration, is of its very essence. Those who are really repelled by it after a fair

trial are being repelled not by its romanticism but by its classicism, for in one sense Morris is as classical as Johnson. Long ago, Mr. Alfred Noyes noticed the self-imposed limitation under which Morris describes nature whether in prose or verse—the birds that are merely "brown," the sea that is never anything more remarkable than "blue" or "green." Morris, in fact, obeys the doctrine of generality; he does not number the streaks on the tulip but "exhibits in his portraits of nature such prominent and striking features as recall the original to every mind." That such "just representations of general nature" can, as Johnson claims, "please many and please long," his own writing, and that of Morris, will prove.

> "I sat down on a bank, such as a writer of romance might have delighted to feign. I had, indeed, no trees to whisper over my head, but a clear rivulet streamed at my feet. The day was calm, the air was soft, and all was rudeness, silence and solitude."
>
> "The road was rough that day, and they went not above a foot-pace the more part of the time; and daylong they were going up and up, and it grew cold as the sun got low, though it was yet summer."

The first sentence is from Johnson and the second from Morris. There are a dozen differences between them, but there are two important similarities; both are content with recording obvious facts in very general language, and both succeed so that we really taste the mountain air. It is, indeed, this matter-of-factness, as Clutton-Brock pointed out, which lends to all Morris' stories their sober air of conviction. Other stories have only scenery: his have geography. He is not concerned with "painting" landscapes; he tells you the lie of the land and then you paint the landscapes for yourself. To a reader long fed on the almost botanical and entomological niceties of much modern fiction—where, indeed, we mostly skip if the characters go through a jungle—the effect is at first very pale and cold, but also very fresh and spacious. We begin to relish what my friend called the "Northernness." No mountains in literature are as far away as distant mountains in Morris. The world of his imagining is as windy, as tangible, as resonant and three-dimensional, as that of Scott or Homer.[1]

But Tolkien need not have learned this generalizing style from Morris. Both were influenced by Northern saga and Old English literature, though Tolkien's knowledge of it is that of a scholar—Morris' that of an amateur.

The contrast between Morris and Tolkien in other respects is interesting. In Morris we find no great struggle between good and evil, but rather personal and somewhat aimless adventuring. There is a certain amount of sex and sensuality in Morris, mild enough now, but extremely uninhibited for the Victorian era in which he wrote. There is something remote and rather impersonal about him. Lewis spoke of Morris' "pastel colors", but I would rather use the image of small, gaily colored figures seen at a distance in space; clear but small. All of this, of course, is unlike Tolkien.

The sense of "geography" Lewis points out in Morris is equally strong in Tolkien, however, and in other respects there is a closeness of atmosphere in Morris and Tolkien despite the differences. Put it this way: Frodo or Bilbo would not be totally out of place in Morris' world, nor would Raymond or Birdalone feel completely lost in Middle-earth.

Comparisons with MacDonald are harder to make. Lewis' "religious" fantasies are both much better written and more successful as presentations of a Christian imagination than

[1] "William Morris", in *The Literary Essays of C. S. Lewis* (New York: Cambridge University Press, 1969), pp. 220–21.

MacDonald's fantasy novels *Phantastes* and *Lilith*. Lewis has, I think, learned nothing about writing or about fantasy from MacDonald. In "straight" religious writing, Lewis may have learned more. In his *Unspoken Sermons* and in the sermons and reflective passages in his potboiling novels, MacDonald explains and illuminates Christian doctrines with extraordinary clarity and beauty. The "holiness" Lewis found in *Phantastes* is hard for me to see there, but it is easy to find, buried under Gothic absurdities, in such long-forgotten MacDonald novels as *A Country Parish* or *Robert Falconer*.

Tolkien shows no signs of being affected by this side of MacDonald, though I think some of it affected him indirectly through Lewis. The atmosphere of *Phantastes* and *Lilith* is quite different from that of Tolkien's books. But MacDonald's children's classics, *The Princess and the Goblin* and *The Princess and Curdie*, are much more like Tolkien; in fact, *The Hobbit*, with its "goblins" (not yet "Orcs") underground, and other similarities to MacDonald may have been directly influenced by the Curdie books, or at least by *The Princess and the Goblin*. Tolkien says of MacDonald, "The Magical, the fairy-story, may ... be made a vehicle of Mystery. This at least is what George MacDonald attempted, achieving stories of power and beauty when he succeeded, as in *The Golden Key* (which he called a fairy-tale); and even when he partly failed, as in *Lilith* (which he called a romance)." [2]

Thus Lewis may have learned something of doctrine and its presentation from MacDonald, and Tolkien *may* have learned something from Morris about making secondary worlds and about a "generalizing" style. But neither

<hr />

[2] J. R. R. Tolkien, "On Fairy-Stories", in *Tree and Leaf*, in *The Tolkien Reader* (New York: Ballantine Books, 2001), p. 52.

influence is certain, and in both cases Lewis and Tolkien could have learned the same lessons elsewhere.

A clearer influence on both Lewis and Tolkien was G. K. Chesterton. Neither resembles Chesterton much in style; indeed, Chesterton's extravagant, exuberant style was *sui generis* both in fiction and in exposition. But in ideas there was a great deal of influence. Both Tolkien and Lewis quote and mention Chesterton with respect. In addition, a sound Chestertonian can detect Chesterton's ideas at work in many places in both Lewis and Tolkien. Both, I think, would acknowledge Chesterton as one of their teachers, one who taught them to see or appreciate things they would not have seen without him.

But this kind of influence, though it may be the most important personally, is the most "transparent", the least useful for understanding Lewis or Tolkien. They have made his ideas their own, and for that very reason they express them clearly and easily. Thus, whether we encounter an idea first in Chesterton or in Lewis or Tolkien matters little: if it is a good idea we can appreciate it equally in any of the three. Often, too, it may be the case that Lewis and Tolkien say Chestertonian things because their own beliefs or attitudes are similar to his, or because they have arrived at the same ideas independently.

Another important influence on Lewis, and perhaps indirectly on Tolkien, was Charles Williams. He was a contemporary and friend who, during the war years, taught at Oxford and was a member of the group of friends who met regularly in Lewis' rooms there. Williams wrote seven fantastic novels in which magic and the occult form the basis of his "secondary world", in the same way that legendary prehistory forms the basis of Tolkien's and the planets and their inhabitants form the basis of Lewis'. He also wrote plays and poetry as well as books on literary criticism, which he himself regards as potboilers.

Williams had a charismatic personality and tended to have disciples rather than friends or students. But in Lewis and Tolkien, he met men who were at least his equals in personality and intellect. There was no question of their becoming his disciples, but they became his friends, and the friendship was evidently a very warm and close one, especially on the part of Lewis.

Some writers have seen Williams as the center of the Lewis-Tolkien circle (for example, Charles Moorman in *Precincts of Felicity*). That the circle existed long before Williams came to Oxford and survived years after his death (until Lewis moved to Cambridge, in fact) is one piece of evidence against this view. Moorman notes that Tolkien himself (and his son Christopher, an ofttimes member of the circle) saw Lewis as the center of the group.

I think Lewis might have said the group had no center, only a circumference: it was like a group of people seated in a circle, each looking at and talking to all the others— not like a group of disciples clustered around a master at the center of the group. But, to continue the metaphor, Williams' accession made the circumference larger; there was one more person to contribute to the circle and receive from it.

With regard to the creation of secondary worlds or to the craft of writing, Williams had more to learn than to contribute. His last novel, which had the benefit of the group's criticism, is technically better than any of his others.

He contributed more, perhaps, in the realm of ideas. Williams had a genuinely original, if somewhat undisciplined, mind. His theological insights, as expressed in his novels and plays as well as in essays and books on theology, are often exciting. But his style is baroque and sometimes confusing. Lewis—whose beautifully clear mind could extract meaning from prose far worse than Williams' and make order out of material even more scattered and diverse than the ideas broadcast throughout Williams' plays, novels, and essays—found Williams fascinating. Tolkien, from the scattered evidence available, liked Williams personally, but was unimpressed by him intellectually.

With Williams, we have mentioned the last of the individual authors who had really strong intellectual influence on both men, at least so far as their published testimony is concerned. The rest is speculation. We can find plenty of material for speculation, of course. Lewis, for example, mentioned his enjoyment of Edith Nesbit's children's stories, and I think I can find some influence of the Nesbit books on the Narnia stories. The Phoenix, in *The Phoenix and the Carpet*, may have contributed to Lewis' idea of Aslan; the characters of Peter, Susan, Edmund, and Lucy may have been suggested in some respects by various Nesbit children. Much more speculatively, I wonder if Lewis was not slightly influenced by Arthur Ransome's *Swallows and Amazons*, especially in the character of Susan.

Tolkien is familiar with a great number of fairy tales from many nations, and their influence can probably be discerned at many points in his books. The influence of *Beowulf*, *Gawain*, and other early English stories on Tolkien is also obvious. But what else Tolkien read, for pleasure or instruction, is not easy to discover.

The influence of Norse mythology (and to a lesser extent of Greek mythology) on both authors is clear. Both Lewis and Tolkien, of course, were influenced by biblical authors (Tolkien translated the Book of Job for the English version of the Jerusalem Bible) and by many great Christian writers of the past. Lewis was fond of Dr. Samuel Johnson, and one suspects that Johnson would be congenial to Tolkien, too. But Tolkien has not told us.

Of their contemporaries, Owen Barfield, for many years Lewis' lawyer, was a member of the circle who met in Lewis' rooms when his work permitted. He was an anthroposophist, and Lewis' own views on many things were clarified by arguing with Barfield. Lewis dedicated a book to him with the inscription: "Opposition is true friendship." Did he also influence Tolkien? Dorothy Sayers was a friend of Lewis and also of Charles Williams. Did she know Tolkien? Such questions cannot be answered, for Tolkien has not told us.

And after all, what does it matter? Lewis and Tolkien are gloriously themselves, whatever they may have learned from others. Let us thank God for them, and enjoy them.

# *That Hideous Strength*: A Double Story

There are two cities, said St. Augustine, a city of God, founded on love of God and our fellow man, and a city of man, founded on love of self. That is the matter of C. S. Lewis' *That Hideous Strength*:[1] the opposition between the society at the Manor at St. Anne's, founded on love and fellowship, and the group at the mansion at Belbury, founded on self-aggrandizement, treachery, and fear. But the manner of telling the story is also based on opposition and contrast; the dialectic of the theme is echoed by the dialectic of the tale. This is obvious enough in the larger structure of the story, the alternation of scenes in which Jane Studdock takes a part and those in which her husband Mark plays a role. But the finer structure of the story also displays an intricate and detailed opposition of scenes and characters; it is this opposition, and the ideas on which it rests, that I wish to examine in what follows.

The opposition begins with the situation of the two protagonists. Jane Studdock is a person who has fled from making a real commitment of herself, either in her marriage or

[1] All quotations are taken from C. S. Lewis, *That Hideous Strength* (New York: Scribner, 2003).

in other areas of her life. She has made her scholarship an excuse not to have children and not to share her life fully with her husband: "She had always intended to continue her own career as a scholar after she was married: that was one of the reasons why they were to have no children, at any rate for a long time yet" (p. 14). But she has no real commitment to her scholarship, although she tries to make herself believe that "if she got out all her notebooks and editions and really sat down to the job, she could force herself back into her lost enthusiasm" (p. 12).

Mark Studdock's problem is not lack of commitment; he has made an "almost heroic sacrifice of nearly every person and thing he actually enjoyed" (pp. 243–44). But his commitment has been to an ideal essentially base and trivial— the desire to be an "insider", to be in the "inner ring". Lewis has written of this desire in an essay: "The lust for the esoteric, the longing to be inside, take many forms. . . . We hope, no doubt, for tangible profits from every Inner Ring we penetrate: power, money, liberty to break rules. . . . But all these would not satisfy us if we did not get in addition the delicious sense of secret intimacy. . . . This desire is one of the great permanent mainsprings of human action." [2] Mark's problem, then, is a wrong commitment as his wife's is a wrong lack of commitment.

In the dialectic of the story, both Mark and Jane eventually free themselves from their ruling vice, but they must first display in their actions what this vice is. Jane's lack of commitment to her marriage is hinted at by her interaction with Mark early in the story. After one of her frightening dreams (which as the story develops are seen to be a sort of

[2] C. S. Lewis, "The Inner Ring", in *The Weight of Glory and Other Addresses* (San Francisco: HarperCollins, 2001), p. 151–52.

vision or "second sight"), Jane meets Mark on his return home frightened and sobbing: "There was a quality in the very muscles of his wife's body which took him by surprise. A certain indefinable defensiveness had momentarily deserted her. He had known such occasions before, but they were rare. They were already becoming rarer. And they tended, in his experience, to be followed next day by inexplicable quarrels" (p. 42).

Similarly, Mark's desire to be an insider is adumbrated in the first few scenes in which he figures. He has newly become a member of the Progressive Element, the "Inner Ring" of his college: "You would never have guessed from the tone of Studdock's reply what intense pleasure he derived from Curry's use of the pronoun 'we.' So very recently he had been an outsider, watching the proceedings of what he then called 'Curry and his gang' with awe.... Now he was inside and 'Curry and his gang' had become 'we' or 'the Progressive Element in College.' It had all happened quite suddenly and was still sweet in the mouth" (p. 15). The loss of real friendship this involves is also suggested in this early scene: "He did not always like Curry either. His pleasure in being with him was not that sort of pleasure" (p. 16).

As the plot develops, Jane's attitude toward Mark and toward her marriage is developed by contrast with the marriages of others—the Dimbles, the Dennistons, Ivy Maggs and her husband. Mark moves from Bracton to Belbury and into the innermost ring at Belbury; at each stage we are shown something of what he has lost and where he is going.

As the action of the story begins, both Jane and Mark encounter people who have been involved in their past lives and who introduce them to a next, crucial, stage in their lives. Jane encounters a former teacher, Dr. Dimble, and his wife, "Mother" Dimble, who had become fond of Jane while Jane was Dimble's pupil. Through the Dimbles, Jane is sent to the Manor at St. Anne's for the next stage of her spiritual journey. Mark encounters Lord Feverstone, not a man he had known well but, as Curry reveals in an early scene, the man who had been influential in getting Mark his fellowship at Bracton. It is through Feverstone that Mark goes to Belbury.

As it turns out both the group at St. Anne's and the group at Belbury would like to make use of Jane's gift of "seeing" or "vision". The difference in their tactics is revealing: Jane is sent to St. Anne's by the Dimbles, who are fond of her. Once there, her gift and its dangers are explained to her, and she is invited freely to become one of the Company at St. Anne's. This first invitation she refuses, and she returns home as freely as she came.

The Belbury group, on the other hand, try to get Jane in their power by first getting Mark. As Wither says on one occasion, "If a mere arrest could have secured the— er—good will and collaboration of Mrs. Studdock, we should hardly have embarrassed ourselves with the presence of her husband" (p. 158). Once having secured Mark, they attempt to make use of him in various ways, but the initial reason for getting him to Belbury is as part of a complicated plot to get Jane's cooperation, as the quote above makes clear. Lord Feverstone has no regard for Mark; when the tormented young man says, "I thought you at least were my friend", Feverstone's reply is, "Incurable romantic!" (p. 110).

Even our early glimpses of the Dimbles on the one hand and Feverstone on the other give us something of their very different atmospheres to which they belong. Dimble is a conscientious teacher. "'There is my dullest pupil just ringing the bell,' he said. 'I must go to the study, and listen to an essay on Swift beginning, "Swift was born." Must try to keep my mind on it, too, which won't be easy'" (p. 31). His wife "appeared to like all Dr. Dimble's pupils of both sexes, and the Dimbles' house, away on the far side of the river, was a kind of noisy *salon* all the term. She had been particularly fond of Jane" (p. 27).

When we first meet Feverstone, he baits Curry, his host and ally, then derides him to Mark after Curry has left to go to a meeting. His conversation reveals that he is on the side of Belbury not because he believes in the publicly proclaimed ideals of the N.I.C.E. (National Institute of Coordinated Experiments) but because he wants power. His appeal to Mark is, "Man has got to take charge of Man. That means, remember, that some men have got to take charge of the rest.... You and I want to be the people who do the taking charge, not the ones who are taken charge of" (p. 40).

The next day Feverstone drives Mark to Belbury, and his driving gives another clue to his character:

> The speed of the car, even in the narrow streets of Edgestow, was impressive, and so were the laconic criticisms of Feverstone on other drivers and pedestrians. Once over the level crossing ... their speed became so great that even on a rather empty road the inexcusably bad drivers, the manifestly halfwitted pedestrians and men with horses, the hen that they actually ran over and the dogs and hens that Feverstone pronounced "damned lucky," seemed to follow one another almost without intermission.... Mark, drunk with air and at once fascinated and repelled by the insolence of Feverstone's driving sat saying, "Yes," and "Quite," and "It was *their* fault." (p. 47)

Once at Belbury, Feverstone abandons Mark to the psychological softening up by Wither and the other powers of Belbury.

Jane's first meeting at St. Anne's is with Camilla Denniston, to whom she takes a liking, but her important contact is with Grace Ironwood, whom she finds stern and unsympathetic. This is one of the few instances, incidentally, where Lewis has painted himself into a corner from a literary point of view. He wanted to show the initial face of Belbury as pleasant and amiable, the initial face of St. Anne's as seemingly repellent. There is a sound tradition behind this move—the straight and narrow path of virtue as opposed to the broad and flowery path to destruction, the stern visage of duty as opposed to the smiling face of vice. But in order to give St. Anne's this initially unsympathetic face, Lewis created a somewhat unsympathetic character, Grace Ironwood, who is a slight embarrassment to him in later scenes. She is absent, on a slight pretext or none, from most of the later scenes involving friendship and companionship. Lewis could, of course, have shown an initially unsympathetic character becoming more sympathetic, but given the many other things he had to do in the book he may be forgiven for having sidestepped the problem by first using Grace Ironwood and then retiring her to the background.

Even the gardens at St. Anne's and at Belbury help the contrast between the two spiritual atmospheres. Jane, even on her first visit, apprehensive and somewhat hostile, finds the garden at St. Anne's delightful: "It was like the garden in *Peter Rabbit*. Or was it like the garden in the *Romance of the Rose*? No, not in the least like really. Or like Klingsor's garden? Or the garden in *Alice*?" (p . 60). For Mark, on the other hand, the garden at Belbury is just another of its torments:

They were not the sort of grounds that anyone could walk in for pleasure. The Edwardian millionaire who had built Belbury had enclosed about twenty acres with a low brick wall surmounted by an iron railing, and laid it all out in what his contractor called Ornamental Pleasure Grounds. There were trees dotted about and winding paths covered so thickly with round white pebbles that you could hardly walk on them.... There were plantations—slabs would be almost a better word—of that kind of laurel which looks as if it were made of cleverly painted and varnished metal.... The whole effect was like that of a municipal cemetery. (p. 99)

This contrast between the gardens may seem purely adventitious, something "dragged in" to darken Belbury and highlight St. Anne's. But Lewis is using the two gardens as a metaphor for the anti-life attitude of Belbury and the pro-life attitude of St. Anne's. All of the St. Anne's people are connected with traditional "natural" activities in some way: MacPhee and Grace Ironwood work in the garden at St. Anne's; the Dimbles' garden at their home is famous for its beauty. Camilla and Arthur Denniston share a taste for weather and nature. Ivy Maggs has a sort of *rapport* with Mr. Bultitude the bear; Ransom has a power over animals gained by his sojourn on Perelandra.

Belbury's attitude is made explicit by Filostrato: "We do not want the world any longer furred over with organic life, like what you call the blue mould—all sprouting and budding and breeding and decaying. We must get rid of it. By little and little, of course. Slowly we learn how. Learn to make our brains live with less and less body: learn to build our bodies directly with chemicals, no longer have to stuff them full of dead brutes and weeds" (p. 171). Earlier Feverstone had suggested the same idea:

"The second problem is our rivals on this planet. I don't mean only insects and bacteria. There's far too much life of every kind about, animal and vegetable. We haven't really cleared the place yet" (p. 40).

The theory behind the St. Anne's attitude toward nature is the idea of man as a link between the animal and the spiritual. Man should not sink to a purely animal level, but it is equally fatal for man to attempt to live as if he were a pure spirit, to attempt to sever his links with the organic. Man's place, as Ransom says, is "between the angels who are our elder brothers and the beasts who are our jesters, servants and playfellows" (p. 376). The image of the world Belbury wants to make is the cold, sterile moon, imagined as inhabited by a race that has denied its organic component, which feeds and even procreates by artificial means. The image of the world St. Anne's wants is the Venus of Lewis' earlier book *Perelandra*, envisioned as an Eden where the manlike inhabitants live in harmony with nature and in partnership with the angelic intelligences who have prepared the planet for their coming.

Interestingly enough, though, Filostrato is a stranger to the full scope and purpose of Belbury, for he knows nothing of the evil angels who are the real force behind its plans and purposes: "He was not an initiate, he knew nothing of the dark eldils. He believed that his skill had really kept Alcasan's brain alive" (p. 352). But Filostrato's dedication to an anti-natural ideal of science makes him a natural tool for the demonic forces who rule Belbury.

MacPhee at St. Anne's is also a partial stranger to the full mission of Ransom's Company. He apparently believes in God (though his model, Lewis' old tutor Kirkpatrick, did not). But he seems not to be a Christian and maintains a sceptical attitude toward the eldils and even toward Ransom's account of his adventures on Mars and Venus. But his concern for truth and his appreciation of Ransom's goodness make him as much a natural ally of St. Anne's as Filostrato is of Belbury. Notice also that Hingest, who is a chemist of international reputation and an agnostic, rejects Belbury as soon as he sees what it is like, because he has his own standards both of science and of personal conduct: "There *are* no sciences like Sociology. And if I found chemistry beginning to fit in with a secret police run by a middle-aged virago who doesn't wear corsets and a scheme for taking away his farm and his shop and his children from every Englishman, I'd let chemistry go to the devil and take up gardening again" (p. 69). The intellectual pride of the physical scientist is well hit off ("There *are* no sciences like Sociology"), but so is Hingest's concern for the ordinary man (and gardening is again a symbol for a pro-life attitude).

The key point here is one that goes very deep in Lewis' thinking. It is the idea that any real and unselfish devotion to an ideal outside oneself leads to God and away from evil, whereas any ideal, no matter how apparently noble, leads away from God and goodness if pursued for the wrong reasons or by the wrong means. (Filostrato's ambition is not to serve science but to become one of the "chosen heads" who will rule the earth, and he will kill and betray to gain his end.)

To return to the adventures of Jane and Mark, we see Mark leave Belbury temporarily and return; on his return he is introduced to the Head, the severed head of Alcasan through which the evil eldils speak. Jane also returns home after her first visit to St. Anne's; on her second visit she meets Ransom, the Director of St. Anne's, and has a momentary experience of the power and strangeness of the good eldils who are the allies of St. Anne's. Mark's experience is terrifying and literally nauseating, and as a result of it he is willing to sacrifice Jane to the aims of Belbury: "Apparently he would *have* to bring her to Belbury. His mind had made this decision for him at some moment he did not remember. He must get her, to save his life.... The first hint of a real threat to his bodily life knocked him sprawling" (p. 183).

Jane, however, has had an experience of great joy and awe: "Her world was unmade: anything might happen now" (p. 141). On her trip home "she was in the sphere of Jove, amid light and music and festal pomp, brimmed with life and radiant in health, jocund and clothed in shining garments" (p. 149). And this experience, though focused on the person of the Director, gives her "new feelings about Mark, feelings of guilt and pity.... It was Mark who had made the fatal mistake; she must, must, must be 'nice' to Mark.... There arose, clouded with some undefined emotion, a resolution to give Mark much more than she had ever given him before" (p. 149).

In the intricate dialectic of the plot, Jane on this return to Edgestow meets a representative of Belbury, "Fairy" Hardcastle, and Mark soon leaves Belbury again to return to Edgestow and meets Dimble, a representative of St. Anne's. Hardcastle tortures Jane and tries to take her back to Belbury; Jane escapes only by accident. Mark finds his meeting with Dimble unpleasant, but only because Dimble shows Mark to himself as he has become: "'Studdock,' said Dimble. 'This is not a time for foolery, or compliments.... I don't trust you. Why should I? You are (at least in some degree) the accomplice of the worst men in the world.... They have corrupted better men than you or me before now. Straik was a good man once. Filostrato was at least a great genius.... Who are you to be exempt?'" (p. 220).

Despite this, Dimble offers to help Mark leave Belbury, knowing that Mark's coming may be a trap, knowing he risks his own life and even the mission of St. Anne's.

It is worth noting the intricate pattern made by the movement of the two Studdocks, a pattern too orderly to be accidental. Jane and Mark each leave home on the same day; Jane goes to St. Anne's, Mark to Belbury. They each return and meet each other. At this stage Mark is happy and confident, Jane worried and apprehensive. Mark returns to Belbury, Jane to St. Anne's; each there meets the real authority of the place. Jane on her second departure from St. Anne's leaves reluctantly; Mark is running in fear on his second departure from Belbury. Their positions are now reversed: Jane is happy, Mark afraid. As we have seen, each meets a representative of the other side, then returns. Jane goes back to St. Anne's gladly, fleeing from "Fairy" Hardcastle's persecution and finding St. Anne's a place of refuge and peace. Mark returns to Belbury a prisoner, afraid and beginning to reject what Belbury stands for. At the end of the book, Jane and Mark are united again both physically and spiritually. In one way, the question of the book has always been, "Will Jane join Mark at Belbury, to their mutual destruction, or will Mark join Jane at St. Anne's, to their mutual salvation?" And it is by staying at St. Anne's that Jane plays her part in the events that lead to the freeing of Mark.

The story here moves on several levels. On one level, it is merely the stock adventure of romance—lovers are separated; will they get back together? At another level, it is about the adventures of any soul and the different ways in which it may choose good or evil. But on an intermediate level, it is a parable of what happens when two people in a relationship begin to go different ways. Jane must not lightly leave Mark; Ransom sends her back to plead with Mark to leave Belbury. But she must not go to him if this means *her* destruction; there is no question of her staying with Hardcastle in order to be reunited with Mark. Her mission of going to plead with Mark is frustrated; she never meets him until all is decided. But her effort bears fruit in unexpected ways: she is tortured by Hardcastle, and the knowledge of this fact probably plays a part in Mark's turnaround.

After the returns to St. Anne's and Belbury, each of the Studdocks faces danger, and each has to face up to the thought of death. Jane meets the real Merlin and the forces he unleashes and does not much like the experience. Mark meets the false Merlin (a tramp) and likes him; without knowing it he finds the right kind of "inner ring" based on friendship and shared danger. Each learns from the experience: Jane is further jolted out of her smug contemporary outfit of ideas and Mark's friendship with the tramp is another point of strength in his growing resistance to Belbury. Both Jane and Mark are offered an opportunity to become more a part of the group they have joined: Jane goes out on the search for the awakened Merlin and later shares with the others in the "side effects" produced by the descent of the eldils on St. Anne's. After her dismaying experience with the dwarfs and the terrestrial Venus, she has a true mystical experience, a sort of brief union with God for which perhaps her gifts as a "seer" especially prepare her. Mark is offered the opportunity to become an "initiate", one of those wholly possessed by the evil eldils who rule Belbury. It is the last and most terrible form of his old temptation to be in the "inner ring": "For here, surely at last (so his desire whispered to him) was the true inner circle of all, the circle whose centre was outside the human race—the ultimate secret, the supreme power, the last initiation. The fact that it was almost completely horrible did not in the least diminish its attraction" (pp. 257–58). But Mark is strengthened by his memory of Jane, by his friendship with the tramp, by his realization (brought on by facing the seeming certainty of death) of how he has wasted his life. Mark resists. He begins to fight back.

In all this, in the eventual defeat of their attempt to control England, in the failure of their attempt to control Mark, the powers of Belbury are the unwitting agents of their own defeat. In trying to invade Perelandra, the evil eldils have broken a sort of treaty that prevented the good eldils from acting directly on earth; the treaty once broken, the eldils can use Merlin as a channel for their power and destroy the evil at Belbury and Edgestow. But even in small things Belbury's own attitude and methods work against its purposes.

A minor villain named Cosser tries to make use of Mark to do some work that is really Cosser's job: visiting and writing a report on a village that is to be wiped out by one of Belbury's schemes. But the village reminds Mark of happy holidays when he was young and an old aunt he was fond of. (The aunt was one of the very type of people Belbury now wants to eliminate.) The visit sows some of Mark's first doubts about Belbury. Cosser's petty bit of meanness, trying to trick Mark into doing some work for him, is on a smaller scale just what the higher-ups at Belbury are trying to do: use Mark for their own purposes. But since people are not tools, attempts to use them for our purposes can backfire, as they do in Mark's case. Belbury, by treating people only as tools, does not even get the best out of them as tools.

St. Anne's, by enlisting the free cooperation first of Jane and then of Merlin, gains two formidable allies, but also two additions to its circle of friends and companions. By getting to know Merlin, both Ransom and Dimble gain an incomparable insight into Arthurian Britain; one cannot imagine Wither or Frost getting to know Merlin in this way or caring about what they can learn from him if it does not help their schemes. By treating Jane merely as an object for her sadistic impulses, "Fairy" Hardcastle frightens her and ensures that she will run straight back to St. Anne's; but each of the people at St. Anne's (except Grace Ironwood) befriends Jane in some way and, though they mainly seem to be giving to her, helping her, they also inevitably gain something in the exchange. Ivy Maggs, for instance, gains at least the knowledge that Jane's situation is worse than her own, for Fred Maggs, though in prison, is not on the side of Belbury. Mother Dimble perhaps finds in Jane the daughter she never had.

Most important for all those at St. Anne's is the fact that they have the opportunity to help someone come closer to goodness, to God. For the really essential struggle between Belbury and St. Anne's is the struggle for souls. As Frost says, "One must guard against the error of supposing that the political and economic dominance of England by the N.I.C.E. is more than a subordinate object: it is individuals that we are really concerned with. A hard unchangeable core of individuals really devoted to the same cause as ourselves—that is what we need and what, indeed, we are under orders to supply" (pp. 239–40). Lewis supposes here, as he does in *The Screwtape Letters*, that the damned want *fresh* recruits in order to feed on them in some way or absorb them; as Wither says in the same scene, "Any fresh individual brought into that unity would be a source of the most intense satisfaction to—ah—all concerned. I desire the closest possible bond. I would welcome an interpenetration

of personalities so close, so irrevocable, that it almost tran-
scends individuality. You need not doubt that I would open
my arms to receive—to absorb—to assimilate this young
man" (p. 240).

This bond of "assimilation" among the lost is a sort of
infernal parody of the unity of Christian love; even some
of the same terms can be used, though with terribly different meanings. So also Wither is a sort of infernal parody
of Ransom. Ransom is the Director of St. Anne's, his own
man, freely obeying the will of God as shown to him by
the eldils. Wither, significantly, is the *Deputy* Director of
the N.I.C.E., the puppet of the real ruler of Belbury, Alcasan's
severed head through which the evil eldils speak. Wither
uses speech to confuse, to bewilder, to mislead. Ransom is
a poet and linguist, a lover and respectful user of language.
After first bamboozling Mark to get him to stay at Belbury,
Wither constantly terrifies and degrades him (for example,
by pretending to forget his name); his attitude toward him
is a cold dislike. Ransom's attitude toward Jane is consistently friendly and interested; he talks to her about books,
shows her the mice that pick up the crumbs, talks with her
about the problems in her marriage. Indeed Ransom seems
alive to and interested in everything, whereas Wither "had
learned to withdraw most of his consciousness from the task
of living, to conduct business, even, with only a quarter of
his mind. Colours, tastes, smells, and tactual sensations no
doubt bombarded his physical senses in the normal manner: they did not now reach his ego" (pp. 247–48).

This last contrast between Wither and Ransom may seem
exaggerated; surely a man can be very evil and yet be alive to
the world around him and appreciative of it. But Lewis intends
Wither to be a picture of man in the last stages of separation
from God, and one of Lewis' most basic convictions is that

ultimately separation from God is separation from everything good. Insofar as a man still has an appreciation of any good thing, whether it be art or nature or other people, that man is not wholly lost. Insofar, on the other hand, as a man is wholly separated from God he loses his appreciation of all good things, which may have first started him on the path away from God. *Any* good thing taken apart from God loses its goodness; it is not a question of God or this good, for without God, "this good" will no longer *be* good.

At this stage, if not long before, the reader not in sympathy, or not entirely in sympathy, with Lewis' theology may find himself rejecting *That Hideous Strength* as a work of fiction. Is it not, he may ask, on my own showing a work of propaganda rather than a work of art, designed to influence the reader by putting a certain way of life or set of values in a good light and the opposing way of life or set of values in a bad light? Is there not, the critic may ask, more to be said for Belbury than Lewis allows, more to be criticized in St. Anne's than Lewis allows us to see?

If the critic merely means that there is more to be said for science, or sociology, or even for scientific planning as applied to society than Lewis allows, then the criticism rests on a misunderstanding. Belbury really cares nothing for science or for human society; it uses its pretended concern for these things as a cloak for its real aims. Nor is Lewis attacking these values as such. As he points out in an essay, he is saying not "scientific planning will certainly lead to Hell", but rather:

> Under modern conditions any effective invitation to Hell will certainly appear in the guise of "scientific planning"—as Hitler's regime in fact did. Every tyrant must begin by claiming to have what his victims respect and to give what they

want. The majority in most modern countries respect science and want to be planned. And, therefore, almost by definition, if any man or group wishes to enslave us it will of course describe itself as "scientific planned democracy." It may be true that any real salvation must equally, though by hypothesis truthfully, describe itself as "scientific planned democracy." All the more reason to look very carefully at anything which bears that label.[3]

If not science or scientific planning, what is Lewis writing against when he pictures Belbury? Just what we have seen: the real face and not the mask of Belbury. And what is this real face? It is seen in the cruelty of "Fairy" Hardcastle, in Filostrato's rejection of nature, in Wither's use of language to confuse and deceive, in Frost's "objectivity", which is a rejection of personhood. It is a rejection of the love of God and neighbor, ultimately a rejection of anything outside ourselves. We sometimes call it, as Augustine does, "self-love". But ultimately it is a hatred of all selves, including one's self. It is saying "*my* will, not Thine, be done" even when my will being done leads and can be seen to lead to loss and destruction. The true face of Belbury is Frost's face as he dies: "The nearest thing to a human passion which still existed in him was a sort of cold fury against all who believed in the mind. There was no tolerating such an illusion. There were not, and must not be, such things as men" (p. 355). As Frost dies, "Escape for the soul, if not for the body, was offered him. He became able to know (and simultaneously refused the knowledge) that he had been wrong from the beginning, that souls and personal responsibility existed. He half saw: he

---

[3] C. S. Lewis, *Of Other Worlds: Essays and Stories*, ed. Walter Hooper (New York: Harcourt, Brace and World, 1966), p. 80.

wholly hated. The physical torture of the burning was not fiercer than his hatred of that. With one supreme effort he flung himself back into his illusion. In that attitude eternity overtook him as sunrise in old tales overtakes [trolls] and turns them into unchangeable stone" (p. 356).

It is against this hatred of the human, this abolition of man, that Lewis writes. If his book is propaganda, it is propaganda against that. It is not argument; the arguments are to be found in his nonfiction, especially in *The Abolition of Man*. Nor is the book propaganda if by propaganda is meant an attempt to sway the emotions by exaggeration and by the selection and suppression of facts. But that it is propaganda in an older sense, *Propaganda fide*—preaching, Lewis would not, I think, deny. *That Hideous Strength* is, if you like, a sermon, preached against certain dangers of our times. It is more than that—it is a fairy tale, a satire on academic life, a commentary on marriage and modern mores. But among all of these things, it is also a sermon, and like all sermons its purpose is to make us repent and change our ways. That it is addressed to our condition is proved by the kind of opposition it has aroused. If we do not take warning from Lewis' tale, it may before long be truth and not fiction that "the shadow of one dark wing is over all Tellus.... The Hideous Strength holds all this Earth in its fist to squeeze as it wishes" (p. 291).

# Did C. S. Lewis Lose His Faith?

In 1986, a well-produced and well-acted television play based on the life of C. S. Lewis entitled *Shadowlands* was released.[1] The average television viewer, knowing little or nothing about Lewis and probably not a great deal about traditional Christianity, would, I think, get the following impression from that television play: a clever and somewhat arrogant Oxford professor thinks he can give an intellectual defense of Christianity. He meets and falls in love with a beautiful American woman who turns out to be dying of cancer. They marry, and she dies shortly after the marriage. His faith is shattered, his intellectual defenses of Christianity now seem worthless. Gradually, he is brought to an acceptance of her death by the beauty of nature and the companionship of his stepson, his wife's child by a previous marriage. It is these natural consolations, rather than his religion, that heal the wound of his wife's death.[2]

---

[1] The television play *Shadowlands* was written by William Nicholson and first broadcast in 1985. It was preceded by a play and followed by a movie, each of which raises somewhat different problems.

[2] Brian Sibley's book *Shadowlands* (London: Hodder and Stoughton, 1985), which was a television tie-in, paints a different and somewhat more satisfactory picture.

Recently the American philosopher John Beversluis has examined Lewis' apologetics and his reaction to the death of his wife in a book, *C. S. Lewis and the Search for Rational Religion*,[3] and in a short article (illustrated with pictures from *Shadowlands*), "Beyond the Double Bolted Door".[4] The book and article both give the same message as the television play: C. S. Lewis' faith and his intellectual defense of the faith could not stand up to the death of his wife. The book also argues that Lewis' intellectual arguments for Christianity are philosophically naïve and will not stand up to close scrutiny by a professional philosopher, and that those who defend or explain Lewis' arguments are uncritical partisans of Lewis.

In his book *The Inklings*,[5] which deals with C. S. Lewis, J. R. R. Tolkien, Charles Williams, and their friends, Humphrey Carpenter tells the story of Lewis' debate with the then young English philosopher Elizabeth Anscombe in which Anscombe severely criticized one of Lewis' key arguments for belief in God. According to Carpenter, it was generally agreed, even by Lewis, that Anscombe won this debate, and Carpenter tells us that after this debate Lewis ceased to give intellectual defenses of Christianity and moved closer to the position that "all we can do is choose to believe." [6]

Now the net effect of the television play, the books, and the article has been to spread a certain general impression,

[3] John Beversluis, *C. S. Lewis and the Search for Rational Religion* (Grand Rapids, Mich.: William B. Eerdmans, 1985).

[4] John Beversluis, "Beyond the Bolted Door", *Christian History* 4, no. 3 (1985): 28–31.

[5] Humphrey Carpenter, *The Inklings: C. S. Lewis, J. R. R. Tolkien, Charles Williams, and Their Friends* (London: Allen and Unwin, 1978). Subsequent quotations from Carpenter's *The Inklings* are taken from the Unwin paperback edition of 1981 and follow the page numbering of that volume.

[6] Ibid., pp. 216–17.

even among people who have not seen the television play or read the books and the article, that C. S. Lewis at least to some extent lost his faith, or at least his faith in the possibility of a rational defense of Christianity. The two key events in this loss of faith were the debate with Anscombe and the death of Lewis' wife.

This general impression is deeply disturbing to many Christians, because for a good many contemporary Christians Lewis is seen as the outstanding, perhaps for some the only, contemporary defender of the position that Christianity can be shown not only to be intellectually defensible against unbelief, but even intellectually superior to unbelief.

If Lewis, the "Defender of the Faith", as one author called him,[7] lost his own faith, or at least his own faith in reason in religion, how can we have any confidence in the rationality of religion? In fact, Beversluis explicitly draws this lesson from Lewis' life; since a rational religion would not stand up to argument and experience, even for Lewis himself, we must abandon the search for "rational religion".[8]

My purpose in this essay is to convince the reader, by evidence and argument, that the general impression given by the television play, the books, and the article is not only false, but perniciously and perhaps deliberately and culpably false. It is in fact part of the counterattack against Lewis' outstandingly successful defense of the rationality and probability of Christianity, and it is a particularly unfair and underhanded counterattack, because it distorts Lewis' work and exploits his personal tragedy.

[7] Richard B. Cunningham, *C. S. Lewis: Defender of the Faith* (Philadelphia: Westminster Press, 1967).

[8] See Chap. 10, "Specimen", in Beversluis, *Search for Rational Religion*, pp. 162–67.

What, then, are the basic components of the counter-attack on Lewis? I have isolated five:

1    That Lewis' faith was unable to stand up to a very terrible but very common human tragedy: the loss of a dearly loved spouse.

2    That in crises such as this, the intellectual justification of religious belief is useless and certainly proved useless to Lewis.

3    That Lewis' justification of Christianity will not stand up to careful and professional philosophical examination.

4    That Lewis was defeated in his argument with Elizabeth Anscombe and that this defeat convinced him that the rational justification of religious belief was hopeless.

5    That since Lewis was the major defender of rational religion, his failure to make out a rational case for religious belief shows that the project of the rational justification of religious belief should therefore be abandoned.

I will begin my rebuttal of the counterattack on Lewis by considering Helen Joy Davidman Lewis' death and C. S. Lewis' reaction to it. Since we are speaking of his private life, I will make bold to speak of C. S. Lewis as "Jack", the name his wife and his close friends used, and to speak of Mrs. Lewis as "Joy", the name she preferred to her given first name, "Helen".

Jack did feel great grief at Joy's death and did love Joy very deeply. The real question is what effect this grief had on his faith. To understand this we must understand more about faith, and for this we can hardly do better than look at what Lewis himself wrote about faith. I will quote from one place in which Lewis examines the problems of faith directly and then from a fictional context in which he illustrates the points he makes in the longer extract.

In the first of two chapters on "Faith" in *Mere Christianity*, Lewis faces the problem of how faith can be a virtue:

> Now Faith, in the sense in which I am here using the word, is the art of holding on to things your reason has once accepted, in spite of your changing moods. For moods will change, whatever view your reason takes. I know that by experience. Now that I am a Christian I do have moods in which the whole thing looks very improbable: but when I was an atheist I had moods in which Christianity looked terribly probable. This rebellion of your moods against your real self is going to come anyway. That is why Faith is such a necessary virtue: unless you teach your moods "where they get off," you can never be either a sound Christian or even a sound atheist, but just a creature dithering to and fro, with its beliefs really dependent on the weather and the state of its digestion.[9]

The fictional context in which Lewis vividly illustrates what he says in *Mere Christianity* is the first chapter of *Perelandra* (also known as *Voyage to Venus*), where a fictionalized version of Lewis himself is going down to a country cottage to visit his friend Elwin Ransom. The whole chapter is well worth reading, but it comes to a culmination in the following passage, where the fictional Lewis begins to have doubts about his friend Ransom:

> He was in league with them! How did I know he was even a dupe? He might be something worse . . . and again I came to a standstill.

[9] C. S. Lewis, *Mere Christianity* (San Francisco: HarperCollins, 2001), pp. 140–41.

The reader, not knowing Ransom, will not understand how contrary to all reason this idea was. The rational part of my mind, even at that moment, knew perfectly well that even if the whole universe were crazy and hostile, Ransom was sane and wholesome and honest. And this part of my mind in the end sent me forward—but with a reluctance and a difficulty I can hardly put into words. What enabled me to go on was the knowledge (deep down inside me) that I was getting nearer at every stride to the one friend: but I *felt* that I was getting nearer to the one enemy—the traitor, the sorcerer, the man in league with "them" ... walking into the trap with my eyes open, like a fool. "They call it a breakdown at first," said my mind, "and send you to a nursing home; later on they move you to an asylum." [10]

So Lewis' idea of faith is this: it is an acceptance of certain beliefs that are not contrary to reason, but are supported by reason. In most cases, what war against faith are not rational considerations, but imagination and emotion. So what we would expect to find in the situation in which Lewis lost his dear beloved wife and had to come to terms with his grief is that he would face a struggle in which imagination and emotion were at war with his reasoned conviction that Christianity is true. And that is precisely what we do find.

The major evidence usually cited for Jack's state of mind after Joy's death is the little book he wrote and published (under a pseudonym) entitled *A Grief Observed*.[11] This is the only piece of evidence cited by those who claim that Lewis lost his faith after his wife's death, and if the book is carefully and objectively examined, it is powerful evidence for exactly the opposite conclusion: that Jack's faith was in fact

---

[10] C. S. Lewis, *Perelandra* (New York: Scribner, 2003), p. 13.
[11] C. S. Lewis, *A Grief Observed* (San Francisco: HarperCollins, 2001).

tested, but in the long run strengthened by his grief at Joy's death.

First let us see what Lewis himself says about the book. In a letter to a Catholic nun with whom he had corresponded for years on literary and religious subjects, and whom he regarded as a good friend, Lewis writes: "I will direct Fabers to send you a copy of the little book, but it may shock your pupils. It is *A Grief Observed* from day to day in all its rawness and sinful reactions and follies. It ends with faith but raises all the blackest doubts *en route*." [12]

There has been some controversy over whether Lewis "distanced" his experience by fictionalizing it somewhat. Are the "sinful reactions and follies" an accurate picture of Jack's own feelings, or are they fictional—or at least a fictionalized picture of what a person who had just lost a beloved wife might feel?

I think that it is possible to answer this question with some certainty because we have letters written by Lewis to close friends at about the time he was writing *A Grief Observed*, and we have another case where Lewis wrote a book on prayer, *Letters to Malcolm: Chiefly on Prayer*, which is closely related to real letters he wrote. [13]

In *Letters to Malcolm*, the correspondent "Malcolm" and his family are fictional. The incidents such as the illness of Malcolm's son are fictional incidents, carefully arranged by Lewis' literary artistry to bring out points about prayer. However, to someone familiar with Lewis' unpublished letters, it is clear that the letters are exactly the kind of letters Lewis often wrote to real correspondents, and major parts of

---

[12] Unpublished letter to Sister Madelva (March 19, 1963).

[13] C. S. Lewis, *Letters to Malcolm: Chiefly on Prayer* (San Diego: Harcourt, 2002).

*Letters to Malcolm* can be exactly paralleled in letters to real correspondents (even little touches like Lewis being able to go upstairs only with difficulty). So what Lewis did in *Letters to Malcolm* was to organize and orchestrate his real opinions and ideas about prayer, and real incidents involving a number of different correspondents, into a united whole that gives literary form to real ideas and incidents.

It seems quite clear that Lewis did exactly the same thing with *A Grief Observed*. He took his real grief in all its rawness, he took the doubts and fears that really came into his mind, and he organized them into a literary masterpiece. At times he certainly heightened the contrast by omitting balancing thoughts and feelings (for example in a real letter he remarks to a friend about the fact that work and sleep, and even food, can temporarily distract us from grief).

The literary form into which Lewis put his story is almost exactly that of his fictional masterpiece *Till We Have Faces*.[14] All the doubts, objections, and anger are expressed in the earlier longer sections, and the reconciliation and understanding come as the "joyous turn" in the final section. (Did those detractors of Lewis who cited *A Grief Observed* as evidence for a loss of faith never read the book all the way through?)

The great body of unpublished Lewis letters in the Marion B. Wade Center at Wheaton College shows that in the years after Joy's death Lewis went on arguing with unbelievers, counseling the doubtful, and (despite his own grief) cheering the despondent—speaking of his own loss only to his close friends and longtime correspondents. Even the published correspondence bears this out for those who take the time and trouble to read it.

[14] C. S. Lewis, *Till We Have Faces* (San Diego: Harcourt, 2003).

So if we look at the facts, at the record, we get exactly the picture Lewis' discussion of faith would lead us to expect: emotion and imagination warred against Lewis' reasoned conviction. But Lewis went on believing and acting on his belief. To quote his vivid description of the war of emotion and imagination on his convictions as evidence of loss of faith is unfair and dishonest in exactly the same way that it would be unfair and dishonest to call a man who had just performed a heroic act "cowardly" because he vividly described the fears he had overcome to do his act of heroism. Courage is overcoming fear to do what you ought to do. Faith is overcoming emotion and imagination to believe and act as you ought to believe and act. And in that battle there is no reasonable doubt that Jack Lewis was the victor.

I turn with some relief from the really despicable attempt to turn Lewis' personal tragedy into an argument against his faith by quoting him out of context, to the related question of whether Lewis found that intellectual justifications of Christianity were of "no use" in facing his wife's death. But again I am genuinely puzzled. What do Lewis' critics expect—that as a safeguard against grief he should rehearse his intellectual grounds for belief? But Lewis had no intellectual doubts about his faith and no new data that might give him intellectual grounds for doubting his faith. He had lost both his parents and several close friends by painful deaths. He was also very well acquainted with the variety and scale of sin and suffering from the great flood of appeals for help that came in letters to him. There is in fact no evidence at all that Lewis was moved to any intellectual doubts at all by his personal loss, and thus there was no need to renew or rehearse his intellectual grounds for belief.

What he did suffer were torments of emotion and imagination. He was unable to feel that Joy still existed after death, he was tormented by imaginings of a cruel God. Against such feelings and imaginings you do not turn to intellectual arguments, you turn to prayer. And there is ample evidence that Lewis did just that.

On the night of Joy's death, he was driven to and from the hospital where she died by a man named Clifford Morris, who had driven Jack for many years, first as a driver for a taxi company, then as the owner of his own car-hire business. Morris had become, as Jack says in a letter, "almost a family friend".[15] In a very moving interview, Morris tells how after Joy's death Jack asked to be driven out into the country, where Jack and Morris prayed together for a good part of the night.[16] Jack's stepson Douglas Gresham recalls how Jack consoled and comforted him, telling him that grief always has an element of selfishness in it, and they should rejoice that Joy was free of her sufferings.[17]

In fact, Jack Lewis did go through a period where all emotional and imaginative support for his faith was temporarily withdrawn. But, of course, many if not all of the great saints and heroes of the Christian faith have gone through such a "dark night of the soul", and Jack himself had written often of the dangers of relying on imagination and emotion in religion. Far from giving rise to any intellectual difficulties, his own experience confirmed and gave

[15] Letter to Arthur Greeves (May 22, 1961), in *They Stand Together*, ed. Walter Hooper (New York: Macmillan Co., 1979), p. 558.

[16] The interview is in the records of the Marion B. Wade Center, Wheaton, Ill.

[17] In a videotaped interview with Douglas Gresham at the Marion B. Wade Center, Ill.

him new insight into the experiences of many great Christians in the past.

What opponents of Christianity believe we Christians believe about pain and suffering in our own lives is often puzzling. If anything is made very clear in the gospels, it is that Christians should expect pain and persecution in this life. But opponents of Christianity seem often to be under the impression that Christians expect to be exempt from suffering because of their faith, and that if they are not then this is an argument against that faith. This is very far from the truth.

Really devoted Christians like Lewis not only expect suffering in this world but are a little worried if things go too easily; for example, Lewis once wrote to a friend: "Pray for me. I am travelling through 'a Plain called Ease'; things are almost too easy for me presently." [18]

We now turn to the charge that a careful philosophical examination of Lewis' arguments for Christianity shows that they do not stand up. In my book *C. S. Lewis' Case for the Christian Faith*[19] I examine these arguments and conclude that they do stand up to criticism. In his book *C. S. Lewis and the Search for Rational Religion*, John Beversluis concludes that they do not. Which of us is right? In a review of Beversluis' book in the *International Philosophical Quarterly* I gave the following characterization of it:

> In his introduction Beversluis divides previous books on C. S. Lewis into two categories: (1) books critical of Lewis which offer "not an assessment but a demolition"

[18] Letter to Sister Penelope (June 5, 1951), in *Letters of C. S. Lewis*, ed. Walter Hooper, p. 410.

[19] Richard L. Purtill, *C. S. Lewis' Case for the Christian Faith* (San Francisco: Ignatius Press, 2004).

and (2) admiring studies of Lewis which are unduly uncritical and adulatory.

Beversluis offers his own book as belonging to neither of
these classes, as an argument not a harangue, an assessment
not a demolition, appreciative of Lewis but not adulatory,
and above all as rationally and judiciously critical of Lewis.
If the book lived up to these promises Lewis would have
been the first to welcome it: he was a man "hungry for
rational opposition" and would have welcomed a rigorous
debate of his arguments. I share Lewis' feelings, and as the
author of one of the books Beversluis puts into his second
category would be glad to be shown important criticisms
of Lewis I had overlooked.

Unfortunately, Beversluis does not fulfill his promises and
in the end what he says of previous critics of Lewis applies
eminently to Beversluis himself: "One begins to suspect that
they have reached these negative conclusions a bit too easily" ... His procedure in criticizing Lewis is typically as
follows: he begins with a straight exposition of Lewis' views,
often with extensive quotation. Then rhetorical negative
characterizations of Lewis' views begin to creep into the
description. Finally actual arguments against Lewis or criticism of his view are given. But these are extremely brief
(ten percent of the total material at a generous estimate),
quite cavalier, and more often than not are based on misinterpretations of Lewis' points. . . .

There is an unfortunate tendency in this book to take
incidents from Lewis' life, interpret them tendentiously, and
use them as against Lewis' arguments. Thus the famous debate
with Anscombe is interpreted as a complete defeat for Lewis'
argument from reason to God, on the alleged evidence of
Lewis' psychological reactions, even though Anscombe herself is quoted in a footnote to the contrary. . . .

It would not be difficult, and may at some future time
be useful, to answer Beversluis's criticisms of Lewis point

by point. When misunderstandings, misinterpretations and irrelevancies are set aside, little of substance remains, however: answering Beversluis is not likely to advance our understanding either of Lewis or of the issues involved. This is, I think, because Beversluis never really enters into dialogue with Lewis, never asks himself how Lewis might reply to his facile and fragmentary criticisms. There is a notable lack of the principle of charity in the logician's sense, as well as of charity in the theological sense, despite much rather patronizing praise of Lewis. In the end, the faults Beversluis sees in Lewis are mainly faults which Beversluis himself possesses in an eminent degree: setting up strawmen, producing false dilemmas, drawing fallacious inferences. And he has characterized his own work in describing that of earlier critics: "not an argument but a harangue, not an assessment but a demolition." [20]

Here we have two professional philosophers disagreeing on the philosophical value of Lewis' arguments. Beversluis claims I am prejudiced in favor of Lewis and criticizes my book; I criticize his book. The best way to settle the issue would be to read carefully both books and the parts of Lewis' writings to which they refer. But even if you were willing and able to do this you could not do it immediately.

So perhaps we can call on a third party, the well-known philosopher of religion Thomas V. Morris of Notre Dame University. Morris is not a partisan of Lewis: in fact he tends to think his success is due to good writing rather than philosophical excellence. But his judgment of Beversluis is in many ways similar to mine, though more moderately expressed. I quote his review:

[20] Richard L. Purtill, *International Philosophical Quarterly* 26, no. 2 (1986), pp. 200–201.

This book actually begins with a measured, judicious, even appreciative tone of presentation. But it soon changes into a somewhat shrill, harsh, strident assault which ends up portraying Lewis as something of a pathetic figure whose blustery posturing as a rational apologist for Christian truth finally gave way at the end of his life to a desperate faith-against-all-odds held onto only by means of blatant philosophical inconsistency.

It is Beversluis's aim to put his readers into a position where they can see Lewis's failures. In representative passages, he characterizes Lewis's "irresponsible writing" as exhibiting "a persistent tendency toward carelessness, inaccuracy, and oversimplification whenever he discusses opposing views", and blasts Lewis's own positive positions and arguments with such epithets as "confused", "wrongheaded", "shipwrecked", "disgraced", "considerably worse than fuzzy", "tendentious", and "desperate". Colorful passages in Lewis are labeled as "bellicose outbursts", and we find that Lewis doesn't just state his opinions on controversial matters, he "gives vent" to them. The overall tone should be evident.

The next assessment is that none of Lewis's reasons for believing there is a God is any good, and that in addition he has no good response to the most popular argument for believing there is no God, the problem of evil. My main overall philosophical criticism of this book is that Beversluis seldom comes anywhere near to digging deep enough to really appreciate a line of thought suggested by Lewis. All too often he gives a facile, fairly superficial reconstruction of a line of argument, and after subjecting it to some critical questioning, declares it bankrupt and moves on.

What is so disappointing to the reader who is trained in philosophy is that in most such instances a few minutes of reflective thought suffice to see that there are very interesting considerations to be marshalled in the direction Lewis was heading, considerations altogether neglected by (Beversluis). There are far too many false alternatives posed for Lewis's arguments, and hasty judgments rendered about their soundness. In short, it seems that Beversluis is guilty of precisely those shortcomings in polemical discussion he attributes to Lewis. I am afraid that it is academically one I cannot highly recommend, either in its tone or in the depth of its philosophical argumentation.[21]

I have quoted from Morris at such length, not only because he does an excellent job of analyzing Beversluis' book, but also because he cannot be called a partisan of Lewis. His own feelings are possibly nearer to those of the philosophers who "having worked hard at philosophy for years are more than a little irritated to see their students and the general reading public idolizing some good writer as a great philosopher".[22] But Morris' very "irritation" insulates him from Beversluis' charge that defenders of Lewis are always merely partisans of Lewis. Lewis' most direct confrontation with a well-known contemporary philosopher was the famous debate with Elizabeth Anscombe, to which we now turn.

First, a little background. The confrontation was at a meeting of the Socratic Club, an organization founded by students with Lewis' help. In an essay about the founding of the club, Lewis says:

> Socrates had exhorted men to "follow the argument wherever it led them": the Club came into existence to apply his principle to ... the pros and cons of the Christian religion. Those who founded it do not for one moment pretend to be neutral. It was the Christians who constructed

[21] Thomas V. Morris, *Faith and Philosophy* 5, no. 3 (1988): 319–22.
[22] Ibid., p. 320.

the arena and issued the challenge. With pains and toil the committee ... scoured [the pages of] *Who's Who* to find intelligent atheists who had leisure or zeal to come and propagate their creed. We expose ourselves, and the weakest of our party, to your fire no less than you are exposed to ours. Worse still, we expose ourselves to the recoil from our own shots; for if I may trust my personal experience no doctrine is, for the moment, dimmer to the eye of faith than that which a man has just successfully defended.[23]

When Elizabeth Anscombe spoke to the Socratic Club in February 1948, she was not an atheist, but a practicing, if somewhat eccentric, Roman Catholic. She and her husband, Peter Geach, had become converts to Catholicism while they were students of the philosopher Ludwig Wittgenstein, and Anscombe combined a Wittgensteinian approach on some philosophical questions with a very theistic one on others. Later she and Geach were to publish a book, *Three Philosophers*, in which they defended Aquinas' arguments for God.[24] So Anscombe was not an unbeliever attacking just any or all argumentation for God, but an honest rational believer attacking an argument she thought inadequate for a conclusion she thought true and justified on other grounds (as Aquinas criticized Anselm's ontological argument).

Anscombe undoubtedly pointed out weaknesses in Lewis' formulation of the argument. Lewis would have endorsed the remark in the club minutes, "in general it appeared that Mr. Lewis would have to turn his argument into a rigorous

[23] C. S. Lewis, "The Founding of the Oxford Socratic Club", in *Timeless at Heart* (London: Collins Fount, 1987), pp. 80, 82.

[24] G. E. M. Anscombe and P. T. Geach, *Three Philosophers* (Oxford: Basil Blackwell, 1961), pp. 109–25.

analytic one, if his motion . . . were to stand the test of all the questions put to him".[25]

Actually, Lewis began this task then and there. In the note of his reply to Anscombe in the Socratic Club minutes, he is already making the distinction that went into his revised chapter of *Miracles*, the relation between CE (cause and effect) and GC (ground and consequent), and he says:

> If an argument is to be verific the conclusion must be related to the premises as consequent to ground. On the other hand, our thinking of the conclusion is an event and must be related to the previous events as effect to cause. It would seem therefore that we never think the conclusion because GC, it is the consequent of its grounds, but only because CE, certain previous events have happened. If so it does not seem that the GC sequence makes us more likely to think the true conclusion than not. And this is very much what I meant by the difficulty in Naturalism.[26]

So Lewis was already fighting back, and when a paperback version of *Miracles* was issued by Fontana Books, Lewis took the opportunity to revise and expand the chapter in question; a very powerful piece of evidence that far from abandoning the argument, Lewis thought it was worth considerable effort to strengthen and restate. Elizabeth Anscombe's account is as follows:

> Rereading the argument of the first edition and my criticism of it, it seems to me that they are just. At the same time, I find them lacking in any recognition of the depth

[25] "A Reply to Mr. C. S. Lewis' Argument that 'Naturalism is Self-Refuting'", in *The Socratic Digest* 4 (1948): 15–16 (reproduced in Lewis, *Timeless at Heart*, pp. 103–4).

[26] "Reply to Miss Anscombe", in *The Socratic Digest* (reproduced in Lewis, *Timeless at Heart*, p. 104).

of the problem. I don't think Lewis's first version itself gave one much impression of that. The argument of the second edition has much to criticize in it, but it certainly does correspond more to the actual depth and difficulty of the questions being discussed. I think we haven't yet an answer to the question I have quoted from him: "What is the connection between grounds and the actual occurrence of the belief?"

The fact that Lewis rewrote that chapter, and rewrote it so that it now has those qualities, shows his honesty and seriousness. The meeting of the Socratic Club at which I read my paper has been described by several of his friends as a horrible and shocking experience which upset him very much. Neither Dr. Harvard (who had Lewis and me to dinner a few weeks later) nor Professor Jack Bennett remembered any such feelings on Lewis's part. The paper that I read is as printed here. My own recollection is that it was an occasion of sober discussion of certain quite definite criticisms, which Lewis's rethinking and rewriting showed he thought were accurate.[27]

As to the fact cited by Carpenter, that Lewis did not publish further apologetic books of the same type as *Miracles*, it is correct but misleading. Lewis wrote controversial books on religion such as *Miracles* reluctantly, and only when he received invitations to do so from publishers or organizations that he did not feel he could refuse. (*The Problem of Pain*,[28] for example, was written for a series published by Geoffrey Bles, Lewis' friend and long-time publisher, at Bles' pressing invitation, and *Miracles*, too, was written at Bles' invitation.) As Lewis' friend Austin Farrer wrote:

[27] G. E. M. Anscombe, *Collected Philosophical Papers*, vol. 2 (Cambridge: Cambridge University Press, 1981).

[28] C. S. Lewis, *The Problem of Pain* (San Francisco: HarperCollins, 2001).

"Philosophy was not Lewis's trade and he had many other irons in the fire.... He was never quite at home in our post-positivist era ... his philosophical experience belonged to the time of his conversion. Philosophy is an ever-shifting never-ending public discussion, and a man who drops out of the game drops out of philosophy."[29] So Lewis had little inclination to argue the whole positivist question. He was wise; our era is now post-post-positivist, and the debates of that era are as dead as mutton.

One valuable piece of evidence is Lewis' essay "On Obstinacy in Belief", published in 1955, seven years after the Anscombe debate. In this essay, Lewis reiterates and reinforces his position in *Mere Christianity*: faith should be arrived at by rational means.

> There is, of course, no question of belief without evidence. We must beware of confusion between the way in which a Christian first assents to certain propositions and the way in which he afterwards adheres to them. These must be carefully distinguished. Of the second it is true, in a sense, to say that Christians do recommend a certain discounting of apparent contrary evidence.... But so far as I know it is not expected that a man should assent to these propositions in the first place without evidence or in the teeth of the evidence. At any rate, if anyone expects that, I certainly do not. And in fact, the man who accepts Christianity always thinks he has good evidence whether, like Dante, *fisici e metafisici argomenti*, or historical evidence, or the evidence of religious experience, or authority, or all these together. For of course authority, however we may value it in this or that particular instance, is a kind of evidence. All of our historical beliefs, most of our geographical beliefs, many of

[29] Austin Farrer, "The Christian Apologist", in *Light on C. S. Lewis*, ed. Jocelyn Gibb et al. (New York: Harcourt, Brace and World, 1966), p. 40.

our beliefs about matters that concern us in daily life, are accepted on the authority of other human beings, whether we are Christians, Atheists, Scientists, or Men-in-the-Street.[30]

In the same connection, contrast Beversluis' earlier-cited picture of a shattered, doubt-haunted Lewis after Joy's death with the serene confidence of his last book, *Letters to Malcolm: Chiefly on Prayer*, completed three years after Joy's death:

> I don't say the resurrection of this body will happen at once. It may well be that this part of us sleeps in death and the intellectual soul is sent to Lenten lands where she fasts in naked spirituality a ghostlike and imperfectly human condition. I don't imply that an angel is a ghost. But naked spirituality is in accordance with his nature: not, I think, with ours. (A two-legged horse is maimed but not a two-legged man.) Yet from that fact my hope is that we shall return and re-assume the wealth we laid down.
>
> Then the new earth and sky, the same yet not the same as these, will rise in us as we have risen in Christ. And once again, after who knows what aeons of the silence and the dark, the birds will sing out and the waters flow, and lights and shadows move across the hills and the faces of our friends laugh upon us with amazed recognition.
>
> Guesses, of course, only guesses. If they are not true, something better will be. For we know that we shall be made like Him for we shall see Him as He is.[31]

In the face of such evidence we can only look at Beversluis' picture in amazement. This is a grief-shattered man

---

[30] "On Obstinacy in Belief" first appeared in *The Socratic Digest* in 1955. It is now available in C. S. Lewis, *The World's Last Night and Other Essays* (San Diego: Harcourt, 2002).

[31] Lewis, *Letters to Malcolm*, pp. 123–24.

with no faith left? This is a man who now doubts all his former certainties?

I turn with some relief to our final question: how much the case for rational religion depends on how successful C. S. Lewis' defense of rational religion was. I say "with some relief" because there is something almost indecent in the attempt to attack a man's plainly expressed views by selective misquotation and misinterpretation of his work and his life story. I have to try very hard indeed to entertain the charitable view that those who do this are sincere and blameless. It is at least clear that they could not do what they do without considerable self-deception.

As to whether the case for rational religion depends on C. S. Lewis' success in defending it, I can imagine very well Lewis' own reaction to the idea. He would laugh, laugh "till the hills rang with laughter". Then he might say something like this: "It's very kind of you to value my work so highly, but you've apparently admired it more than you've read it. Over and over again I've emphasized the richness of the Christian tradition; told my readers to read at least one old book for every new one they read."

"Among my contemporaries and near contemporaries, there are many great defenders of Christianity. It's come to a pretty pass if the whole weight of the case for rational religion is supposed to fall on poor Jack Lewis, a teacher of English literature who reluctantly wrote some popular books on religion in his spare time. Look to Aquinas, look to Chesterton, look to your own contemporaries. If this fellow Beversluis wants to make a case against rational religion, why does he attack me; why doesn't he take on some of his philosophical peers who can correct his misreadings and answer his attacks? I'm praying hard for him of course, but it really does seem a little like Falstaff pretending to triumph over the corpse of Percy, who in life would have made Falstaff run like a rabbit."

Now Lewis, if he said that, would be as usual too modest. Lewis was for many ordinary Christians the prototypical "defender of the faith" for our times. He had powerful philosophical abilities, but because he was not a professional philosopher, he did not use the jargon of the professionals nor was he caught up in the transitory controversies of the academic philosophers. He was a fine writer; one of the foremost prose writers of our time, with an almost unequalled combination of clarity and energy. If you were allowed to read only one twentieth-century defender of rational Christianity, Lewis would be the best choice by far.

However, we are not confined to reading only Lewis, and if we read only Lewis we are ill-equipped even to appreciate Lewis himself, much less his message. It is certainly true that on all levels of the rational defense of religion there are several contemporary "defenders of the faith" who command our respect: philosophers such as Richard Swinburne and John Lucas come to my mind; some preacher or teacher who has been of help to you in thinking and living your faith might come to yours. But Lewis does have a special position in the minds and hearts of many of us, and it would be a blow, though by no means a fatal blow, if he had really lost his faith, or even his faith in reason. That is why I have taken the trouble to show in perhaps excessive detail that he did no such thing.

Finally, let me conjecture, as charitably as I can, on the motives of those who spread these untruths about Lewis. First, I think that there is a considerable element of plain envy in the attack on Lewis. Why should Lewis be so successful at winning converts to Christianity when my efforts are so unsuccessful; why should his faith be so robust when mine is so feeble? Envy delights to see the object of envy falter or fail and is prone to exaggerate the faltering or failure.

Second, Lewis' message is profoundly out of step with the conventional wisdom of our times. Christians are supposed to be on the defensive, not on the offensive. Christians are allowed to have their faith if that faith is admittedly irrational and sufficiently tentative and agonized, but a rational and confident faith? No "modern man" can be allowed to have that!

Finally there is a motive very well exposed by Lewis himself in his last book, *Letters to Malcolm*. He is speaking of those who object to the supernaturalism of his religion, his refusal to explain away the miraculous and the divine, but it is equally true of those who object to his rational approach:

> Don't, however, misjudge these "liberal Christians." They genuinely believe that writers of my sort are doing a great deal of harm.
>
> They themselves find it impossible to accept most of the articles of the "faith once given to the saints." They are nevertheless extremely anxious that some vestigial religion which they (not we) can describe as "Christianity" should continue to exist and make numerous converts. They think these converts will come in only if this religion is sufficiently "demythologised". The ship must be lightened if she is to keep afloat.
>
> It follows that, to them, the most mischievous people in the world are those who, like myself, proclaim that Christianity essentially involves the supernatural. They are quite sure that belief in the supernatural never will, nor should, be revived, and that if we convince the world that it must choose between accepting the supernatural and abandoning

all pretence of Christianity, the world will undoubtedly choose the second alternative. It will thus be we, not the liberals, who have really sold the pass. We shall have re-attached to the name *Christian* a deadly scandal from which, but for us, they might have succeeded in decontaminating it.[32]

Simply replace "supernatural" with "rational" in some of this:

> They themselves find it impossible to accept [a rational religion].... It follows that the most mischievous people in the world are those who, like myself, proclaim that Christianity [is essentially rational, and more rational than any alternative]. They are quite sure that [rational religion] never will, nor should, be revived, and that if we convince the world that it must choose between accepting [a rational Christianity] and abandoning all pretence of Christianity, the world will undoubtedly choose the second alternative.... We shall have re-attached to the name *Christian* a deadly scandal from which, but for us, they might have succeeded in decontaminating it.

I think Lewis is quite right; this is why both in the case of the supernatural in religion and in the case of the rational element in religion, Lewis' most determined opponents are "liberal" Christians. He is disliked by the atheists as a formidable opponent. But there is an element of distaste almost amounting to hatred in some of his opponents who call themselves Christians. Some of course fight with "covered shields"; for example, it is difficult if not impossible to discover from Beversluis' book whether he is an anti-rationalist Christian from the liberal camp or a complete agnostic.

Attacks on Lewis from within Christianity please the opponents of Christianity: as Lewis said, an attack on religion

---

[32] Ibid., pp. 119–20.

from within is "news". However, we cannot dismiss such attacks merely because they give "aid and comfort to the enemy"; if the charges they make were true, that would have to be honestly admitted. But as I have tried to show, the charges are not true.

What can we learn from all this? First, I think, not to pin too much of our faith on any one "defender of the faith". We should preach Christ crucified and resurrected, not Lewis, even though his agony and his recovery of both confidence and peace in the faith he never lost together echo Christ's death and Resurrection. Next we should make very sure that in thinking about the faith we are really thinking with the aid of great men like Lewis, not merely parroting their arguments without making them our own.

Finally, we should let our thoughts and our prayers work together, as they did for Lewis, and bring hope and charity to the aid of faith, until we can say with Lewis:

> Our opponents, then, have a perfect right to dispute with us about the grounds of our original assent. But they must not accuse us of sheer insanity if, after the assent has been given, our adherence to it is no longer proportioned to every fluctuation of the apparent evidence. They cannot of course be expected to know on what our assurance feeds, and how it revives and is always rising from its ashes. They cannot be expected to see how the *quality* of the object which we think we are beginning to know by acquaintance drives us to the view that if this were a delusion then we should have to say that the universe had produced no real thing of comparable value and that all explanations of the delusion seemed somehow less important than the thing explained. That is knowledge we cannot communicate. But they can see how the assent, of necessity, moves us from the logic of speculative thought into what might perhaps

be called the logic of personal relations. What would, up till then, have been variations simply of opinion become variations of conduct by a person to a Person. *Credere Deum esse* turns into *Credere in Deum*. And *Deum* here is this God, the increasingly knowable Lord.[33]

---

[33] C. S. Lewis, "On Obstinacy in Belief", in *World's Last Night*, pp. 29–30. The Latin translates as follows: *Credere Deum esse*: "to believe God exists", and *Credere in Deum*: "to believe in God".

# Basic Lewis–Tolkien Bibliography

## A. Essential Books

TOLKIEN: *The Hobbit*
*The Fellowship of the Ring*
*The Two Towers*
*The Return of the King*
*Smith of Wootton Major*
*Farmer Giles of Ham*
*The Tolkien Reader*
*The Silmarillion*
(Available in Ballantine Books paperbacks)

LEWIS: *Out of the Silent Planet*
*Perelandra*
*That Hideous Strength*
(Available in Scribner paperbacks)

*The Great Divorce*
*The Screwtape Letters*
(Available in HarperCollins paperbacks)

*The Lion, the Witch and the Wardrobe*
*Prince Caspian*
*The Voyage of the Dawn Treader*
*The Silver Chair*
*The Horse and His Boy*

The Magician's Nephew
The Last Battle
(Also available in HarperCollins paperbacks).
The best edition is the 50th Anniversary
Collector's Edition, which features color
illustrations by Pauline Baynes.

B. Other Important Books
(Inclusion of a book about Lewis or Tolkien implies at
least qualified recommendation. Books with useful bib-
liographies or summaries are noted.)

BY TOLKIEN:
"Beowulf: The Monsters and the Critics". In *An
Anthology of Beowulf Criticism*, ed. Lewis E. Nich-
olson. Notre Dame, Ind.: University of Notre Dame
Press, 1963, paperback.
*The Road Goes Ever On: A Song Cycle*. Poems by
J. R. R. Tolkien, music by Donald Swann. Boston:
Houghton Mifflin Co., 1967. Notes by Tolkien.

ABOUT TOLKIEN:
Bassham, Gregory, and Eric Bronson, eds., *The Lord
of the Rings and Philosophy*. Chicago: Open Court
Press, 2003.
Isaacs, Neil D., and Zimbardo, Rose A., eds. *Tolkien
and the Critics*. Notre Dame, Ind.: University of
Notre Dame Press, 1968. Bibliography, paperback.
Kreeft, Peter. *The Philosophy of Tolkien*. San Francisco:
Ignatius Press, 2005.
Pearce, Joseph, ed. *Tolkien: A Celebration*. San Fran-
cisco: Ignatius Press, 2004.
Pearce, Joseph. *Tolkien: Man and Myth*. San Francisco:
Ignatius Press, 2003.

By Lewis: *Mere Christianity*
*Miracles*
*The Problem of Pain*
*The Abolition of Man*
(Available as HarperCollins paperbacks)
*The Four Loves*
*Surprised by Joy*
(Available in Harvest Paperbacks from Harcourt)

About Lewis:

Bassham, Gregory, and Jerry L. Walls, eds. *The Chronicles of Narnia and Philosophy*. Chicago: Open Court Press, 2005.

Downing, David C. *Planets in Peril: A Critical Study of C. S. Lewis' Ransom Trilogy*. Amherst: University of Massachusetts Press, Reissue Edition. 1995.

Gibb, Jocelyn, et al., eds. *Light on C. S. Lewis*. New York: Harcourt, Brace and World, 1966.

Gibson, Evan. *C. S. Lewis: Spinner of Tales*. Grand Rapids, Mich.: William B. Eerdmans Publishing Co., 1980.

Kirk, E. J. *The Chronicles of Narnia beyond the Wardrobe*. New York: HarperCollins, 2005.

Kreeft, Peter. *C. S. Lewis for the Third Millennium*. San Francisco: Ignatius Press, 2001.

Schultz, Jeffrey D., and John G. West, eds. *The C. S. Lewis Readers' Encyclopedia*. Grand Rapids, Mich.: Zondervan, 1998.

## C. Other Sources of Information

Collections:

The Marion Wade Collection at the Library of Wheaton College, Wheaton, Illinois, has a fine collection of material by and about Lewis, Tolkien, and related writers, including unpublished letters by Lewis and unpublished doctoral dissertations on Lewis and Tolkien.

SOCIETIES:

The Mythopoeic Society is devoted to the writings of Lewis, Tolkien, Charles Williams, and other fantasy writers. The society publishes a monthly newsletter, *Mythprint*, and periodically issues *Mythlore*, which contains articles, artwork, and information pertaining to these writers. For information see: www.mythsoc.org.

D. Of Related Interest

Purtill, Richard L. *C. S. Lewis' Case for the Christian Faith*. San Francisco: Ignatius Press, 2005.

Purtill, Richard L. *J. R. R. Tolkien: Myth, Morality, and Religion*. San Francisco: Ignatius Press, 2003.

Purtill, Richard L. *Reason to Believe*. Grand Rapids, Mich.: William B. Eerdmans Publishing Co., 1974.

E. Other Books by Richard Purtill: Selected Bibliography

*The Golden Gryphon Feather*
*The Stolen Goddess*
*The Mirror of Helen*
*The Gryphon Seal*
*The Eleusinian Gate*
*Enchantment at Delphi*
*The Parallel Man*
*Murdercon*

For more information, please visit Richard Purtill's official site at www.alivingdog.com.

# ACKNOWLEDGMENTS

# INDEX

*The Abolition of Man* (Lewis),
    48–49, 176, 226
Ainur, 125–27
*Akallabêth* (Tolkien), 132
Alcasan, 216–17, 223
*Alice in Wonderland* (Carroll), 6
*The Allegory of Love* (Lewis),
    28–29, 35, 118–19
allegory
    Lewis on, 28–29, 35, 118–19,
        136–37, 156, 161
    in Lewis' works, 17, 27, 135,
        179
    loose/strict, 5–6, 117–18, 135
    Tolkien on, 17, 117
    in Tolkien's work, 117–18, 122
angels
    Ainur as, 125–27
    fallen, 68, 73, 93, 114, 126
    Lewis' use of, 116–17
    power of, 67, 93, 126, 144
    Tolkien's use of, 113–14,
        116–17
Anscombe, Elizabeth, 228–30,
    238, 241–45
Anselm, St., 242
apologetics, Christian, 7, 37–39,
    64, 77, 134–37, 165, 173–83,
    228
appreciative fantasy, 6–7, 11–12,
    19

Aquinas, St. Thomas, 118, 242,
    247
Aragorn, 94, 100, 104, 119–21,
    165, 192
Aristotle, 35, 119
art, 4, 10, 21–26, 27, 32–40
Arthurian legend, 16, 48, 51–53,
    80, 91
Arwen, 94, 119–21
Aslan
    after death, 90, 159–60
    Christ resemblance of, 118–19,
        136, 156, 159–64, 166
    lion image of, 159–61
    Lucy and, 82–83, 162
    nature of, 43, 160–62
Atlantis legend, 111, 113, 132
Augustine, St., 84, 141, 144, 164,
    209, 225

Baggins, Bilbo, *See* Bilbo
    Baggins
Baggins, Frodo. *See* Frodo
    Baggins
Balrogs, 100, 115–16, 127, 132
Barfield, Owen, 207
Baynes, Pauline, 161
Beagle, Peter, 26nn17–18, 26–27
Bede, 87
*Beowulf and Its Analogues*
    (Garmonsway), 54n10

"Beowulf: The Monsters and the Critics" (Tolkien), 50n8, 86–87, 105–6

*Beowulf*
  author of, as Christian, 87, 105–6
  influence of, 34, 51, 53–56, 85–89, 100, 105–6, 207
  Tolkien on, 50, 59, 105–6
Bernardus Silvestris, 28–29
Beversluis, John, 228–29, 237–41, 246–47, 250
"Beyond the Double Bolted Door" (Beversluis), 228
Bible
  on being like God, 143–45, 163
  Christ in, 96, 143, 163, 194
  Jerusalem Bible, 207
  Job translated by Tolkien, 207
  on morality, 194
  personal responsibility in, 143, 194
  Satan in the, 163
  on speech as character, 47
  the Tempter in, 138, 142–43, 145
  *See also* religious references
Bilbo Baggins, 14, 41, 45, 95–96, 99, 186–87
Bill Sykes, 45
Bles, Geoffrey, 244
Boswell, James, 34
Bunyan, John, 5, 136

Calormenes, 41, 44
Capon, Robert Farrar, 147
Carpenter, Humphrey, 124, 129n43, 228, 228n5, 244

Carroll, Lewis, 6
character and language, 42–46, 50–51, 58
Chesterton, G. K., 12, 91, 147, 191, 205, 247
choice theme, 16–18, 68, 72, 84, 101–2, 142–43, 146, 172–73
Christ
  in the Bible, 96, 143, 163, 194
  character resemblances to, 118–19, 136, 156, 159–64, 166, 186, 194
  dismissal of, as teacher only, 180–81
  story of, 10, 13, 89–90, 165, 170
  suffering and, 147, 166, 173, 236–37
  *See also* God
*The Christian Apologist* (Farrer), 173–75, 245
Christianity
  apologetics, 7, 37–39, 64, 77, 134–37, 165, 173–83, 228
  courtesy as virtue, 192–93
  modern world views *vs.*, 72, 77, 180–82, 189, 195
  moral code of, 96, 189–93
  proofs of God, 72, 175–78
  suffering and, 96, 147, 166, 172–74, 181–82, 197, 236–37
  truth of, 174–83
co-inherence doctrine, 166
*Cold Comfort Farm* (Gibbons), 26
Common Speech, 41, 46
*Confessions* (Augustine), 164
Cosser, 75, 221

*A Country Parish* (MacDonald),
204
courtesy theme, 192–93
creation myths, 125–29
*C. S. Lewis and the Search for Rational Religion* (Beversluis), 228,
229n8, 237–41, 246–47, 250
*C. S. Lewis' Case for the Christian Faith* (Purtill), xii, 237
*C. S. Lewis: Defender of the Faith* (Cunningham), 229n7
Cunningham, Richard B., 229
cup incident, 54–55

Dante, 12, 37, 39, 145, 245
*De Futilitate* (Lewis), 174–75
death
    characterized, 120–22
    immortality and, 43, 49, 111,
        119–21, 130
    life after, 90–91, 105, 111–12,
        159–60, 179, 236
    resurrections from, 90, 115–19,
        160
Denethor, 50, 95, 99
the Dennistons, 211, 214–15
"Dethronement of Power"
    (Lewis), 155n2
devils, 74–76, 103–4, 114, 139
    *See also* evil; Satan
devotion theme, 217
dialects, 44–46
    *See also* language
"Did C. S. Lewis Lose His
    Faith?" (Purtell), xiii
the Dimbles, 70, 76, 211–13, 215,
    218–19, 222
*The Discarded Image* (Lewis),
    156–57

diversity of characters, 185–86
Dodson, Charles. *See* Carroll,
    Lewis
Dostoyevsky, Fyodor, 37, 65
Dwarves
    ancestry of, 94, 125
    Christ imagery and, 186
    Dwarvish, 13n, 31, 41, 42n1
    as fallible, 14, 93, 95–96
    Gimli, 93–94, 100, 104,
        187–88
    limbo for, 120–21

ecology theme, 13–14, 56, 171,
    187
Eden, 65, 216
Edmund Pevensey, 82–83, 161,
    207
Elbereth (Varda), 107–12, 117–18,
    127, 130, 131
eldils
    evil (bent), 15, 92, 135, 217,
        220–21, 223
    Maleldil, 64, 118–19, 134–35
    as rulers, 71, 112, 135, 145,
        220, 223
    as spiritual beings, 92, 116–17,
        155, 158
Ellman, Mary, 38n31, 42n1, 100
Elvenhome (Eressëa), 111–12,
    121, 130–31
Elves
    Elvish, 31, 41, 46, 58, 108,
        110, 114–16, 140
    Gimli befriended by, 93–94
    High Elves, 90, 106–7,
        114–15
    Legolas, 6, 31, 88, 100, 104,
        120, 187

Elves (continued)
  nature of, 49, 111, 119–20,
    121, 130, 132
Elwin Ransom. See Ransom,
  Elwin
emotion vs. faith, 232–33, 235–36
ends vs. means theme, 69–71,
    101–2, 142, 144, 161, 188–89,
    221
English Literature in the Sixteenth
  Century excluding Drama
  (Lewis), 29n23, 88
Ents, 13, 43, 92–93, 99
Eressëa (Elvenhome), 111–12,
    121, 130–31
Eru, 114, 125, 130
eucatastrophe (happy endings),
    10, 13, 89
Eustace Scrubb, 82–83, 162, 181,
    187
evil
  absolute, 88, 140, 250
  devils, 74–76, 103–4, 114,
    139
  ends vs. means and, 69–71,
    101–2, 142, 144, 161,
    188–89, 221
  as a free choice, 16–18, 68, 72,
    84, 101–2, 142–43, 146,
    172–73
  nature of, 88, 101–4, 139–40,
    250
  problem of, 129, 170, 172–74,
    240
  relationships of, 74–76, 103–4,
    114
  in That Hideous Strength
    (Lewis), 71–73, 75–76, 138,
    146–47

  as uncreative, 74, 93, 101–2,
    126–27, 129, 131–32
  See also Satan
Evil and the God of Love (Hick),
    173
existentialism, 87–88, 178,
    189–95
experience, arguments from,
    170–71, 179–80
An Experiment in Criticism
  (Lewis), 12, 20–25, 32–40,
    128

faith
  Anscombe's, 242
  Beversluis on Lewis', 227–30,
    237–39, 246–48
  defined, 231–32, 235–37
  imagination and emotion vs.,
    232–33, 235–36
  lack of, 76
  rationality of, 72, 174–83,
    227–32, 237–42, 243–52
  Wain on, 190
  Walsh on, 167
Faith and Philosophy (Thomas V.
  Morris), 239–41
the Fall, 72, 141–44, 192
fallen creatures
  angels, 68, 73, 93, 114, 126
  Balrogs, 100, 115–16, 127,
    132
  individuals vs. races, 22, 93,
    132, 169
  Maiar, 127, 133
  Men, 71, 91–92, 132, 173
  Ringwraiths, 94
  unfallen creatures, 42, 64–67,
    69, 71, 92, 94, 113, 135

*fana* (Elvish for "veil"), 114–15, 116

fantasy
  creativity and, 4–5, 8
  kinds of, 6–7, 11–12, 19, 21–26, 27, 32–40
  Lewis' writings as, 26–29
  purposes of, 8–10
  Tolkien's writings as, 29–32
  Wain on, 3

Farrer, Austin, 172–73, 175, 244–45

*The Fellowship of the Ring* (Tolkien), 93, 99, 101, 103–4, 107–11, 115, 117–21, 192

Feverstone, Lord, 49, 75, 77–78, 212–16

films, 7, 99, 227n2

Filostrato, 215–18, 225

*A Fine and Private Place* (Beagle), 26n17

Francis, St., 63

free will theme, 16–18, 68, 72, 84, 101–2, 142–43, 146, 172–73
  *See also* personal responsibility theme

Frodo Baggins
  Christ resemblance of, 118, 166, 194
  death of, 90
  as fallible, 97, 109
  heroism of, 88–89, 95–100, 165–66
  as religious, 109–10

Frost, Professor, 73, 75, 78, 222, 225

Fry, Christopher, 122

Fuller, Edmund, 114n16

Galadriel, 31, 94, 100, 108, 140–41

Gamgee, Sam, 95, 97–98, 109–10, 120, 186, 194

Gandalf
  Beagle on, 26
  Christ resemblance of, 118
  on evil, 93
  nature of, 88, 95, 99–103, 109, 113–16, 192
  resurrection of, 115–18, 119

Gawain, 50–53, 100, 207
  *See also* *Sir Gawain and the Green Knight* (Tolkien and Gordon, eds.)

Geach, Peter T., 242

gender, treatment of, 116–17, 127

*George MacDonald: An Anthology* (MacDonald), 201

George MacDonald (character), 73–74, 78, 147

Gibbons, Stella, 26 -28, 44, 144

Gimli, 93–94, 100, 104, 187–88

goblins, 13, 13n17, 41, 95, 204

God
  being like, 143–46
  death as exploration into, 122
  Elbereth as, 107–12, 117–18, 127
  Eru as, 114, 125, 130
  on evil tools, 69–71, 101–2, 142, 144, 161, 188–89, 221
  Ilúvatar as, 125
  Maleldil as, 64, 118–19, 134
  proofs of, 72, 174–78
  as source of all goodness, 72–74, 83–84, 101, 148, 178, 217, 223–24
  *See also* Christ

*The Golden Key* (MacDonald), 204

Golden Rule, 191

Golding, William, 6

Gollum, 14, 53, 95, 97, 101–2, 194

the good
  devotion to, 217
  separation from God and, 72, 223–24
  source of, 72–74, 83–84, 101, 148, 178, 217, 223–24

Gordon, E. V., 50n8

Grace Ironwood, 80, 214–15, 222

*The Great Divorce* (Lewis), 73–74, 78, 147, 158, 201

Green Lady, 47, 68, 116, 140–44, 187

Greeves, Arthur, 236n15

Gresham, Douglas, 236, 236n17

*A Grief Observed* (Lewis), 232–34

"Growing Up Hobbitic" (Ellman), 38n31, 42n1

Halflings, 94
  *See also* hobbits

Hamilton, Edith, 200

happy endings (eucatastrophe), 10, 13, 89

Hardcastle, 73, 75–76, 218–20, 222, 225

heaven, 111–12, 121, 130–31, 158–59

hell
  Lewis on, 74–75, 158, 180, 224
  nature of, 36, 74–76, 139, 145, 158

heroism themes, 86–89, 95–100, 165–66, 188

Hick, John, 173

Hidden Fire, 133

hierarchy, 71–72, 104, 135, 142–44, 165, 192

High Elves, 90, 106–7, 114–15
  *See also* Elves

Hillegas, Mark R., 89

Hingest, 217

Hitler, 224

*The Hobbit* (Tolkien)
  *Beowulf* influence in, 34, 51, 53–56, 85–89, 100, 105–6, 207
  reader participation in, 26, 34
  summary, 95–99

hobbits
  language and, 41, 45, 94
  nature of, 14, 93–95, 99–100, 186, 194
  as religious, 108–9

"The Homecoming of Beorhtnoth, Beorhthelm's Son" (Tolkien), 86

Homer, 24, 34–36, 39

Housman, A. E., 12

*hross*, 43, 79

Hume, David, 170–71

hymns, 107–11

*I See by My Outfit* (Beagle), 26n17

The Ides of March (Wilder), 200

*The Iliad*, 24

illustrative fantasy, 6–7

Ilúvatar, 125

images and metaphors, 155–62, 165–67
  *See also* mythology and myths

imagination, 58, 167, 232–33, 235–36

"Imaginative Writing" (Gibbons), 27n19

immortality, 43, 49, 111, 119–21, 130

*See also* life after death

"Impact on America" (Walsh), 167

induction, Hume's problem of, 171

*The Inklings* (Carpenter), 228, 228n5

*"The Inner Ring"* (Lewis), 78, 210–11, 220

invented fact (stiffening), 28–29, 31, 46, 91, 106, 130, 132, 145, 165

Ironwood, Grace, 80, 214–15, 222

Istari (Wizards), 113, 133

Ivy Maggs, 71, 193, 211, 215, 222

Jadis, 15, 41, 161, 181

Jane Studdock, 15, 71, 76, 80–81, 156–57, 209–14, 217–23

Jerusalem Bible, 207

Jill Pole, 33, 162, 181, 187

Job, book of, 207

Johnson, Samuel, 34, 208

joy theme, 147, 179–80

*J. R. R. Tolkien: Myth, Morality and Religion* (Purtill), xii

*J. R. R. Tolkien* (Stimpson), 38n31, 42n1

justice, common standards of, 174–78

Kilby, Clyde, 133

Kirkpatrick (Lewis' old tutor), 216

language
alphabetical letters *l* and *k*, 42, 42n1

Common Speech, 41, 46

description, 29–31, 58, 201–3

dialects, 44–46

Elvish, 31, 41, 46, 58, 108, 110, 114–16, 140

evolution of, 50–51, 56–57

Hobbits and, 41, 94

invented, 28–29, 41, 51

Latin, 29, 51, 252n33

loss of, as punishment, 43

magical theory of, 42, 46–48, 58, 113

names and, 31

Orcish, 41–42, 42n1, 45–46, 58, 140

originality and, 33–37, 48–51, 199–205

personality and, 42–46, 50, 58

of poetry, 42, 45, 49

Ransom and, 28, 41–42, 43, 49, 57

rationality and, 42–44, 58

translation and, 29, 44, 53–54, 57, 108, 120, 207, 252

uses of, 44, 50–51, 58, 111, 223, 225

*The Last Battle* (Lewis), 83, 158, 162

Lawrence, D. H., 30

"Leaf by Niggle" (Tolkien), 6, 122–23, 153–54, 164, 187

legends
Arthurian legend, 16, 48, 51–53, 80, 91

Atlantis legend, 111, 113, 132

legends (*continued*)
  definitions of, 27
  *See also* mythology and myths
Legolas, 6, 31, 88, 100, 104, 120,
  187
letters, 51n9, 136–37, 141,
  233–36, 255
*Letters of C. S. Lewis* (Lewis,
  W. H.), 51n9, 136–37
*Letters to Malcolm* (Lewis),
  155–56, 183, 233–34, 246, 249
Lewis, C. S.
  allegory in works of, 17, 27,
    135, 179
  on allegory, 28–29, 35, 118–19,
    136–37, 156, 161
  Anscombe and, 228–30, 238,
    241–45
  Beversluis' critique of, 228–29,
    237–41, 246–47, 250
  conversion of, 164, 167, 179
  good characters, 64–67, 69–71,
    78–84
  letters from, 51n9, 136–37,
    141, 233–34, 236–37
  on meaning, 58–59
  personal life of, 164, 167, 179,
    227–28, 230–36, 246
  as professor, 28–29, 34, 56–59
  Protestant influence, 7, 63,
    111, 118–19
  *Shadowlands* and, 227, 227n2
  villainous characters of, 72–77
  writing style, 25–26, 47–49
Lewis, Helen Joy Davidman, 164,
  229–30, 232–36
Lewis, W. H., 51n9, 136–37
life after death, 90–91, 105, 111–
  12, 120–22, 159–60, 179, 236

*Lilith* (MacDonald), 204
limbo, 120
*The Lion, the Witch and the
  Wardrobe* (Lewis), 159, 181
literary value criteria, 21–26, 27,
  32–40
Lord Feverstone, 49, 75, 77–78,
  212–16
*Lord of the Elves and Eldils*
  (Purtill), xii
*Lord of the Flies* (Golding), 6
"The Lord of the Hobbits:
  J. R. R. Tolkien" (Fuller), 114
*The Lord of the Rings* (movie), 99
*The Lord of the Rings* (Tolkien)
  influences on, 34, 51, 53–56,
    85–89, 100, 105–6, 207
  invented fact in appendices of,
    31, 106, 132
  languages in, 34, 51
  Lewis on, 154–55
  religious references in, 108–12,
    113–21, 122–23
  secondary world of, 13–14
  themes in, 17–18, 88–89, 92,
    192–94
Louis of France, St., 118
Lucas, John, 248
Lucifer, 126
Lucretius, 12, 37
Lucy Pevensey, 82–83, 153–54,
  160–62, 181, 187, 207

MacDonald, George (author),
  167, 201–4
MacDonald, George (character),
  73–74, 78, 147
MacLeish, Archibald, 58
MacPhee, 76–77, 215–16

Madelva, Sister, 233n12

Maggs, Ivy, 71, 193, 211, 215, 222

magic
  language as, 42, 46–48, 58, 113
  witches', 41, 161, 181

Maiar, 127, 133

Malacandrians
  genders of, 116–17
  as unfallen, 64, 67, 69, 71, 92, 113

Maleldil, 64, 118–19, 134

Marion B. Wade Center (Wheaton College), 234, 236n16

Mark Studdock
  growth of, 79, 83, 210, 218–19, 221
  weaknesses of, 15, 75, 78–79, 210–14, 217–20, 223

master plan theme, 88, 121, 125, 175

means vs. ends theme, 69–71, 101–2, 142, 144, 161, 188–89, 221

medieval world view, 42, 128, 136, 145, 156–57
  See also modern world views

Melkor, 125–27, 130–32

Men (characters)
  as ancestors, 94, 120–21
  evil and, 94–95, 113
  fallen race, 14, 71, 91–92, 94, 132, 173
  languages of, 41, 93–94
  prayers of, 110–11
  shape of, 113–14, 117, 125–26
  See also Saruman

Mere Christianity (Lewis), 7, 137, 169, 175–77, 179, 191–92, 231, 245

Merry Brandybuck, 46, 95, 99, 99n19, 104, 186, 192

Milton, John, 35–36, 49, 75, 125, 129, 138, 141–45, 159

miracles, 170–71

Miracles (Lewis), 7, 171, 174, 243–44

modern world views
  Christianity vs., 72, 77, 80–182, 189, 195
  errors of, 44, 77, 154, 157, 165, 170–71, 190
  escape sought from, 9, 13–19, 48
  existentialism, 87–88, 178, 189–95
  heroism, 86–87
  medieval world views vs., 42, 128, 136, 145, 156–57
  pagan, 13, 89–91, 128, 136
  style, 47–48, 56
  See also philosophy

Moorman, Charles, 89–91, 206–7

moral argument as proof of God, 175–78

morality, 63–65, 76–77, 166–67, 176–78, 189–95

Morgan Le Fay, 52

Morris, Clifford, 236

Morris, Thomas V., 237–39

Morris, William, 201–3

movies, 7, 99, 227n2

music, 45, 81, 107–11, 125–26

mythology and myths
  creation, 125–29

mythology and myths (*continued*)
  described, 22–23, 25, 27–28,
    128
  value of, 154–57, 159–62,
    166–67
  *See also* legends

narrative, 22–23, 32, 128
naturalism, 44, 174–75, 243
nature, 13–14, 56, 171, 187
Nesbit, Edith, 207
N.I.C.E. (National Institute of
  Coordinated Experiments),
  70, 78, 146, 213, 222–23
Nicholson, William, 227n1
*Nineteen Eighty-Four* (Orwell), 11
*Notes from Underground*
  (Dostoyevsky), 65
Notre Dame University, 239
" 'Now Entertain Conjecture of a
  Time'–The Fictive Worlds of
  C. S. Lewis and J. R. R.
  Tolkien" (Moorman), 89
Noyes, Alfred, 202
Numenor, 111
numinosity, 22, 28, 128

obedience, 72, 135, 142–44, 192
*Of Other Worlds: Essays and Stories*
  (Lewis), 224–25
*Omar* (Fitzgerald), 12
"On Fairy-Stories" (Tolkien), 4,
  30, 89–90, 129, 133, 155,
  183n15, 201
"On Obstinacy in Belief"
  (Lewis), 169n1, 245–46, 252
Orcs
  ancestry of, 132, 204

capitalization of name of,
  13n17
as evil, 45–46, 49, 55, 92–93,
  101, 132, 140
Orcish, 41–42, 42n1, 45–46,
  58, 140
originality, 33–37, 48–51, 144,
  199–205
Orual, 148, 166, 173–74
Orwell, George, 11
Ousiarches, 28–29
*Out of the Silent Planet* (Lewis)
  the eldils in, 15, 145, 158
  invented fact in, 29
  language use in, 41–43, 57
  nature in, 57
  Ransom in, 28, 64, 66–69,
    185–86
  religious references in, 134–38
  the *sorns* in, 77, 79, 185–86
Oyarses, 28–29

pain. *See* suffering
*Paradise Lost* (Milton), 125, 138,
  141
Penelope, Sister, 237n18
*Perelandra* (Lewis)
  fallenness in, 67–69, 141–45
  fallibility in, 67–69, 92, 138
  genders in, 116–17
  Ransom and, 79–80, 83, 90,
    139–41, 215, 231–32
  secondary world of, 14–15,
    58–59
  Un-man in, 47, 139–40,
    143–45
personal responsibility theme,
  102, 143, 187–89, 192–95, 225
  *See also* free will theme

personality and language, 42–46, 50, 58

Peter Pevensey, 161, 187, 207, 214

*Phantastes* (MacDonald), 204

philosophy
Anscombe and, 228–30, 238, 241–45
apologetics and, 7, 37–39, 64, 77, 134–37, 165, 173–83, 228
existentialism, 87–88, 178, 189–95
experience, arguments from, 170–71, 179–80
generally, 168–70
naturalism, 44, 174–75, 243
problem of evil and, 104, 129, 170, 172–74, 240
in proofs of God, 72, 174–78
Satanism defined, 72, 78, 144
unbelief, flaws of, 72, 76–77, 174–78
universal moral law, 166–67, 176
verifiability, 170–72, 180–81

*The Phoenix and the Carpet* (Nesbit), 207

*Pilgrim's Progress* (Bunyan), 5, 136

*Pilgrim's Regress* (Lewis), 6, 135, 179

Pippin Took, 89, 95, 99, 99n19, 103–4, 186

plan theme, 88, 121, 125, 175

Plato, 119

*Playboy*, 26

*Poems* (Lewis), 183

poetry
Chesterton's, 91
language of, 42, 45, 49

Lewis', 164, 183
originality in, 34–36
purposes of, 100
science fiction and, 27
Tolkien's, 58, 110
Williams', 206
see also *Beowulf*

Pooh and Piglet, 51

"Power and Meaning in *The Lord of the Rings*" (Spacks), 121

prayer, 107–11, 134, 155–56, 183, 233–34, 236, 251

*Precincts of Felicity* (Moorman), 206

*A Preface to Paradise Lost* (Lewis), 35–36, 129, 141

*Prince Caspian* (Lewis), 82

*The Princess and Curdie* (MacDonald), 204

*The Princess and the Goblin* (MacDonald), 204

problem of evil, 104, 129, 170, 172–74, 240

*The Problem of Pain* (Lewis), 7, 129, 148, 169, 173, 244

Puddleglum, 77, 181–83

Purgatory, 122

Purtill, Richard L., xii, xiii, 237

*Quenta Silmarillion* (Tolkien), 127, 129–32

Raffell, Burton, 30n57

Ransom, Elwin
faith and reason, 231–32
language and, 28, 41–42, 43, 49, 57
nature of, 79–80

Ransom, Elwin (*continued*)
  in *Out of the Silent Planet*, 28,
    64, 66–69, 185–86
  power over animals, 215
Ransome, Arthur, 207
rational religion, 72, 174–83,
  227–32, 237–42, 243–52
rationality
  naturalism and, 44, 174–75,
    243
  of religion, 72, 174–83,
    227–32, 237–42, 243–52
  scientific reasoning *vs.*, 171
  speech and language and,
    42–44, 58
reader participation, 21–26,
  32–34, 39, 153–54, 167
Ready, William, 38n31
realism, 24–25, 28, 32, 44
Red Book of Westmarch, 31
redemption, 65–67, 69, 92, 166,
  169, 180
religion
  elements of, 105
  permanence of ideas in, xi–xii
  rationality of, 72, 174–83,
    227–32, 237–42, 243–52
  redemption, 65–67, 69, 92,
    166, 169
  as wish-fulfillment, 39, 170
  *See also* Christianity
religious references
  angels, 113–14, 116–17
  hymns, 107–11
  implicit, 105–6, 109, 121–22,
    123, 124, 134–38
  life after death, 90–91, 105,
    111–12, 120–22, 159–60,
    179, 236

prayer, 107–11, 134, 155–56,
  183, 233–34, 236, 251
resurrections, 90, 115–19, 160
  *See also* Bible
"Reply to Miss Anscombe"
  (Lewis), 243n26
"A Reply to Mr. C. S. Lewis'
  Argument that 'Naturalism is
  Self-Refuting'" (Anscombe),
  243n25
responsibility, theme of personal,
  102, 143, 187–89, 192–95,
  225
resurrections, 90, 115–19, 160
  *See also* life after death
*The Return of the King* (Tolkien),
  109
*Of the Rings of Power and the
  Third Age* (Tolkien), 132
Ringwraiths, 94, 96, 109
*The Road Goes Ever On: A Song
  Cycle* (Tolkien and Swann),
  110, 114
*Robert Falconer* (MacDonald),
  204
*The Roman Way* (Hamilton), 200
Rose, Stephen and Lois
  hierarchical objections by,
    71–72, 165–66
  on Lewis as Christian
    apologist, 7, 64, 77,
    134–37, 165, 173–75
  on Lewis' lack of originality,
    33–37
  on passivity of Lewis'
    characters, 64–67
  propaganda accusation by,
    37–39
  psychoanalysis and, 73–74

on religion as wish-fulfillment, 39, 170

Rougemont, Denis de, 147

Sale, Roger, 85n1, 85–89, 91

Sam Gamgee, 95, 97–98, 109–10, 120, 186, 194

Sartre, Jean-Paul, 87, 88, 178

Saruman
  as evil, 14, 49, 101, 103–4, 113–14, 187
  Gandalf as, 116
  moral struggles of, 95
  speech of, 46–47, 49

Satan
  in the Bible, 145, 163
  eldils as, 135
  Eve and, 142–43
  as fallen angel, 68, 93
  as God's tool, 142, 144
  Melkor as, 125–27, 130–32
  Milton's, 138
  obedience to, 72, 78, 135, 144
  and the problem of evil, 129
  Sauron as, 93, 100, 103–4, 113–14, 132
  as spoiler, 93, 126–27, 129, 131
  temptation by, 78, 100, 138, 142–47, 163
  Un-man as, 143
  Weston and, 68, 138–39
  See also devils; evil; Saruman

Satanism, defined, 72, 78, 144

Sauron, 93, 100, 103–4, 113–14, 132

Sayers, Dorothy, 207

science fiction, 26–27, 63–64, 144

The Screwtape Letters (Lewis), 74–75, 158, 199, 222

Search for Rational Religion (Beversluis), 228–29, 229n8, 237–41, 246–47, 250

Secret Fire, 133

secret intimacy (inner ring), 78, 210–11, 220

Sense and Nonsense in Religion (Stenson), 170

separation from God theme, 72, 223–24

Shadowlands (Sibley), 227n2

Shadowlands (television play), 227

Shadows of Imagination (Hillegas), 89

The Shattered Ring (Rose and Rose), 64–65, 71, 73

Sibley, Brian, 227n2

The Silmarillion (Tolkien), 105n, 124–28, 129–33

The Silver Chair (Lewis), 83, 181–82

Silvestris, Bernardus, 28–29

Sir Gawain and the Green Knight (Tolkien and Gordon, eds.), 50–53, 207

Smaug, 14, 43, 45–47, 54–55, 95

smiles, devilish, 139

"Social Morality" (Lewis), 191

social morality theme, 189–95
  See also personal responsibility theme

Socratic Club, 241–44

song, 107–8, 110–11

the sorns, 77, 79, 185–86

Spacks, Patricia Meyer, 121

speech. See language

Spenser, Edmund, 88

*Sprightly Running* (Wain), 190

Stenson, Sten H., 170–72

stiffening (invented fact), 28–29, 31, 46, 91, 106, 130, 132, 145, 165

Stimpson, Catherine, 38n31, 42n1, 45

Studdock. *See* Jane Studdock; Mark Studdock

*Studies in Words* (Lewis), 56–59

subcreator theme, 4, 126, 165

subordination, 71–72, 104, 135, 142–44, 165, 192
*See also* hierarchy

"sudden joyous turn" (eucatastrophe), 10, 13, 89–90, 234

suffering
acceptance of, 96, 166, 194, 237
of Christians, 147, 166, 173, 236–37
grief and, 230–37
problem of evil and, 104, 129, 170, 172–74, 240
purpose of, 166, 172–74, 181–82

*Surprised by Joy* (Lewis), 164, 167, 179

Susan Pevensey, 82, 162–63, 207

*Swallows and Amazons* (Ransome), 207

Swann, Donald, 110

Swinburne, Richard, 248

Sykes, Bill, 45


temptation theme, 78, 100, 138, 142–47, 163

Teresa, St., 162

*That Hideous Strength* (Lewis)
evil in, 71–73, 75–76, 138, 146–47
good characters in, 64–67, 69–71, 80
invented fact in, 91, 145
secondary world of, 14–17
summary of book, 209–26

themes
courtesy, 192–93
devotion to good cause, 217
ends *vs.* means, 69–71, 101–2, 142, 144, 161, 188–89, 221
free choice, 16–18, 68, 72, 84, 101–2, 142–43, 146, 172–73
heroism, 86–89, 95–100, 165–66, 188
joy, 147, 179–80
life after death, 90–91, 105, 111–12, 120–22, 159–60, 179, 236
master plan, 88, 121, 125, 175
modern failure, 13
nature, 13–14, 56, 171, 187
personal responsibility, 102, 143, 187–89, 192–95, 225
separation from God, meaning of, 72, 223–24
social morality, 189–95
subcreator responsibilities, 4, 126, 165
temptation, 78, 100, 138, 142–47, 163
world of wonder, 13
*See also* evil

Thomas Aquinas, St., 118, 242, 247

Thorin, 95, 120
*See also* Dwarves

*Three Philosophers* (Anscombe and Geach), 242

*Till We Have Faces* (Lewis), 148–49, 173, 234

"Tolkien and Frodo Baggins" (Sale), 85n1

*Tolkien and the Silmarillion* (Kilby), 133

*Tolkien* (Carpenter), 124, 129n43

Tolkien, Christopher, 124, 130, 206

Tolkien, J. R. R.
  allegory in works of, 117–18, 122
  on allegory, 17, 117
  *Beowulf* influence and, 34, 51, 53–56, 85–89, 100, 105–6, 207
  Book of Job translated by, 207
  Catholic influence, 7, 63, 108, 111, 118–20
  as literary writer, 25–26, 128
  on meaning, 58–59
  as philologist, 31, 50–51, 58–59, 111, 203
  writing style, 47–49

*Tolkien's Magic Ring* (Beagle), 26n18

"Transposition" (Lewis), 161

Treebeard, 92–93, 99

trolls, 13, 13n17, 41, 45, 55, 92–93, 103, 226

*The Two Towers* (Tolkien), 46, 88, 93, 115–16, 188

unbelief, flaws of, 72, 76–77, 174–78

unfallen creatures, 42, 64–67, 69, 71, 92, 94, 113, 135
  *See also* fallen creatures

uniformity of nature, 171

universal moral law, 166–67, 176

Un-man, 47, 139–40, 143–45

unoriginality, Lewis accused of, 33–37

*Unspoken Sermons* (MacDonald), 204

*Valaquenta* (Tolkien), 125, 127

Valar, 106, 111–17, 126–27, 130–31

Varda, 108–10, 127, 130, 131
  *See also* Elbereth (Varda)

verifiability, 170–72, 180–81

*The Voyage of the Dawn Treader* (Lewis), 17, 82–83, 153–54

*Voyage to Venus* (Lewis), 231

Wain, John, 3–5, 8, 10, 190–91

Walsh, Chad, 167

Webb, C. C. J., 29

"The Weight of Glory" (Lewis), 72, 78, 161, 195

Wells, H. G., 77

Weston, 15, 57, 68, 135, 138–39

Wheaton College, 234, 236

Whitehead, Alfred North, 171–72

Wilder, Thornton, 200

"William Morris" (Lewis), 201–3

Williams, Charles, 166, 205–8, 228

Wilson, Edmund, 17

Wither, Deputy Director, 73, 75, 78, 212, 214, 222–23, 225

Wittgenstein, Ludwig, 242

Wizards, 113–14, 133

world of wonder theme, 13

world views. *See* medieval world view; modern world views

writer's tasks, 3–8, 10–12